Heritage Interpretation

The *Issues in Heritage Management* series is a joint venture between Routledge and English Heritage. It provides accessible, thought-provoking books on issues central to heritage management. Each book within the series is designed to provide a topical introduction to key issues in heritage management for students in higher education and heritage professionals.

Heritage Interpretation is an essential guide to present practice and policy concerning issues in heritage management. The UK has an international reputation for the excellence of its heritage interpretation. During the 1980s and 1990s the UK developed innovative public presentation of heritage sites in the increasingly competitive cultural tourism market. UK heritage organisations developed ideas pioneered by the US National Park Service in the 1960s and applied these to cultural heritage sites.

This volume draws on this accumulated expertise to describe and analyse best practice in heritage interpretation within the UK. The contributors are all responsible for developing best practice in a range of heritage organisations, such as English Heritage, The National Trust, Historic Scotland, Cadw and National Parks. Looking at subjects from public art to twentieth-century military remains and from cathedrals to urban heritage, the contributors discuss the enormous range of interpretative options available to them and how these can be sensitively and appropriately tailored to specific places and specific audiences.

Alison Hems is Head of Interpretation at English Heritage.

Marion Blockley, a freelance consultant, was formerly the Director of the Ironbridge Institute, Ironbridge, UK.

ISSUES IN HERITAGE MANAGEMENT
Published by Routledge in association with English Heritage

Series editor: Peter Stone, University of Newcastle

Managing the Historic Rural Landscape
edited by Jane Grenville

Managing Historic Sites and Buildings
edited by Gill Chitty and David Baker

Education and the Historic Environment
edited by Don Henson, Peter Stone and Mike Corbishley

Heritage Interpretation
edited by Alison Hems and Marion Blockley

Heritage Interpretation

edited by
Alison Hems and Marion Blockley

Routledge
Taylor & Francis Group

LONDON AND NEW YORK

First published 2006
by Routledge
2 Park Square, Milton Park, Abingdon,
Oxon, OX14 4RN

Simultaneously published in the USA and Canada
by Routledge
711 Third Avenue, New York, NY 10017

Routledge is an imprint of the Taylor & Francis Group

Transferred to Digital Printing 2011

© 2006 English Heritage

Typeset in Bell Gothic and Perpetua by
Florence Production Ltd, Stoodleigh, Devon

British Library Cataloguing in Publication Data
A catalogue record for this book is available from the
British Library

Library of Congress Cataloging in Publication Data
Heritage interpretation/edited by Marion Blockley.
    p. cm.
    Includes bibliographical references and index.
    1. Historic sites – Interpretive programs.
    2. Historic sites – Great Britain – Interpretive
    programs.   3. Great Britain – Antiquities.
    4. Great Britain – History, Local.   I. Blockley,
    Marion R.
    CC135.H459 2005
    363.6'9'0941–dc22   2005003080

ISBN10: 0–415–23796–3 (hbk)
ISBN10: 0–415–23797–1 (pbk)

ISBN13: 9–78–0–415–23796–3 (hbk)
ISBN13: 9–78–0–415–23797–0 (pbk)

CONTENTS

ILLUSTRATIONS

Illustrations

Figures

Table

Contributors

CONTRIBUTORS

Brian Bath, Interpretive Design Limited, 36 Carlisle Road, Hove,
BN3 4FS
bath_brian@hotmail.com

Marion Blockley, 6 Cherry Tree Hill, Coalbrookdale, Telford,
TF8 7EQ
blockley@aol.com

Margi Bryant, TellTale (Interpretation Consultants), 83 Corbar Road,
Buxton, SK17 6RJ
margib@lineone.net

Tim Copeland, The International Centre for Heritage Education,
University of Gloucester, Francis Close Hall, Swindon Road,
Cheltenham, GL50 4AZ
tcopeland@glos.ac.uk

Rona Gibb, Project Manager, Paths for All Partnership, Inglewood
House, Tullibody Road, Alloa, FK10 2HU
rona.gibb@pathsforall.org.uk

Brian Goodey, Harvard Consultancy Services, 112 Malling Street,
Lewes, East Sussex, BN7 2RJ
brian@harvardcs.com
brian.goodey@btopenworld.com

Alison Hems, Museums Libraries and Archives Council, 16 Queen
Anne's Gate, London, SW1H 9AA
alison.hems@mla.gov

Peter Humphries, Cadw: Welsh Historic Monuments, Crown Building,
Cathays Park, Adeilad Y Goron, Parc Cathays,
Cardiff, Caerdydd, CF10 3NQ
peter.humphries@wales.gsi.gov.uk

Carol Parr, 8 Kenyons, West Horsley, Leatherhead, Surrey,
KT24 6HX
carol.parr@ukgateway.net

Jon Price, Cultural Management Unit, School of Arts and Social Sciences, Northumbria University, Newcastle upon Tyne, NE1 8ST
jon.price@unn.ac.uk

Andrew Robertshaw, National Army Museum, Royal Hospital Road, Chelsea, London, SW3 4HT
arobertshaw@national-army-museum.ac.uk

John Schofield, English Heritage, 23 Savile Row, London, W1S 2ET
john-schofield@english-heritage.org.uk

Chris Tabraham, Historic Scotland, Longmore House, Salisbury Place, Edinburgh, EH9 1SH

Dr Ruth Taylor, Learning Advisor – Interpretation, The National Trust, Heelis, Kemble Drive, Swindon, SN2 2RA
ruth.taylor@nationaltrust.org.uk

FOREWORD

This book is the fourth volume in the series *Issues in Heritage Management*. The series, a joint initiative between the English Heritage Education Service (EHES) and Routledge, is based on discussions at professional seminars and conferences where those involved in particular aspects of the heritage met and exchanged views, ideas and approaches. It is important to note that the seminars and conferences were conceived as educational, rather than policy-forming, events. The seminars that provided the information for the first two of these volumes (*Managing the Historic Rural Landscape* and *Managing Historic Sites and Buildings*) and this one were organised and facilitated by the EHES. *Education and the Historic Environment* was based on a conference hosted by the Council for British Archaeology.

Marion Blockley, then of the Ironbridge Institute, helped the EHES to organise the seminar from which this book came but then had to hand the project over owing to pressure of other work commitments. I am extremely grateful to Alison Hems for stepping in to help with the rest of the process and to the authors for their understanding and patience during what has been an overlong gestation period. My apologies and thanks to you all. Especial thanks must also go to Liz Bell, a research student at the University of Newcastle, without whom the book would almost certainly not have seen the light of day.

The following chapters provide a 'snap-shot' of policy and practice at the start of the twenty-first century. They are intended to actively encourage debate of the *issue* of the relationship between heritage and interpretation. They do not put forward a particular English Heritage view or policy but rather try to reflect how professionals are trying to grapple with the complexities of heritage interpretation in the early years of a new century.

Peter G. Stone
July 2005

INTRODUCTION: BEYOND THE GRAVEYARD – EXTENDING AUDIENCES, ENHANCING UNDERSTANDING

Alison Hems

> Nobody really knows their ancestors, even if they're living beside the graveyard where their great-great-grandparents are buried, or in the house which their family built and lived in for generations. They may possess papers, objects, maybe money and property. But they don't possess the lives of the past, any more than you do.
> But they may possess stories . . .
>
> Helen Dunmore, *Mourning Ruby*, 2003

Whether by accident or design, the essays that follow throw down a number of challenges for those who seek to interpret the historic environment – to tell its stories. These challenges are both practical and philosophical, and they relate, above all, to the nature of our understanding – of the sites, monuments and places with which this book is concerned, of the processes that underpin their interpretation, and of the techniques we may use in so doing. They relate equally to our understanding of audiences and visitors, and of those who may never visit an historic house or castle, but who will nonetheless encounter the broader 'historic environment' in a whole variety of ways and contexts, perhaps without really noticing that they have done so. They relate, too, to the idea of significance and the value we place upon the once accidental survivals from the past, as well as upon those buildings and monuments we now consciously designate, list and conserve. They relate, perhaps above all, to the kind of stories we choose to acknowledge and to tell, and to the ways in which the significance of each place will change in their retelling.

Some of the challenges outlined in this book stem from our changing ideas about nature of the historic environment, its conservation and its interpretation. Here, a number of chapters anticipate the thinking encapsulated in *Power of Place*, which was published well after most of them were written. *Power of Place* was published in December 2000 following a comprehensive review of relevant policies, and contained a series of recommendations to government on the future management, regulation and use of the historic environment. English Heritage co-ordinated the review for the Department for Culture, Media and Sport and the Department for the Environment, Transport and the Regions. The government's response to the recommendations arising from the review was published by DCMS in December 2001, under a title *The Historic Environment: A Force for our Future*.

The review involved extensive consultation with a wide range of heritage bodies, agencies and charities, and a large-scale research project that looked at attitudes towards, and perceptions of, the historic environment – what it was, and meant, to the general public. Its principal conclusion was that 'the historic environment is all around us – people value places, not just individual sites and buildings'. This, and the recommendations emerging from this, have long been recognised by those who try to interpret it.[1]

The challenge here is to find ways of making meaningful and explicable the wider historic environment, beyond and between the formally designated structures of ancient monuments, ruinous castles or historic houses and landscapes. It is a challenge touched upon in Brian Goodey's chapter on interpreting 'urban heritage' and, from a different perspective, in Rona Gibb's essay on the consultative processes underpinning interpretative planning in the Scottish Highlands. At the same time, heritage interpreters, working at traditional sites, are faced with the familiar challenges of creating sustainable displays in the absence of adequate revenue funding, of keeping up with rapidly changing technologies and rising visitor expectations, and of working within a discipline which is still, from time to time, obliged to justify its very existence.

Andy Robertshaw's chapter on live interpretation neatly sums up one of the major barriers to meeting the challenges inherent in our work. In describing the lack of an intellectual framework for 'living history' in the UK, and the weaknesses and inconsistencies that have stemmed from this, he also describes a problem common to all forms of interpretation and to all its practitioners.

Despite borrowing from related disciplines in education, museums and the arts, adopting many of the concepts familiar to us from Tilden and John Veverka, and notwithstanding an emerging body of audience and other research, professional interpreters working in the UK still lack a coherent framework within which to place their ideas and to test their assumptions.[2] Professional interpreters also lack a coherent framework within which to deal with the ideas and assumptions of audiences and visitors, who bring with them their own notions of the past, their own values and their own sense of place. Thus we still talk about 'bringing the past to life' when what we are really doing is trying to engage with our visitors in the present. Interpreters must begin with what they have: Stonehenge in its twenty-first-century landscape, with or without the buzz of major roads; the mills, workshops and machinery of industrial archaeology set now in a post-industrial England. 'Bringing the site to life' is thus a more rational proposition, since it opens up a whole range of opportunities for exploring it in different contexts, using different media and giving voice to different ideas about meaning and significance.

But there is something here that the profession has not yet quite resolved, and that leads us, with the best of intentions, into both ethical and practical difficulties. It is here that the supposed tension between preserving the historic environment and presenting a historic attraction becomes most apparent. It is here, too, that notions of authenticity begin to conflict, however unintentionally, with the development of real understanding and appreciation.

The essays here indicate a fairly clear divide between those who work for the large, national institutions – the heritage agencies of Historic Scotland, Cadw and English

Heritage, for example – and those who work with smaller, community-based organisations or, yet still, in the commercial sector or the universities. There is, for example, in Chris Tabraham's chapter on the work of Historic Scotland, a strong emphasis upon the aim of providing the visitor with a stimulating and enjoyable experience, 'while fully respecting the historic fabric and the setting of the monument'. English Heritage, for its part, promotes the concept of 'non-intrusive' interpretation and of 'discreet' signage. This is partly why audio tours are so popular among many heritage interpreters – they disappear when the visitor does, and leave no trace among the walls and mossy banks, the drawing room or the conservatory.

All this is unexceptional, and exactly what one would expect from bodies whose primary responsibility is the conservation of the historic environment. But there is a dilemma here. The heritage agencies have a parallel responsibility to promote access and understanding, and this may be more fully discharged by consciously intruding upon the historic building or monument. The intention is not to cause irreversible damage or to mislead, but to challenge preconceptions and encourage greater engagement – or at least the possibility of taking this further. The means of doing so may be temporary – an arts project or community theatre; story-telling or re-enactment – but it may nonetheless be the means by which we acknowledge other notions of significance – those of the visitor rather than of the archaeologist or the architectural historian – and promote more meaningful forms of understanding and engagement.

Another difficult idea is that of authenticity. Jon Price tackles the issue in relation to interpreting industrial heritage, while Peter Humphries for Cadw presents a different, but allied perspective of the related notions of authenticity and accuracy. In Chapter 5, Peter Humphries offers a useful account of the processes through which Cadw goes in researching, designing and producing the interpretative panels provided at its sites. He describes the value of reconstruction drawings in illuminating a site for its visitors and, as at English Heritage, in providing architectural historians with new insights into a building's design and development. Reconstruction drawings and computer models can suddenly reveal a previous misapprehension about a roof line or window detail, particularly if earlier drawings have been only in plan. The process itself is useful, and can support a continually evolving understanding of a building's form and function. Yet this may create a problem for the interpreter charged with commissioning the panels upon which the drawings will appear, and ensuring that they are installed on time.

> Therein lies the dilemma which all practitioners of reconstructions face: people will believe what is presented to them in the name of authority, and it is particularly incumbent upon a public body to take the utmost care over interpretation such as this.

English Heritage would doubtless take a similar view, when its real, or at least equal responsibility, might be to help visitors to understand that ideas may change over time or as new evidence is revealed. Above all, its overarching responsibility may be to help them examine that evidence for themselves. It has recently gone some way towards doing this, through temporary exhibitions and publications that explore the process of reconstructing the past, and the dilemmas and uncertainties that the process contains.[3] Such an approach is unusual, however, and the overwhelming tone remains simply authoritative, rather than truly involving and participatory.

An alternative approach is outlined by Tim Copeland in Chapter 6. Here, he draws a distinction between positivist and constructivist approaches to interpretation. The first usually offers 'ready constructed facts and a fixed view of the site as it "was"', while the latter involves 'portraying the complexities of the site and how constructions about it have been made'. Copeland recognises, exactly as Peter Humphries does, that the visitor will bring ideas and assumptions with them, but then turns this notion upon its head. These ideas and assumptions will necessarily inform the visitor's view of a particular site, so they must become part of its interpretation, either challenged or confirmed by the assessment of evidence. This, together with the use of Copeland's 'big concepts', allows the visitor to

> gain incremental knowledge of the evidence of the past in the landscape. It helps ensure that visitors do not see every heritage venue as a special or unique case separate from the evidence of all the other heritage sites that they have seen, but as part of the wider historic environment existing all around them.

After *Power of Place*, this is an important idea, and a challenging one for those bodies whose promotional material and marketing campaigns are intrinsically linked to the notion of special places.

The National Trust has long been associated with 'special places' and, erroneously, as Ruth Taylor makes clear in Chapter 7, with a particularly discreet and non-intrusive form of interpretation offered either through a guidebook or the quiet interventions of volunteer room stewards. By way of contrast, she lists the wide range of interpretative approaches used by the Trust that transcend the stereotype. Nonetheless, many of its properties are still presented 'as if their occupants have just left the second before the visitor arrives'. The same approach has been used by English Heritage at Down House, where the illusion is that Charles Darwin and members of his family have just stepped into the garden or disappeared upstairs.

This is a pragmatic response to the problem of 'peopling' now empty rooms, however authentic and well-researched the furnishings might be. The sound of music playing in a next-door room, or of logs crackling in a grate; the casually discarded notebook or scattered collection of natural history specimens all represent a form of 'interpretation', without the intrusion of costumed mannequins or the expense of costumed interpreters. But if this is a pragmatic response, and one much appreciated by visitors, then it is also a problematic one.

The previous inhabitants of historic houses have manifestly not just left the room, to busy themselves elsewhere; by pretending that they have, we avoid the need to deal with the changes in values and perceptions that have occurred between the actual then and the fictitious now. To preserve the illusion and the authentic interior, we may do this in an introductory exhibition located elsewhere, in an audio tour or in a carefully worded paragraph in the guidebook. Yet this careful separation of the monument from its interpretation may be too cautious, too respectful – of the building in its past, rather than of its significance in the present. The use of first-person interpreters, particularly where they are the only form of interpretation on offer, poses a similar dilemma.

The recreation of period interiors from which all traces of modern intrusion have been carefully excluded may also obscure the very meaning and significance that good interpretation should seek to reveal – the stories that otherwise go untold and the connections that remain unmade. As Stuart Hall so succinctly put it: 'Heritage is a powerful mirror. Those who cannot see themselves in it feel excluded.'[4]

Every historic interior, each recreated landscape, will contain layers of meaning and significance. Many of these will not be immediately apparent to the visitor, but once-hidden links and connections may well hold the key to attracting new audiences and sustaining existing ones. The lesson has long been learnt by museums and galleries,

experienced in providing alternative ways of seeing the same objects and in contextualising objects in different ways. In 2002, for example, Tate Britain encouraged its visitors
to re-examine paintings by Thomas Gainsborough, and to look again at the pastoral idyll
he depicted in light of prevailing social and economic realities – it was important, thought
the exhibition's curators, to understand where the money had come from, to support
and sustain the great estates of eighteenth-century England. Such approaches are increasingly used by heritage bodies, particularly as the larger national agencies begin to adopt
the insights and perspectives of smaller, community-based groups: places, like objects,
have multiple meanings. The challenge, perhaps inevitably, is to make other meanings
explicit even within the confines of the period interior, allowing both its atmosphere to
be enjoyed, and its links and connections to be explored.

Heritage may be a powerful mirror; it is also a distorting one, through which past
events and experiences can be reduced to a kind of nostalgic dressing-up or bland description of people, places and processes. Jon Price outlines some of the pitfalls in relation
to industrial heritage, although curiously makes little mention of the casualties of industrial change. While he does refer to economic decline as a spur for heritage-based
regeneration, he has less to say about changing employment practices, trades unionism
or the battle of Orgreave – now itself a subject for re-enactment. Industrial change is
manifest in real places, in factory architecture and in call-centre design, in monumental
sculpture and in the debate about the future of the headquarters of the National Union
of Miners in Sheffield. Its impact, however, is not simply upon places, but upon those
people whose lives, and sense of self, are changed as a result. The authors of *Power of
Place* might thus have usefully added that people value people, and that the significance
of place stems from those who once created or experienced it.

Ideas about significance, and the importance of recognising alternative views about what
constitutes significance, are nonetheless fundamental to *Power of Place*. Alongside its
recommendations on conservation-led regeneration and rationalised planning procedures,
the review recognised that

> the historic environment is part of everyday life. It is accessible to everyone. It
> is around us every time we travel to work, drive to the supermarket or go to
> school. Studying it, being able to read and interpret it, enriches people's lives as
> much as literature, music, or history. Access creates interest, interest stimulates
> understanding, understanding brings enjoyment, enjoyment leads to commitment.
> All contribute to the quality of life.

Heritage interpreters have always known this, and extending and enhancing access has
always been fundamental to their work. A number of chapters here deal explicitly with
the challenge of interpreting the historic environment beyond the castle moat or estate
lodge, as well as with access, understanding and enjoyment within the castle or estate.
Brian Goodey, for example, considers ways of interpreting the urban environment, while
Carol Parr describes the use of public art in interpreting both urban and rural landscapes.
She outlines a tradition of public art in this country that runs from Celtic crosses to
commemorative statues, and onto the contemporary commissions of the present. A slightly
broader perspective would include war memorials and our changing attitudes towards the
monumental sculptures of once familiar public figures. It would also include the outcry
that sometimes greets suggestions that such figures might be moved to make way for
more recognisable ones, and the responses and reactions to the empty plinth in Trafalgar
Square. The history of public art contains its own narrative, played out in our cities and
town squares. The value of interpretation lies in reminding passers-by of the now forgotten

achievements of once familiar men and women, and in encouraging debate about changing fashions in public art and changing definitions of greatness.

Brian Goodey takes a slightly different approach, considering ways by which we might come to understand the urban landscape as a whole, rather than the isolated monuments within it. Looking beyond the medieval street patterns and great Minster of a city such as York, or the Georgian crescents and squares of eitheenth-century Bath, his answer lies in the greater use of the internet and electronic media, as a means of interpreting non-traditional urban spaces. As with the authors of *Power of Place*, the aim is to encourage and enable participation in the processes of conservation and decision-making. This is a vision that links interpretation to education and empowerment, and which does not rely upon a nostalgic affection for a vaguely remembered high street or half-imagined market place. Interpretation, again, is rooted in the experience of the present, not in the recreation or reconstruction of a past.

Thus, interpretation becomes an exciting, if not dangerous activity. Its possibilities are most apparent in John Schofield's chapter on 'presenting and interpreting recent troubles'. Here, places become significant because of the human stories associated with them. They are clearly not places of outstanding natural beauty or human artistry, although ingenuity, ruthlessness and inhumanity may all be present, along with political ideologies and particular views of the world.

Much of this will be invisible without interpretation, although the building may retain its own power and the resonance of memory. For those who lived through the events that took place there, the preservation of the building as a memorial may well be enough. Yet recent events pass rapidly into history, and the carefully preserved structures and original features can equally rapidly lose their significance – unless one knows what it was, and can acknowledge changes in significance and understanding, as time passes. Thus, John Schofield describes the conservation of the Cold War experimental site at Orford Ness in Suffolk, and its preservation within the landscape. In this way, he argues, its 'symbolic value will . . . be maintained for future generations'. Yet the symbolic value of Cold War sites is already different for different audiences, and will change again as the rival perspectives of, say, nuclear protestors and government scientists pass beyond living memory and into history. A policy of non-intervention goes a long way in preserving an 'aura of mystery' or in presenting 'cold, grey structures [from] which visitors depart feeling chilled', but it may not offer them the insights they need to place the monument in its broader context or to deal with their emotional response to its creation and survival.

Schofield's essay concludes with some useful recommendations on the interpretation of recent events. He makes a plea for accuracy, and 'not some sanitised or diluted version or fabrication of the truth'. He encourages active involvement and participation, so that visitors can develop 'their own appreciation of significance' and, in the case of very recent events, so that those who lived through them can share their perceptions and experiences. He advocates 'emphasising human experience' as the most effective means of presenting the 'troubled past', and reinforces the importance of place as the foundation for relating its human stories. Its 'atmosphere or character . . . and its material remains' may be the most powerful means of engaging with visitors and of drawing them into an understanding of past events.

In many respects, John Schofield sums up the qualities that one would expect of good interpretation anywhere, irrespective of place, period or media. Effective interpretation must involve audiences in hearing *and* telling past stories; it emphasises human experience, and places it at the core of those stories. Adopting such approaches, in the context of landscape management or the conservation of the built heritage, is enormously difficult to do. The practical difficulties outlined at the beginning of this short introduction often conspire to limit true audience involvement or to reduce the options to a single story, however well told. We should, perhaps, borrow another phrase from *Power of Place*, and use it to develop an approach to interpretation that is built upon understanding and involving audiences, and which puts their knowledge and experience alongside that of the professional: 'Involving people means working locally, project by project, community by community. It takes time and effort, but brings long term reward. It means creating trust and sharing knowledge.'[5] It means, in other words, bringing the site, or street or city square to life by beginning the process with those who do just that – its visitors, residents and passers-by. It means respecting the present, as well as the power of the past, and extending the range of stories we might tell to encompass those traditionally omitted from the dialogue. Few of us will have a direct connection with those sites and monuments we might visit – the graveyard, as it were, or the family home passed down through the generations – but the connections are many and varied. Good interpretation – timely, well-researched, imaginative, challenging – is the means by which we make them.

Notes

1   *Power of Place: the future of the historic environment* (London, 2000); *The Historic Environment: a force for the future* (London, 2001)
2   See also, Margi Bryant, *Tilden's Children: interpretation in Britain's national parks* (Chapter 12, this volume)
3   See, for example, Brian Davison, *Picturing the Past* (London, 1997) and Mark Redknap, *Re-creation: visualizing the past* (Cardiff, 2003); and the outreach work by Peter Dunn, reconstruction artist at English Heritage
4   Stuart Hall, *Whose Heritage?* Manchester conference proceedings, The Arts Council, November 1999
5   *Power of Place*, p. 28

Author's note

This volume has taken a number of years complete, during which time the introduction has been revised several times, to take account both of textual changes in the essays that follow and in the real world. This version stands as a broad analysis of the options open to heritage interpreters, and the different frameworks within which we may choose to work. It is my hope that I have succeeded both in describing these choices, and in accurately representing the ideas expressed by other contributors, notwithstanding the passage of time.

I should also like to record my thanks to Liz Bell of the University of Newcastle, who succeeded in keeping track of all the contributions over this same period, and who was unfailingly helpful in dealing with requests for yet another copy.

Chapter 1

INTERPRETING URBAN HERITAGE

Brian Goodey

Goodey

At first it was difficult to believe graffiti that appeared in view of steel framing rising over the former site of our local, Banbury, bus station, itself located on the in-filled canal dock. 'Heritage Woz Here' seemed less a popular protest than a contrivance waiting for camera to record it. But there it was, a modest protest against the obliteration of the town's defensive works, canal and early manufacturing industry beneath enclosures for parking and shopping, all wrapped in a pastiche of anywhere nineteenth-century-styled maltings façade devices. Or it may be a regret at the political demise of the concept of 'heritage' in a brave new Britain (see Goodey, 1998).

Since the mid-nineteenth century much of the UK has looked to its market towns and cities for the vitality and context that sustain life. Within the next hundred years, people moved from describing their geographical position as a village or rural location, to the proximity to town or city. Gradually the urban agglomeration drew them in – factories, shop jobs and administration providing a ticket to suburban residence within one or two generations. We are all urban dwellers now – with abstract postal codes that reinforce that relationship.

But what do we know, and care, of the urban areas within which we live, or visit? Newspaper surveys suggest that over 50 per cent of urban residents would, if given the chance, retreat to discernably rural areas, rejecting proximity, crime, grime and other presumed urban disadvantages for the, possibly false, freedom and arcadia of rural residence. Potential densification of our towns and cities, the development of 'brownfield' sites, and a presumption against development in the countryside or greenbelt, mean that an increased percentage of the population will be added to the residents of urban places (Urban Task Force, 1999).

Some new developments will, no doubt, be built on semi-urban locations. Estate titles will reflect field, vegetation, wildlife and village titles, often denying centuries of urban history. But when new residents receive family visitors, or instruct children, they may look to nearby urban areas which, they assume, are 'on ice' for their pleasure and learning.

It is this 'pleasure and learning' that is fundamental to the understanding of interpretation in urban areas. Interpretation should not be primarily for the overseas visitor or the informed national traveller, but for the suburban, or catchment resident, who chooses to explore the neighbouring town, not just as a retail target, but as a comfortable resource for family learning. The belief that the essence of urbanism is in the provision of effective democratic learning spaces guided such writers as Lewis Mumford, Kevin Lynch (1972) and Colin Ward (Ward and Fyson, 1973).

This local, civic seeking clientele is very seldom considered in the programmes and facilities that local authorities propose for visitors (though see Parkin *et al.*, 1989 on the mutual visitor/resident relationship). Heritage turns its back on recency, seldom is the suburb connected to the urban centre, seldom is the twentieth-century experience that brought people to an area heralded in the themes that are explored in urban place.

We are slow off the mark. In Lowell, Massachusetts the US urban National Park, events and museum space are dedicated to introducing new immigrant groups from Asia to previous arrivals in this community mosaic. Interpretation is, and must be a gateway to civic experience – with all the value problems thus implied.

Although we have a fairly clear idea of what visitors want from urban areas, and the techniques that might be used to link visitors and place, that link is seldom made. The bottom line for interpretive investment in most towns is that local people are drawn into designing an emotional relationship with the life, history and fabric of the town, that they join organisations that sustain historic environments, events and activities, and that the sundered status of local and regional identity is repaired.

It is not really important that a local resident recognises Pevsner's *Buildings of England* architectural world of fourteenth-century towers and sixteenth-century monuments – or even the more impressive recent city-based volumes. Rather, that local events and features that have evolved in the townscape, many of them recently, strike a personal chord.

The best interpreter in this context is still probably the historian, allowed free rein in the local paper, using photographs, interviews and a pointed text, to link both casual and deep-felt personal experiences or memories with more rooted information (see Hayden, 1995). If that 'historian' is, in fact, a composite of the community, as in Stratford's 'Eastside Community Heritage' project in London then so much the better. This workshop project has over 5,000 participants, eighteen exhibitions, five publications and an audio documentary to its credit since 1993.

With assistance and/or initiative, such local schemes can become visitor attractions as evidenced in South Africa's Township Tours, or more instructively in the communities of Barcelona.

For public or private investment in interpretive provision to work for visitors and residents there must be an underpinning of knowledge, availability and exchange that stimulates interest and resources.

Contemporary approaches and attitudes towards urbanism

There has probably been no generation where 'the city' has been an undisputed attraction to the entire population. Urban places have always represented power and an association with power, innovation and the risks of innovation, freedom and a context for individual expression.

Today, differing perceptions of the city may depend on income, life-style and expectation. For the young, unencumbered with family, '24 hour city' vitality beckons. For the suburban family it is a quick purposeful day trip, and for the retired a chance to explore within a limited, comfortable, and often nostalgic context. Movement patterns, perceived access and lifestyle, in both physical space and in the electronic world have stimulated new patterns (and academic understandings, e.g. Westwood and Williams, 1997) and have led to a new concern for legibility (see Kelly and Kelly, 2003) after the success of a Bristol project.

In a working lifetime, those born around the Second World War have seen a remarkable sequence of urban changes. First, wartime damage, emergency housing

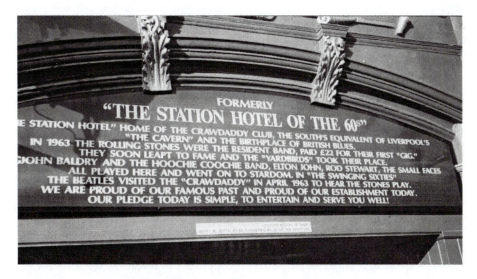

Figure 1.1   Station Hotel, Richmond. A message of rock hunters; commercial interpretation of recent cultural history

provision and belated Modern Movement central area experiments such as Coventry and Basildon, the latter one of many brave 'new' towns. Then phases of slum clearance, 'decanting' to new communities, tower blocks and peripheral estates. More Modern Movement centres trapped, as in Birmingham, by throttling road rings. From a concern with 'Traffic in Towns' (Buchanan, 1963), traffic became towns and from the 1970s retail vitality began to shift to 'edge city' leaving 'historic town centres' to fend as they may. It was only ministerial concern at the contrast between the brash Merryhill shopping centre and sad Dudley nearby that began to put real clout behind government's re-emphasis on traditional town centres, though as some recent public protest concerning modifications to Milton Keynes' shopping centre have shown, modern shopping structures do have their aesthetic, as well as retail, supporters.

A wide range of scenic beauties that had been pilgrimage centres since the medieval period and mass, red book, tourist destinations since the railways, were established purveyors of the UK's heritage. Through the significance of their built form, early local interest in conservation, established events programmes (as with the Three Choirs Festival) and international visibility, cathedral, spa and early resort towns set the pace for 'interpretation' long before that term arrived in Britain. Even nineteenth-century guidebooks promote selected walking routes (the earlier 'perambulations'), key buildings open to the public, official guides and an array of specialist publications. These latter offered an ecclesiastical or academic authority that is not entirely removed to this day although it now serves to distance, rather than relate, visitor to site.

Such established traditions of urban heritage presentation and interpretation were shaken by the 1975 European Architectural Heritage Year, a Council of Europe campaign in which the UK, largely through the Civic Trust, played a major part. A post-1969 European theme of cultural democratisation played through into the Campaign's concern with environmental education in schools, with participation by communities in the management of their heritage, and with telling others – interpretation – in which all could join (see Percival, 1979). This was the period of Heritage and Urban Studies Centres, of trails and walks for schools, and of industrial archaeology. 'Architectural' heritage turned out to be rather more – boundaries into concern for public artefacts, spaces, even meanings, began to be broken and although, as Wood (1996) has noted, the building preoccupation still survives, it is now alongside a much wider interest in context.

Since the 1970s there has been increasing recognition that all aspects of urban change, development, management . . . and even interpretation, require a multi-agency and -area, rather than site-specific, approach. With a commitment that began long before ministries or departments were dedicated to the urban condition, the Civic Trust began its sequence of initiatives through a network of local amenity groups. Recognising the need for an holistic approach to urban revival, with interpretation as an integrated element, the Trust's Regeneration Unit (at www. civictrust.org.uk) has pioneered the development of local partnerships, an early

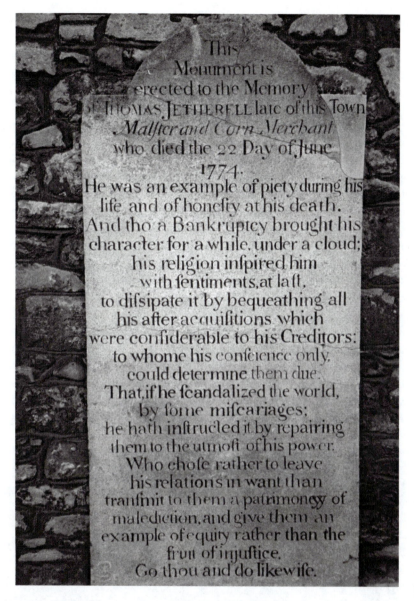

Figure 1.2 Huntingdon. Putting a life's record straight in the eighteenth-century and providing easy access to the past

example of which focused on Wirksworth in Derbyshire. The Wirksworth experience generated several important interpretive studies (including Civic Trust/CEI, 1983; Civic Trust, 1987) that developed themes and methods still evident in the Trust's approach in former industrial cities and agricultural market towns.

The 'former' of the previous sentence is significant. We are all aware of living in a post-industrial world where lone examples of the commonplace (such as a pot-kiln in the Staffordshire Potteries) now provide modest employment as relics. Similarly post-war generations have seen animals leave town, first for a new market on the periphery, and then for sale by video if there are any buyers. The open stalls of former market towns trade on plastic, textiles, fruit and vegetables from around the world, with the novel concept of 'Farmer's Markets' now (re-)introduced from North America.

The rationale for contemporary urban places is no longer a simple matter of location and centrality. Though places remain known for a single manufactured product, the firm has probably diversified and is owned elsewhere. If of value in heritage development the identifiable product may be plundered. Bird's Custard moved from down-at-heel Digbeth in Birmingham to Banbury in the great post-war decanting and is still manufactured there, though in a factory whose name has passed through several ownerships. In Digbeth, The Custard Factory is a new 'quarter' venue.

Quarter? From the French *quartier* – as in the Paris Latin Quarter, not a fourth part of a town, and not – in translation at least – a living community of interest. Closer, it usually appears, to the North American 'district' – as in New York's Garment District, or to what has been termed an 'epitome zone' (by Clay, 1973). It is inevitable that a term that has dominated urban interpretation has come to mean all things to all people. In order to stimulate regeneration outside any established historic core, it has become necessary to characterise former inner industrial areas by what marketing might term the Unique Selling Proposition, reflected in an acceptable title (there is a Jewellery Quarter but no promoted Gunmaker's Quarter in Birmingham), with logo, street furniture, re-named public transport

Figure 1.3   From Albert Dock, Liverpool. The regrettable implication of making a secure urban quarter is the severing of selected history from its context

destinations, visitor centres and the rest. As a 'district', such as the Harbour District of Baltimore, the model scheme upon which many UK projects were based, the idea of a public–private regeneration partnership originated in the US. Heritage interpretation played a key role in such tourist-led regeneration (see Law, 1992). In Britain the idea was established in such areas as Manchester's Castlefields (promoted as Britain's first urban heritage park) and Chinatown. Another early designation was Glasgow's Merchant City, although its rival Edinburgh, like many other British towns, already had conserved epitome zones such as the New Town quietly functioning as interpreted visitor attractions.

The 'quartering' of the UK's cities and towns continues apace, with some evident advantages for the spread of visitor spend, and for raising the profile, and possibly the business confidence, of previously neglected areas (see Goodey, 1993). The reader might wish to visit the Ancoats district (surely a quarter in waiting) north of Manchester's city centre to see whether the re-branding of this sad hearth of the industrial revolution has progressed, or if its proposal as a World Heritage site has meant much.

From being a jostling pattern of streets where traffic, pedestrian and even animals moved, towns and cities are becoming a mosaic of bounded private retail and branded public spaces, linked by pedestrian ways, ringed by traffic. The gradual plot by plot evolution of townscape is replaced by major schemes and new designations, history is served up as photographic (or in the case of one Stoke example, artefact) decoration to fast-food outlets.

In this new urban scene partially planned and integrated interpretation is likely to turn up in all sorts of places, from the 'rooting powder' of an illustrative historic plan in a new shopping centre, to the paid access to a church tower for the bird's eye view, from the museum exhibition on a local company to the use of an historic vehicle or costume by that company. Public art, Britain in Bloom, a voluntary display for funds or a local guide may all bring local history into the high street.

What do we want to know about towns?

The heritage thus presented is likely to be short on theory or explicit values, and strong on character, economically brief, but criminally and militarily rich. And with the fragmentation of the urban fabric into quarters and centres, it is fair to admit that we know less and less about the overall form and function of urban places.

Living close to a complex web of private investments and public services, the former urban resident was, at least, casually aware of the holes in the road that revealed service runs, the complexity of public transport provision and the servicing of shops and offices. With so few central city residents, these activities take place in a 'town centre managed' world that is safeguarded for shoppers, rather than regarded by residents. Most people want to know the availability of retail outlets, but are little concerned by the presence of services or of the infrastructure of urban places as long as they appear to function. There is an increasing knowledge gap between the use of towns and cities, and any understanding as to how they have evolved.

Probably the best way to understand the fundamentals of urbanism is by examining the location, form and purpose of isolated, small settlements. Anyone who has seen the twelfth-century Sinagua cliff dwelling, Montezuma's Castle National Monument in Arizona, and has been guided by exemplary US National Park Service interpretive practice, will have the roots of urban living. In the UK, urban morphology and growth are best sensed in villages or small towns where the visual language of building age and type remain coherent (see Goodey, 1992; also RUDI) and where walk or trail leaflet tells the story that is submerged in larger centres.

Enjoying, and possibly understanding, the city has always involved marvelling at landmark structures (recently Bilbao's Guggenheim and the Millennium Dome). The biggest marvel was, before air travel miniaturised plans, a matter of urban scale and morphology (as introduction, see Aston and Bond, 1976). Mounds, towers, viewpoint sites, belvederes and wall walks all provided, and still provide, an essential interpretive opportunity overlooking, but often overlooked. In the case of Edinburgh, The Outlook Tower, still a visitor attraction adjacent to the castle, houses a camera obscura, a facility that Patrick Geddes promoted in his advocacy of urban involvement.

While the need to understand urban growth and scale may still exist for some, especially within the educational curriculum, the negative public attitude towards plans, planning and planners has reduced interest in interpretation that encourages an evolutionary approach to urban places through maps, plans and models, though computer animation and simulation offer largely unexplored possibilities in this area. In a 1999 survey of interpretive professionals, urban interpretation was seen as the most poorly developed aspect of the field.

Saving and presenting a commonplace that is no longer accessible has been a developing theme in both conservation and interpretation. In 1982 the National Trust for Scotland purchased 145 Buccleuch Street, Glasgow as an early twentieth-century example of a tenement (see Robinson and Ritchie, 1990). The English National Trust, English Heritage and local authorities have all invested in what might formerly be seen as 'ordinary' homes for presentation to new generations to whom the conditions and contents are far from ordinary.

New buildings deserve as much explanation as old. The city of Columbus, Indiana, has prided itself on the assemblage of works by contemporary architects and interprets within the frame of their work (see van Heeswijk, 2002, for an excellent guide).

Today, two parallel strands of interest in towns and cities persist. There is a latent interest in understanding the temporal and spatial aspects of urban change, matters glimpsed in daily life but clearly no longer as learned in school texts. More evident is a desire to understand the who and how of urban living through the

Figure 1.4   Gas Street Basin, Birmingham. Only the barges hold together the traditions of this Birmingham quarter

lives of former and present urban residents, a theme explored through the famous in Nottingham Castle's city presentation, and through a more accessible mixed-media exhibition in Croydon in the 1990s.

As with all interpretation, the contact point is the participant's own life experience together with the known areas of popular enquiry – the biggest, the fattest, the oldest, the most heinous, the dirtiest . . . sewers and secret sub-service runs are a good place to start the story of above ground! (Wurman, 1971 and 1972, represents an under-utilised resource here).

How are towns interpreted?

The most obvious, and available, form of interpretation (aside from the buildings and places themselves), is signage. Since the 1960s two unrelated systems of urban signage have developed, the one provided for drivers, the other, belatedly, for pedestrians. Never the twain shall meet, and woe betide the pedestrian who believes that traffic signage provides a convenient route to a goal.

In Britain, pedestrian signage systems have a reputation for heavy-handed statement of the obvious. The majority are now in a stock nineteenth-century industrial form, gold on black (or local option 'heritage' colours), and require that each post is encircled with an array of heritage and service directions. As with so many aspects of hard landscaping in public places (especially the ubiquitous CCTV cameras) the initiative has been captured by manufacturers, with less interest in designs and texts that reflect local identity of interests. As Bateson (1999) illustrates in the context of London's Bankside, it is possible to break out of the traditional signed framework.

In many key cities the next most obvious sign of interpretation is the continual passage of decapitated double-decker buses with either a headset or human text available to passengers. The quality of the interpretation often depends on the exigencies of traffic management within the town or city, as do the items chosen for interpretation. The proposed image of Oxford changed fundamentally in 1999 when a radical traffic-management scheme routed all buses along several back-dominated peripheral streets. In terms of energy consumption this interpretive technique should be low on national priorities, but interpretation has never been subject to such analysis and visitors often expect such a tour to be available. The advantage is often a wider exploration than would be achieved on foot.

On foot, the standard repertoire should be the hand-held map or trail leaflet, linked to key interpreted sites and facilities. Although there is usually no shortage of such leaflets or booklets available in the Tourist Information Centre, I very seldom see either local leaflets or standard published guides in use except in set-piece buildings, although the increasingly popular axonometric, illustrated map in text or brochure helps (as in the 'Citimap' series, for example in Brixton, London). Some towns may include informative waymarks in support of their published trails, such markers frequently have to obey planning and other regulations which lead

Figure 1.5 Urban evolution. The Millennium Dome under construction in 1998. The dereliction in the foreground is forgotten

to obscure locations. While published trails perhaps have a life of five years, markers can survive much longer and a frustrating mismatch between published and on site interpretation may result.

Many visitors will arrive with their own coach guide. Here, the form and quality of a walking tour is very much geared to the other attractions of the day and may only allow time for two or three unmissable attractions, or at least features that have been claimed as essential in the tour literature. The advantage is often the use of visitors' native language, the disadvantage is the suspect information on offer. Local, badged, guides offer a more effective service but their themes and stories are, inevitably, generalised and may rely heavily on embedded local myths with more emphasis on characters and traditions than on buildings or, especially, recent events.

In addition there is much casual interpretation in towns, often associated with the food and drink industries – Oxford pubs where Tolkien drank, or where *Inspector Morse* was filmed. Every filming leaves behind an array of signed photographs that sets in train the dominance of a mythical, over the original, place.

Established heritage cities and towns, and especially those areas that have been brought into the visitor market place in the past fifteen years, are likely to reflect an attempt at coordination in signage, information provision and on-site interpretation. Many more urban places suggest spasmodic interest in interpretation tuned to bursts of capital funding and officer enthusiasm. This leads to false promise, where the presence of a panel advertising neighbouring attractions or continuity is no longer linked to any system of provision. Fragmentation and discontinuity are the major frustrations of urban interpretation.

The growth of organisations of historic towns (notably the English Historic Towns Forum, 1994 and 1999) has allowed the interpretive message to be promoted and integrated with a wider range of management and conservation issues. The parallel growth of Town Centre Management as a sub-profession does not seem to have incorporated interpretive ideas.

Urban museums and study centres

To suggest that museums or visitor centres may be the most effective means of interpreting an urban area is unreasonable. Much of what is open to interpretation in an urban area is the built context itself, with spaces and façades, if not the interiors of buildings, available free to public view. There is seldom the sensitivity to ecology or conserved rarity that led, quite sensibly, to the establishment of visitor centres in natural sites.

An exception, which was developed from this very rationale, was the Oxford Experience, where Oxford's colleges contributed through the University to the establishment of a compact presentation of the city's, but largely the university's, history so as to reduce the pressure of visitors on college precincts which needed conservation as places of learning. In this role it has only been partially successful as many visitors quite properly want an experience of what goes on behind closed doors.

On a world scale many cities, both great and new, have seen a museum dedicated to their evolution, design and history, as an essential contribution to civic awareness. The Museum of London is one successful example in England, though it singularly fails to draw its visitors onwards to some comprehension of the design intentions behind the modernist complexity of the Barbican in which it is located. Amsterdam's city museum occupies a cunningly integrated sequence of existing buildings and through its use of original artefacts in association with models and architectural illustration is an interpretive success; the Bath building museum adopts a similar approach (reviewed by Goodey, 1993a). The Chester Heritage Centre, product of 1975 innovation, managed to link a focus to external trails.

There are clearly many elements of urban evolution that must be presented within a controlled, secure and well interpreted context – archaeological remains, art works, textiles and documents for example, and here the museum, or heritage centre, a more participatory environment located so as to provide a focus for visitor attention, scores well. Most local museums include some elements of urban history, while an increasing number draw on the cultural and collecting interests of the urban population, often revealing hidden interests and groups within the community (Digger, 1995). What museums should not do is pre-empt the visitors' encounter with the urban place. All too often a well-organised collection explaining the evolution of place fails totally to provide the maps, literature or guidance that allow users to reconnect with the world outside.

As established elements in heritage provision, museums must play a significant role in interpreting their local communities, and many do so. Too often, however, their 'outreach' stops at educational and in-house programmes and fails to connect with residents and users of their urban hosts.

In the 1970s, environmental education interests developed Urban Studies Centres as resource bases for educational exploration. Two or three dozen survived that decade into the 1980s, but curriculum restriction and cuts in educational funding closed most of them. In many ways they offered the ideal context for exploring the background to a town or city, with the advantage that interpretive materials focused on social data, oral histories and other people – rather than buildings – were available. Recent discussion with regard to the conclusions of the Urban Task Force may see their revival. City farms, a product of the same period, seem to have fared rather better.

Any conserved buildings can, of course, be more than a time capsule. In the 1980s the National Trust was persuaded, through local community pressure, to abandon plans for the residential conversion of Sutton House in Hackney in favour of a locally managed and inspired resource and cultural space where weddings and salsa concerts cohabit with an accessible local history centre (Lambert, 1999). Millennium and Heritage Lottery funding criteria have both advocated community responsive facilities based on heritage resources, and English Heritage has gradually moved to a community-based policy. We should be seeing a flush of essentially novel projects where community derived activities and uses, including local interpretation, dominate over the conserved fabric. Only confirmation of revenue budgets and the economic viability of community-based heritage will, however, ensure their survival.

Urban trails and walks

The logic of marked paths and trails is indisputable. Link a sequence of existing and available walking paths, key locations and structures around a theme, ensure that waymarks or signs are interconnected, produce a guidance leaflet, publicise and maintain the route, and long-distance walkers and stroll dippers will come. That, at least, is the idea.

A Thames Path was first suggested in the 1930s, a trail declared by the River Thames Society and Ramblers' Association in 1989, and a 180-mile path between the source in Gloucestershire and the Thames Barrier at Woolwich was inaugurated in 1996 (Rowe, 1999). But in its most used portion, overlapping with a waymarked Jubilee walkway south of the river in central London, the experience

Figure 1.6 Clerkenwell historic trail. A good waymarked urban trail on the northern edge of the City of London: photographed on opening day. How is it holding up?

is increasingly chaotic. Development opportunities and the push for river frontage have twisted the path in all directions and through cavernous environments that hold little attraction to the determined, or casual, user.

The potential of London for self-guided or waymarked trails is considerable and a diligent search through architectural and topographic sources would reveal many. Few visitors have access to such texts, and commercial publishers or tourist interests see little advantage in promoting essentially free facilities, especially when the use of any route is likely to lead to complaints that at least suggest diversions and hazards, and may lead to personal insecurity.

This author, a collector of trails since the 1970s (see Goodey, 1974), has a dogged interest in the design and pursuit of such routes, but in some twenty-five years walking them in Europe and the Americas I have yet to find a published trail route that correctly links with waymarks, or offers precisely what is implied by the text. Though this does not mean that I have given up on this cheap, and potentially effective method of urban interpretation, it does mean that I now recognise the limitations.

There are limits in what text can be included in terms of technical detail, the complexity of access and location, dates and cross references to other sites. There are limits, too, on any expectation that features on the route will remain as they seem, for even if conserved, access opportunities can change. Within a short period aspects of the route may become unrecognisable, and new elements deserving of interpretation appear. Outlets for the booklet are likely to change, revisions will take longer than expected and a waymarked trail will be stranded without a text. Add to this the fact that far more people are likely to collect the leaflet than use the trail, and far more people are likely to encounter random waymarked sites without having the leaflet, and this most basic of interpretive strategies begins to have problems. As with most interpretation, the answer is not in the initial research, design or capital investment, but in the maintenance of text and route, its regular monitoring for change, and integrated promotion with the range of local interpretive opportunities.

Trails are, however, a very effective community development device, a means of recording, structuring and presenting a community as it wishes to be seen. Thus far it is usually the established British educated middle class that has promoted its world in trails – architecture and history the key elements of that world. But there are other worlds. A recent visit to Ipswich revealed a set of local historic trails, but also one devoted to public art, featuring a dedication to the cartoonist Giles, and a Women's History Trail which, as so often, uncovered a largely hidden world. In the 1970s the, then new, University of Salford introduced its students to the area through an essentially social trail the like of which has not been seen since, though the Salford example remains in use. Currently, financial support seems to be with the natural environment, a fruitless search for any Milton Keynes building trail revealed several popular park trails. Newham's Central Park Tree Trail replaces botanical labels with an accessible and concise introduction to twenty-five species.

Urban markers

Although there has been considerable investment in the impedimenta and staffing of formal urban interpretation, informal assessment suggests that many more visitors are touched by urban markers than by the structured presentation of urban history. Some such markers are integral to historic structures – decoration, date stones, relic advertising and conserved images – while the contributions of the arts community have a signal impact (see Flemming and von Tscharner, 1987).

The vast majority of urban interpretation is not done by interpreters. My own working definition of interpretation is a process that adds value to the experience of place. In that regard the street performer and artist, whose work is frequently more evident and engaging than that of the interpreter, are very much part of the same team. Heritage? Interpretation? Culture? . . . visit the Vietnam Veterans' Memorial in Washington, DC administered by the US National Park Service and consider whose messages are being conveyed to whom.

Elsewhere, I have explored some aspects of public art in place making and interpretation (Goodey, 1994a) and here it is impossible to outline the range of intentions, contexts and products involved. One example must suffice.

An exhibition such as the figurative sculpture display mounted in Stafford's Victoria Park in 1998 (Goodey, 1994b) underlined a number of key roles for public art as community interpretation, although only one image, that of W.G. Grace (founder of the English Bowling Association in 1903), had any direct relationship

Figure 1.7   The open-topped bus. An integral element in future public transport, or so it seems from this appearance in the City of London's Lord Mayor's Procession, 1998

Figure 1.8   Interpretive sculpture, Stafford. W.G. Grace surveys the Victoria Park bowling greens, an element in the town's sculptural experiment, 1998

with the site, being situated next to the bowling green. The sculptures were part of a programme of four exhibitions leading to 2000 (Edwards, 1998), they were created by local students, sponsored by both local authority and industry, involved passers-by in selection, and *were* maintained as part of a positive public space. By late 1999 it was reported that local authority staff changes had, however, stranded this exemplary scheme.

Urban interpretation seldom admits the role of sculpture, decoration and hard landscaping, yet the casual presence of a clearly designed zone of public space can draw many who would not consciously enter an interpretive facility, as evidenced in Newport, South Wales, Birmingham's extensive public zones, or the readily adopted public art of Milton Keynes.

Formally researched and designed interpretation is often too heavy-handed for the dynamic, catch-phrase and instant, urban world. In a truly living urban area – not the brown signed 'Historic Market Town' – the pace of life only allows occasional thoughts as to the past and context. Sculpture, graphic arts and landscape design, like architecture, can achieve casual and sensed reference for people on the move (see Miles, 1997). Castelo's (1999) guide to sculpture and markers in the 1960s' Brazilian capital of Brasilia, complete with satellite coordinates, begins to convey the new language of the extraordinary deserving of attention by the urban visitor.

Innovation in urban interpretation

Urban interpretation is in crisis. Its major techniques have derived from an age where explanation of the past was sufficient to engage a population that linked with pre-war housing, industrial and commercial conditions. A new generation of visitors, both native and immigrant, is now emerging with few, if any, personal links to the dominant forces that shaped our city centres. The historic chain has been broken by the demise of industrial employment and the re-definition of urban centres as themed alternatives to out-of-town shopping centres. Going to town is a very different experience from ten or twenty years ago when patterns of urban interpretation were established.

Interpretative practice never managed to bring the visitor and information to an urban site. The key tools were complex evolutionary displays, contained in museums or centres, or trails that required that the potential user obtain the leaflet from some marketing centre. This latter has proved appropriate for a minority, but most people will only connect to the urban fabric if information is provided in situ.

There is now considerable potential to link immediate local information with the visitor through video points that are being explored as information and participatory elements in the urban system. The recent Exchange Square in Manchester provides immediate public evidence, although the nearby purpose-built urban experience – Urbis – has had less success (see Goodey, 2004). Before advocating their widespread

video in the context of #1

use it is as well, perhaps, to identify at least three, increasingly contrasting, urban interpretive contexts.

First, the historic town centre or character quarter (see Tiesdell *et al.*, 1996 and Bell and Jayne, 2004), or even the 'tourist-historic city' (as defined by Ashworth and Tunbridge in 1990). Here, survival is achieved through the exploitation of a conserved fabric, the incorporation of appropriate retail outlets, functions and events, the use of costume, period sound and a largely traffic-free ambience. This is at least a well-managed (see Meethan, 1997 on York) or even a contrived, but often essential, environment for the generation of employment and income. The range of interpretive provision must remain 'in keeping' with period hardware, first-person presentation, and sufficient historic detail to engage both the knowledgeable and the leisure visitor. There is some innovation here, especially in the management of movement and impacts (see Glasson *et al.*, 1995), but there are limits to the use of electronic sources that may be out of keeping with the prevailing theme.

#2

Second, the living city, the everyday environment that has historical and environmental contexts, but which largely reads as a commonplace world where sufficient is known to allow navigation and goal achieving. In such environments interpretation per se currently finds little place. Vandalism and space constraints often restrict the use of panels or other hardware, while first-person interpretation may look out of place. But such areas are often located at the heart of the historic site, and offer opportunity to consider the past and current nature of urbanism. Given secure and efficient video points and other electronic devices, this is where they will serve best, especially in likely combination with marketing or survey activities. Here is a chance to develop an essentially new area of interpretation, the contemporary and future city (explored further in Goodey, 1999a).

#3

Third, the residential suburbs, and the edge city beyond. Characteristically residents or users have to wait until a first generation has reached retirement when one or more decides to offer a history of their 'pioneer' lives. Only when the first flush of retail enthusiasm has passed will commercial interests dip into local history and context in the search for new interest, but the evolution of electronic facilities associated with retailing and suburban living should hint at the possibilities for on-line interpretation of disparate, non-place, areas. Unless interpretation explores such contexts and media it will be doomed to the reproduction of panels in historic centres (but recently, see Sawyer, 1999; English Heritage, 1999).

Underwriting the urban experience

In moving to the future of urban interpretation, we have to consider the future of the city in public life. A negative perception might suggest that the city core is a left-over relic, used by office workers and shoppers during the day, and by 24-hour city users at night. What is its heritage future?

Figure 1.9 Wor Jackie. Adopted public art, the sculpture to Jackie Milburn, hero of Newcastle United, in the city's centre

It is certainly multi-media, multi-dimensional and experienced in real, virtual and cyber time and space. The revealing exhibition 'Cities on the Move' opened in Vienna in 1997, arrived in London in 1999, and was an attempt to evoke and contain the dynamism of Asian cities as presented by the Dutch architect Rem Koolhaas. As Worsley (1999) notes:

> When it comes to cities, Koolhaas takes a very post-modern approach. Instead of trying, like Le Corbusier and the classic modernists, to stamp order on chaos, he celebrates that chaos. Instead of seeing the city as a series of threats – social, moral, sanitary – to be swept away and replaced with a nice, logical plan and clean rational buildings, Koolhaas realises that the city cannot be constrained, particularly not the dynamic cities of the Far East.

There is an exciting tension in the world of urbanists as to how we intervene in city making and managing processes, and to what end. Koolhaas would not enjoy general support in the UK, where there is a determined political effort to retain traditional cities as places worth being, and creating, in.

There is increased professional interest, too, in urban design, in the spaces between the buildings not just being the leftovers from privatised retail containers (for pioneer interpretation of such spaces, see Taylor, 1979). After a very productive, and re-usable, research enquiry (see especially Comedia, 1999), the Urban Task Force report (1999) identifies four key initiatives likely to be adopted by government and with a direct contribution to urban interpretation.

Figure 1.10 Thoughtful interpretive design, Halifax, Nova Scotia. District markers with interpretive detail on their face, and district logos below, unobtrusive and effective

Design competitions will be promoted to raise public and professional interest in urban change. Urban design and urban management techniques for regeneration will be introduced at all *education* levels. Twelve *architectural resource centres* in major cities will be opened by the end of 2001 with advice facilities and as a forum for debate and for exhibitions. *Demonstration projects* exhibiting good practice in urban design will be endorsed and publicised.

Interpretation in urban areas has developed within urban landscape, design, heritage and tourist management programmes. Seldom has an effective interpretive plan (as explored, for example, in Goodey, 1994, 2003; Carter, 1997) that harnesses even part of the interpretive potential of a town or city been designed or achieved. With the potential for electronic media, and an increasing involvement of stakeholding communities in their futures, the basis for local urban management is likely to shift considerably over the next decade. Within what may emerge as a cultural planning process, it should be possible to raise the visibility of interpretation, linking conservation, the community and education (as attempted in Copeland, 1999) to a level where the successes of the 1970s can be repeated, though with new media and, quite probably, new messages.

Rapid reappraisal of the role of artists and the cultural industries in the image of cities (see Goodey, 2002, for a leading example) is having a major impact on the recovery and generation of urban meaning. Current focused public art plans for the expansion of Milton Keynes city centre involve an artist-designed 'Information Box' which may emerge as both icon and interpretation.

■   ■   ■

References

Ashworth, G.J. and Tunbridge, J.E. (1990) *The Tourist-Historic City*, London: Belhaven

Aston, M. and Bond, J. (1976) *The Landscape of Towns*, London: J.M. Dent

Bateson, K. (1999) ' Signage of the times', *Building Design*, 8 Oct., 18–21

Bell, D. and Jayne, M. eds (2004) *City of Quarters: Urban Villages in the Contemporary City*, London: Ashgate

Buchanan, C.D. (1963) *Traffic in Towns*, Harmondsworth: Penguin with HMSO

Carter, J. ed. (1997) *A Sense of Place: An Interpretive Planning Handbook*, Inverness: Tourism and Environment Initiative, Highlands and Islands Enterprise

Castelo, R. (1999) *Brasilia: Monumentos, Marcos e Esculturas*, Brasilia: Editora Cavaleiro dos Pireneus

Civic Trust (1987) *The Wirksworth Story: New Life for an Old Town*, London: The Wirksworth Project – Civic Trust

—— (1999) *Civic Trust Regeneration Unit*, London: Civic Trust

—— and Centre for Environmental Education (1983) *Up Greenhill and Down Dale: An Interpretive Plan for Wirksworth, Derbyshire*, London/Manchester: CT/CEI

Clay, G. (1973) *Close-up: How to Read the American City*, New York: Praeger

Comedia (1999) *The Richness of Cities: Urban Policy in a New Landscape*, London: Comedia/Demos

Copeland, T. ed. (1999) *Our Street: Learning to See*, London: Royal Fine Art Commission

Digger, J. (1995) 'The People's Show', *Museum Visitor*, 5–11

Edwards, A. ed. (1998) *Park Life: An Exhibition of Figurative Sculpture in Stafford's Victoria Park*, Stafford: Stafford College

English Heritage (1999) *London Suburbs*, London: Merrell Holberton and English Heritage

English Historic Towns Forum (1994) *Getting it Right. A Guide to Visitor Management in Historic Towns*, Bristol: EHTF

—— (1999) *Making the Connections: A Practical Guide to Tourism Management in Historic Towns*, London EHTF/English Tourism Council/English Heritage

Flemming, R.L. and von Tscharner, R. (1987) *Placemakers: Creating Public Art that Tells You Where You Are*, New York: Harcourt, Brace, Janovich

Glasson, J., Godfrey, K. and Goodey, B. (1995) *Towards Visitor Impact Management: Visitor Impacts, Carrying Capacity and Management Response in Europe's Historic Towns and Cities*, Aldershot: Avebury

Goodey, B. (1974) 'Towards new perceptions of the environment: using the town trail', *Bulletin of Environmental Education*, No. 51 (July), 9–16

—— (1975) *Urban Trails*, CCC/DC(75)6, Strasbourg: Committee for Out-of-School Education and Cultural Development, Council of Europe

—— (1992) 'Pubs, plots and parades: the physical character of small towns', *Environmental Interpretation*, Feb.

—— (1993) 'Urban design of central areas . . . and beyond', in R. Hayward and S. McGlynn (eds) *Making Better Places: Urban Design Now*, Oxford: Butterworth Architecture, 53–8

—— (1993a) 'Beauty of Bath', *Town and Country Planning*, April, 93

—— (1994) 'Interpretive planning', in R. Harrison (ed.) *Manual of Heritage Management*, Oxford: Butterworth Heinemann and AIM, 303–11

—— (1994a) 'Art-full places: public art to sell public places', in J.R. Gold and S.K. Ward (eds) *Place Promotion: The Use of Publicity and Public Relations to Sell Towns and Regions*, London: Belhaven, 153–79

—— (1994b) 'Kept up to the mark (Stafford)', *Town and Country Planning*, Dec., 344 (also in *Midlands Landscape Quarterly*, Summer 1994)

—— (1998) 'New Britain, new heritage: the consumption of a Heritage Culture', *International Journal of Heritage Studies*, 4: 3/4, 197–205

—— (1999) 'Mediating the shock of the new: interpreting the evolving city', in D. Uzzell and R. Ballantyne (eds) *Contemporary Issues in Heritage Interpretation: Problems and Prospects*, London: HMSO – National, 133–51

—— (1999a) 'No more market', *Town and Country Planning*, Jan., 30–1

—— (2002) 'The ceramic work of Francisco Brennand in Recife, Brazil', *Glazed Expressions*, No. 45 Autumn, 8–9

—— (2003) 'Interpretive planning in a historic urban context: the case of Porto Seguro, Brazil', *Urban Design International*, 8: 85–94

—— (2004) 'Takes a turn round Manchester's Urbis', *Landscape Research Extra*, No. 34, Jan., 16–17

Hayden, D. (1995) *The Power of Place: Urban Landscapes as Public History*, Cambridge, Mass.: The MIT Press

Kelly, A. and Kelly, M. (2003) *Building Legible Cities: Making the Case*, Bristol: Bristol Cultural Development Partnership (www.bristol2008.com)

Lambert, A. (1999) 'A surprising urban portfolio', *The National Trust Magazine*, 86: Spring

Law, C.M. (1992) 'Urban tourism and its contribution to economic regeneration', *Urban Studies*, 29: 3–4, 597–616

Lynch, K. (1972) *What Time is this Place?*, Cambridge, Mass.: MIT Press

Meethan, K. (1997) 'York: managing the tourist city', *Cities*, 14: 6, 333–42

Miles, M. (1997) *Art, Space and the City: Public Art and Urban Futures*, London: Routledge

Parkin, I., Middleton, P. and Beswick, V. (1989) 'Managing the town and city for visitors and local people', in D. Uzzell (ed.) *Heritage Interpretation: the Visitor Experience*, London: Belhaven, 108–14

Percival, A. (1979) *Understanding our Surroundings: A Manual of Urban Interpretation*, London: Civic Trust

Roberts, M., Marsh, C. and Salter, M. (1993) *Public Art in Private Places: Commercial Benefits and Public Policy*, London: University of Westminster Press

Robinson, P. and Ritchie, W.K. (1990) *The Tenement House*, Edinburgh: The National Trust for Scotland

Rowe, M. (1999) 'Slow motion along the Thames path', *The Independent on Sunday*, 12 Sept., p. 12

RUDI *Resource for Urban Design Information*, web site, www.rudi.herts.ac.uk

Sawyer, M. (1999) *Park and Ride: Adventures in Suburbia*, New York: Little, Brown

Taylor, L. ed. (1979) *Urban Open Spaces*, New York: Cooper-Hewitt Museum/The Smithsonian Institution/Rizzoli International

Tiesdell, S., Oc, T. and Heath, T. (1996) *Revitalizing Historic Urban Quarters*, Oxford: Architectural Press

Urban Task Force (1999) *Towards an Urban Renaissance*, London: Department of Environment, Transport and Regions (summary at www.detr.gov.uk)

van Heeswijk, J. (2002) *Face your World*, Amsterdam: Artino

Ward, C. and Fyson, A. (1973) *Streetwork: The Exploding School*, London: Routledge & Kegan Paul

Westwood, S. and Williams, J. eds (1997) *Imagining Cities: Scripts, Signs, Memory*, London: Routledge

Wood, L. (1996) 'The conservation and management of historic urban space', *International Journal of Heritage Studies*, 1: 2, 111–25

Worsley, G. (1999) 'Far out but not Far East', *Daily Telegraph*, 26 May

Wurman, R.S. (1971) *Making the City Observable*, Cambridge, Mass.: The MIT Press

—— (1972) *Yellow Pages of Learning Resources*, Cambridge, Mass.: The MIT Press

Chapter 2

HIGHLAND INTERPRETIVE STRATEGY PROJECT

Rona Gibb

Introduction

The Highlands and Islands of Scotland have some of the most outstanding landscape, wildlife and cultural heritage in Northern Europe. The area has a rich natural resource, with a rural economy that relies heavily on primary production from fisheries, forestry and agriculture. Much of this is internationally important for landscape and wildlife and significant sections are protected through a range of conservation designations. Add to this the rich cultural and historic aspects and you have a unique destination. Many people living in the area value this and it is the major reason for tourism being the biggest single employer in the area.[1]

Interpretation of the culture, history, people, wildlife, landscape and industry is important in sustaining communities and plays a vital part in the visitor experience of the area. It crosses a wide range of providers from the private, public and voluntary sectors. Good interpretation leads to a better visitor experience, which has benefits for many other sectors of the tourism industry. Interpretation is not the preserve of any one agency and is utilised in many forms by all of the public and private sector agencies within the Highlands. Raising people's awareness, increasing their enjoyment and making sure that this heritage is passed on to future generations are vital to all communities and to the long-term success of tourism. Through *good interpretation* much of this can be achieved, recognising the distinct and special character of the different parts of the Highlands.

An *Interpretive Strategy* offers a method of doing this. By providing a structure for the co-ordination and implementation of interpretation, relevant agencies can work together, in partnership, leading to a commitment by them to the process and to provide resources where joint working is appropriate.

The 'Highlands & Islands Single Programming Document' – the planning document for the ERDF (European Regional Development Fund) Objective One Programme (1994–99) recognises that, 'the natural environment and traditional culture underpins the tourism resource of the region and contributes to the quality of life and thus the stability of the communities'. It seeks to

> promote initiatives which maintain and *interpret* the natural and cultural heritage: to increase the geographical availability of *heritage interpretation facilities*: to raise public understanding of the natural and cultural heritage and to contribute to increased visitor numbers, length of stay and season.

The Project

The Highland Interpretive Strategy Project (HISP) was in existence from 1994 to 2001 and was jointly funded by the Highland Council (HC), Highlands and Islands Enterprise (HIE), Scottish Natural Heritage (SNH) and has had ERDF Objective 1 funding under the Highlands & Islands Partnership Programme. The Highlands of Scotland Tourist Board (HOST) and the Scottish Tourist Board (STB) are non-funding partners.

The Project was established to deliver the objectives within the 'Interpretive Strategy for the Highland Area of Scotland' that was adopted by the then Highland Regional Council in 1994. There were three phases of the Project. The first phase worked extensively with local communities on locally targeted *Local Interpretive Plans* (LIPs) with the remit for the second and third phases being changed to concentrate on larger strategic area plans that bridge the gap between the local plans and the overall strategy. This strategic approach aimed to give greater co-ordination and direction to future interpretive provision.

Interpretive Strategy
for
The Highland Area of Scotland
↓
Area Frameworks for Interpretation
(8 geographic areas of the Highland Council area)
↓
Local Interpretive Plans
(18 completed to date)

The Project focused on promoting good practice in interpretation; promoting proper appraisal and planning of interpretation; working with local communities, public agencies and commercial interests throughout the Highlands to continue to encourage and support the production of LIPs and the development of *Area Frameworks for Interpretation* (AFIs).

The key objectives[2] of the Project are:

* to promote the understanding, appreciation and enjoyment of the natural and man made resources of the Highlands, including not only the physical fabric of the area but also the social, cultural and historic heritage of the area;

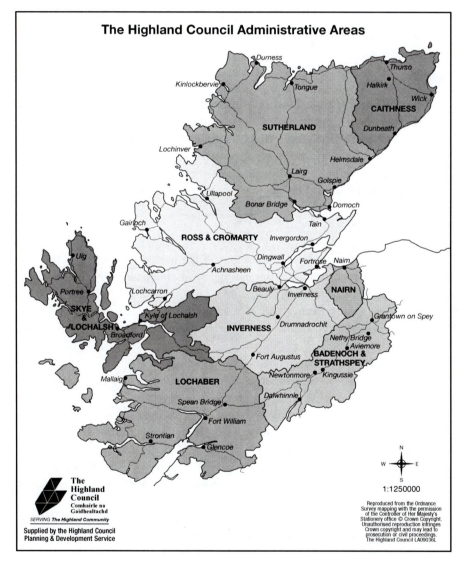

Figure 2.1   The Highland Council administrative areas (with permission from the Highland Council)

- to promote care and regard for the area's heritage among all visitors, residents and land managers;
- to promote 'good practice' in the planning, provision operation and maintenance of interpretive facilities;
- to further the social and economic aspects of community development by establishing a stronger linkage between communities and their heritage resources;
- to encourage community involvement in the planning and implementation of interpretive projects;
- to promote effective partnerships between those responsible for the planning and provision of heritage interpretation in the Highlands.

Phase I

The Project Officer for Phase I was Bill Taylor on secondment from Scottish Natural Heritage. This phase concentrated on the development of LIPs. These were developed on a community basis and reflect the individual character and development objectives of each locality particularly for tourist development and for the protection of heritage resources. Local communities, groups and associations helped in the development of these LIPs in relation to their knowledge about *their local heritage.*

The LIPs involved:[3]

- the preparation of a detailed inventory of the heritage resources of the area. This is developed primarily through the local community (by the use the of Planning for Real process);
- developing strong themes that will form an identifiable image that can be used to promote the area and provide links between the various elements of interpretation;
- assessing the visitor characteristics for the area;
- stating what the wider provision of interpretation is to achieve and identifying the main objectives of any interpretive provision;
- reviewing the current provision against these themes;
- identifying those sites that can support interpretive facilities and also those that should not be interpreted;
- identifying the type and scale of provision that will be appropriate and proposing locations for the new developments or for the upgrading of existing facilities;
- drawing up a programme of implementation and seeking funding assistance;
- monitoring the success of the interpretation.

During this phase there were eighteen LIPs developed or assisted through the Project. The implementation of these LIPs, to date, has been varied.

The LIP for Abernethy, near Aviemore, provides the best example of the process. Following the completion of the LIP the community employed a part-time Project Officer to take the findings of the LIP forward. Elspeth Grant, who had co-ordinated the development of the LIP, took on this role and through her determination and that of the community secured £50,000 Rural Challenge Funding.

This has been used, along with assistance from the Council and other agencies to develop a path network, leaflet and visitor facility. The 'Explore Abernethy' room is within the community centre and is aimed at local residents and school children as well as visitors, providing information on what is on, displays and exhibits and a community corner which has reference books and space for future Internet access points. The interest within the community has grown and further developments are planned linking and complementing their facility to existing path networks and facilities. This is being achieved with the help of various agencies.

A Sense of Place

Working with the *Tourism and Environment Initiative* (TEI)[4] and others, the Project assisted in the production of a handbook called *A Sense of Place – an Interpretive Planning Handbook*. The aim of this handbook is to guide groups from the planning to development and evaluation stages of interpretation. This was seen as a worthwhile tool to assist communities, individuals and agency officials through the planning process.

> Producing interpretation which balances the needs of the visitors who will use it, the conservation of the place which is its subject, the desires of those who produce it, and the interests of those who will live with it, is not a simple matter. If interpretation is to be really effective, it needs to be planned with both sensitivity and creativity. This handbook is an introduction to doing that . . . Within Scotland, and particularly in the Highlands and Islands, there are many projects which aim to present local heritage to visitors. The examples and case studies included in the book reflect this, but they are relevant to projects anywhere in the world.[5]

This handbook is widely regarded as an example of 'good practice' and is extensively used in the UK and abroad, by countryside and tourism staff and by individuals and community groups who wish to take work forward themselves. It was awarded an Interpret Britain Commendation in 1999.

Phases II and III

These phases of the Project had a different emphasis from the First phase. There was still the promotion of 'good practice' and encouragement for the implementation of the existing LIPs as well as the production of new LIPs. However the main emphasis was now to develop eight strategic AFIs using the old District

Council boundaries within the Highland Council area. These bridged the gap between the overall Interpretive Strategy and the LIPs.

The purpose of the AFIs was to ensure that the objectives of the Strategy were achieved; that the full interpretive potential of the Highlands was recognised and utilised; and that unnecessary duplication of facilities was avoided. The development of AFIs effectively guided the use of resources (Highland Council, the Enterprise Companies and Scottish Natural Heritage are the main funding sources for interpretive provision in the area) and opportunities in relation to agency policies and procedures. They gave broad guidance regarding the location of interpretive facilities and services, but retained flexibility in order to accommodate opportunism, particularly where private sector developments were concerned. The development of networks and linkages between communities and agencies was a vital part of the development of the AFIs.

The AFIs were designed to:

- Identify the main themes for the area. It should identify the principal interpretive resources to be found in the area and should seek to develop a consensus among the agencies as to the key issues to be addressed through interpretation.
- Identify the 'gap' areas and topics for interpretation.
- Help the agencies (Local Enterprise Companies, Highland Council, SNH, etc.) better determine grant provision – a more planned and structured basis. This will aid the securing of support from ERDF or other European funding who support the development of interpretive facilities where a 'need is demonstrated through *local strategies*'.
- Provide guidance to the agencies involved with respect to new developments and relate this to existing agency management structures.
- Promote linkages and networking between attractions, sites etc.
- Link with the existing Local Interpretive Plans (LIPs), Local Plans (HC Planning and Development Department), Tourism Action Plans (HOST) and other relevant strategic documents – site-specific or subject-based plans.
- Promote interpretive planning as a fundamental aspect of any heritage development. The AFI will follow the principles contained within the Highland Interpretive Strategy, in terms of good practice in planning and in the design and development of quality interpretive facilities.

There was an AFI developed for each of the eight geographical areas of Highland Council, e.g. Sutherland, Nairn. They not only formed a framework to which the agencies could work, but encouraged the networking and integration of interpretive facilities *within* each of the areas as well as *between* each of the areas in a pan-Highland set-up.

This aimed to promote better continuity, linkages and a less confusing overall picture for the visitor to the Highland area. The AFIs aided planners and developers to target their product more precisely and encourage a planned approach to their interpretation.

The process for producing the Framework in each area varied, adapting to local circumstances. This was seen as a strength of the process and ensured that a rigidly applied procedure was avoided, with every effort being made to ensure the ultimate success of the process and the development of a rational approach to the future provision of heritage interpretation in the Highlands

The inventory

To enable the process of developing the AFIs to progress it was felt that an *inventory* of all existing interpretation was required. If we do not know what we have now, how can we plan for the future? This was the first time that such an exercise had been carried out in Scotland and was an exciting development, that kept the Highlands at the forefront of interpretive planning. The process has since been refined and used in several areas of the UK, most significantly by the National Trust for Scotland which undertook a complete review of all their sites.

The inventory provided, for the first time, a clear picture of the interpretive provision in the Highland Council area. As with other areas of the UK the 'perception' of what interpretation is available has always been a problem with no real way of quantifying what media and topics were being used and addressed and, more importantly, what the standard of the interpretation is. Much of the information has relied on individuals' knowledge of their local working area.

The quality of interpretation

The quality of the interpretation was another vital part of the data gathering process. An integral function of the AFIs was to raise standards in interpretation and to recommend a minimum standard below which funding should not be given to projects. The inventory data showed a huge disparity between the different ends of the scale and gave a much clearer indication as to the priority areas, showing that complacency is not a luxury that can be afforded by anyone involved in interpretation in the Highlands. Much of the interpretation was considerably older than five years and time (and weather) had taken its toll.

Qualitative research in this inventory highlighted the major problems of refurbishment and replacement. Most agencies and organisations involved in funding interpretation have, regularly and enthusiastically, given funding for new provision over many years. This has perpetuated the 'scent marking by various bodies' but it also has current implications as to the age and state of the stock.

Many visitor centres, museums, panels, leaflets, etc. need attention. If repeat visits and new custom are to be the goals then regular updating and replacement of interpretation, print and exhibits is an essential factor of the planning process. The agencies must now look to address this issue in a positive manner. The continuing trend to only fund new developments is constantly stretching the economically tight situation that the facilities find themselves in. The capacity for this new product needs to be analysed and the refurbishment of many sites addressed.

Priority in the *National Strategy for Tourism in Scotland* is given to improving existing facilities rather than new visitor attractions and suggests that staged investment be investigated. This would give a percentage of the overall funding in year one and some capital held back to, maybe, year three to reflect the need to 'freshen' interpretive facilities to secure repeat visitors and attract new business. The Visitor Attraction Review undertaken by Scottish Enterprise, Scottish Tourist Board and Highlands & Islands Enterprise confirmed this view and that of the staged payments.

The Highland Interpretive Strategy Project achieved many things over its life span, from the community aspects of the LIPs to the co-ordinated approach of the strategic AFIs.

Interpretation, of whatever kind, continues to be a vital part of the jigsaw that makes up the 'experience in the Highlands'. The planned approach to interpretation that the Project was so successful in promoting, has continued to influence planning across the Highlands. With the continued support of the agencies involved, and the enthusiasm and support of many communities, it is hoped that this will ensure that the quality of both the interpretation and the visitor experience is greatly enhanced.

Notes

1   The Scottish Tourist Board statistics for 1997/8 show that 13.6 per cent of all employment in the Highlands is tourism related (10,247 jobs). The Highlands account for 18.5 per cent of the value of UK-based tourism to Scottish destinations and 14 per cent of the value of overseas tourism to Scottish destinations

2   From 'An Interpretive Strategy for the Highland Area of Scotland', 1994, revised 1997

3   From HISP 'Report of Activity – Phase 1' Bill Taylor, Project Officer 1995–97

4   The Tourism and Environment Initiative is a Scotland-wide initiative by several agencies. Their mission is: 'To bring long-term business and environmental benefits to the Scottish tourism industry through encouraging sustainable use of our world-class natural and built heritage'

5   *A Sense of Place – An Interpretive Planning Handbook*, Tourism and Environment Initiative, 1997, www.scotinterpnet.org.uk – full download

Chapter 3

LIVE INTERPRETATION

Andrew Robertshaw

In 1895 H. G. Wells published *The Time Machine* a fictional account of time travel. The book remains a classic of the time travel genre. It is not difficult to see its appeal and large numbers of us have considered what it would be like to have the opportunity to travel in time, possibly into the future, but particularly into the past. Many young people have their interest in history awakened not in a classroom, but by reading novels in which the key figure is able to travel back in time. So far the scientific reality of time travel has eluded us, but it has not prevented some people from claiming that it is almost possible to achieve this goal without technology. This is what Jay Anderson asserted in *Time Machines* (Anderson 1984). What he described was not the blue-print for travel in the fourth dimension, but 'living history' an interpretative method familiar to him from museums, such as Colonial Williamsburg and Plimoth Plantation in the US, in which costumed performers recreate incidents or activities from the past.

During the past few years similar techniques have also become common at British museums, galleries and historic sites. Institutions such as the Historic Royal Palaces, The Science Museum, London Transport Museum, The National Railway Museum in York and Llancaiach Fawr House in Wales all now use costumed performers as interpreters on a daily basis. A glance at the massive programme of events staged by the Special Events Department of English Heritage featuring living history displays, battles and re-enactments is sufficient to convince even sceptics that this new method, not found in Britain before 1970, has become a significant interpretative technique.

The question remains what is 'live interpretation'? Confusingly, in Britain, the term 'living history' has been applied to battle re-enactment, steam rallies, morris dancing and poetry recitals. Raphael Samuel has used the term to describe activities ranging from the Jorvik dark ride to 'the Art Deco revival pioneered by the avant-garde boutique Biba' (Samuel 1994: 194). In fact, the term 'living history' was first used by the United States National Park Service in the 1970 publication 'Keep it Alive! Tips on Living History' (Kennon 1970). Ironically this term was already being used by the American Psychiatric Association to describe a form of reminiscence therapy.

Initially 'living history' meant using performers wearing appropriate clothing to simulate life in an earlier time. The term was distinct from other interpretative methods used in museums, galleries and historic sites. Since that time 'living history' has been applied so freely in the UK that it is now almost meaningless. Otherwise knowledgeable curators, authors and participants talk about 'role-play', 'first-person interpretation', 'theatre in education', 're-enacting' and 'living history' without ever making clear the boundaries between these terms and frequently without being aware of the differences between the methods described. For the purpose of this chapter I propose to define 'live interpretation' as being any presentation using people, usually costumed, whether in an historical environment or not, which aims to place artefacts, places or events in context against the background of the human environment of the past. The interpretation must be based on historical facts, have an educational intent and rely upon sound performance/presentational skills. Under this umbrella term we can encompass first- and third-person interpretation, some forms of drama and theatre in education, costumed guiding and craft demonstration. Essentially any project to be defined as live interpretation requires a balance of four elements – historical content, educational intent, presentation skills and interaction with visitors. Pure drama is obviously high on presentational skills, but might not be educational or historical and might have little interaction with the public. Battle re-enactment is frequently strong on some aspects of presentation (drill and weapons handling), but is often historically weak, without education intent and discourages public interaction.

The first use of the technique now known as live interpretation took place in Europe, not America, just over 100 years ago. Artur Hazelius (1833–1901) the pioneer of the open-air museum, founded Skansen the Museum of Scandinavian Folklore in Stockholm in 1873. Despite the popularity of the museum, he felt that something was lacking; essentially, he had created an architectural park devoid of human context. In 1898 he began to bring in musicians and crafts people to bring the site to life. Initially those involved were recreating the customs and activities of their own experience, but later this became the recreation of past activities and ways of life. This advance in interpretation was largely ignored in Europe. By 1974, there were 314 open-air museums in 21 European countries, but live interpretation found a limited role in the interpretative repertoire of these sites.

It was in the US that the approach received a wholehearted welcome and in the US and Canada sites using 'living history' have a long and successful history of co-existence with formal museums. By and large, in comparison with the US, the use of live interpretation in Britain lacks both the status and methodology it has achieved on the other side of the Atlantic. Many museum professionals remain sceptical about, or even hostile towards most forms of live interpretation. One reason for this situation is the lack of a common vocabulary to describe the various techniques that go to make up live interpretation. In the US the umbrella organisations such as the Association for Living Historical Farms and Agricultural Museums (ALHFAM) and the International Museum Theatre Alliance (IMTAL) have been instrumental in establishing a philosophy, terminology and methodology for, what they call, living history. Until recently this framework has been largely absent in the UK and the many weaknesses and inconsistencies apparent in live interpretation projects in Britain can be traced to the lack of any common clear philosophical framework.

This situation is made worse by low standards of presentation and historical accuracy common to battle re-enactment, the first experience most people have of 'living history'. Since 1968, when Brigadier Peter Young established the Sealed Knot, the number and variety of battle re-enactors has exploded. Hardly a summer weekend goes by without a mock battle, skirmish, siege or historical camp being organised by enthusiastic groups of volunteers somewhere in Britain. In 2004 there were over 600 re-enactment groups listed in the British journal *Call to Arms*, an increase of more than 150 since the start of the twenty-first century. Although entertaining, most of these re-enactments are hampered by the simple fact that the participants are indulging in a hobby, giving up time and spending their own money to enjoy themselves. Many offer no more than a nodding acknowledgement of the presence of the public and some simply ignore them completely. If response from the public is mixed, historians are almost universal in condemnation of this 'historical hooliganism on Bank Holiday weekends' (Hewison 1987: 43). This attitude served to reinforce the view among professional interpreters that battle re-enactment might be entertainment, but it is not a form of interpretation suitable for museums and galleries. In the US battle re-enactors became known as 'Farbs' among museum professionals. This was supposedly based on the curator's initial response to mock battles of 'Far be it from me to comment, but . . . !'.

It was from this inauspicious beginning that a small group of British battle re-enactors began to experiment with a technique that would develop into live interpretation. The first recognisable 'living history' event was held at Doddington Hall, Lincolnshire, in 1976. Charles Kightly, a leading member of the English Civil War Society (a battle re-enactment group), was given the opportunity to people the house and estate as it may have been in the 1640s. Although he was aware of Colonial Williamsburg, and other US projects, he used the term 'practical history' to describe these activities. Following the popularity of Doddington with the re-enactors and public, this was repeated in 1977 and a more ambitious event was run at Kentwell Hall, Suffolk, in the same summer. This set off a succession of similar events arranged by members of the English Civil War Society and others. Within two years these enthusiasts began to use the term 'living history' for various military/domestic events in castles and fields all over Britain and the 'authentic campsite' began to be a feature of most battle re-enactments. For many re-enactors the repetitive nature of mock battles and the emphasis on male roles has resulted in the development of a large number of 'living historians' involved in craft and other skills-based demonstrations. These volunteers have shown that public involvement in history can be beneficial and the standard of historical research and presentation is very high in a minority of groups. If this development was popular with some of the more committed and enthusiastic members, other battle re-enactors sought to restrict 'authenticity' in case it spoilt the battles.

Perhaps influenced by this lack of historical accuracy in such battle re-enactments many British museum professionals in the 1970s, especially open air museums directors, were still convinced that 'living history' was not appropriate for their sites, although many admitted that North Americans did well with the technique. As a result, when, in 1980, an American commentator G. Ellis Burcaw reported on European open air museums he announced: 'On the living history continuum, history on the Continent is dead; beautifully embalmed, but dead. The farmhouses are empty husks of peasant culture, collected as curiosities not as settings for the explication of social history' (Burcaw 1980). However, even when this was published the situation in Britain had begun to change. The idea of 'interpretation' had arrived and museums began to establish new departments to translate the work of curators into public exhibitions and displays. One result of this came in the early 1980s when, possibly encouraged by example of the very best of British Living History, sites gradually began to apply American Living History ideas to interpretation on a full time basis. Among the early examples of this process were Littlecote House in Wiltshire, where Mark Wallis ran a team of actors and interpreters from 1987–89, and Wigan Pier in the Midlands. At this innovative site Peter Lewis employed a small team of actors who used a mixture of scripts and improvisation to role-play a variety of characters in settings appropriate to the year 1900. Here 'heritage with a difference' as it was called offered performers who were 'trained to record authentically the sight, sense, smell and feel of the past' (Leaflet, 'The Way We Were', Wigan Pier 1988). This was, perhaps, the first example of full-time, first-person interpretation in Britain. The idea was also taken up by the Museum of the Moving Image in 1988, where actors, members of an in-house company, functioned as costumed guides. They were stationed in appropriate galleries as historical characters able to demonstrate artefacts such as an 1890s' Magic Lantern, putting them into the context of their original function. Here, the plan was to use role-playing performers, as the then director Neil Potter said, 'to look at the social and political background to the moving images' (Malcolm-Davies 1990).

This concept of drama and role-play was taken up by The Science Museum and it became the largest institution to experiment with live interpretation when it too began to use actors in its galleries in the mid-1990s. Their role was to interpret the exhibits and they were stationed in the galleries performing scripted pieces to a general audience. While this is an example of incorporating live interpretation

Figure 3.1 Explaining the workings of Great War airfield defence at the Royal International Air Tattoo, 2004 (courtesy of Mr Norm Reeve)

into an existing space, the new Royal Armouries building in Leeds incorporated special stages and arenas for the actors to work on or in. As the subject matter was military and the site included an area for jousting, some performers demonstrated techniques of warfare rather than simply talking about them. The approach at the Blist Hill site of Ironbridge Museum was different. The decision was made not to employ actors, but to train a team of full-time and volunteer demonstrators, wearing period clothing, in a variety of craft and performance skills and allow them to deal with visitors without the use of role-play: a good example of third-person interpretation. At Callendar House, near Falkirk in Scotland, the decision to adopt third-person interpretation in the early 1990s resulted from a curatorial visit to sites in the US. At Callendar House, the 'interpreters' also functioned as craft demonstrators, although they were not expert in those crafts. A similar approach was adopted at Beamish but, although there were efforts in the early 1990s to get the museum to adopt first-person interpretation, internal politics and fear of the new technique among management, not the demonstrators, led to the experiment being abandoned. The Historic Royal Palaces use a different approach and the professional interpreters bringing to life sites such as the Tower of London and Hampton Court are not actors, but historians with performance training. These interpreters work without scripts and use either first- or third-person approaches and act as costumed guides. Llancaiach Fawr in Wales is a rare example of the full-time use of first-person interpretation on a British site. Here, a team of specially trained 'actor/interpreters' appear as the servants of Colonel Edward Pritchard in the year 1645. There are many more examples of the technique in sites as varied as zoos and art galleries, but each of these projects has added to our knowledge of the strengths and weaknesses of live interpretation.

The decision of sites to use live interpretation full time has led to the creation of a new group of professionals working in museums and galleries. These staff members, distinct from the curatorial and warding staff, call themselves variously 'actors', 'performers' or 'interpreters' depending upon their background or train-ing. Sometimes employed directly, more often as members of a company, they are employed full or part time to work in museums and galleries nationally. Early experiments highlighted the divisions between those that were concerned about the advent of museum theatre and those that welcomed the opportunity to use a dramatic approach. This resulted in a number of acrimonious debates between 'actors/interpreters' and those who saw themselves as non-actor 'historian/interpreters' at the conferences held to discuss live interpretation in Liverpool in 1993 and Bradford in 1994. More recently bodies such as the Centre for Environmental Interpretation (CEI) have run courses on live interpretation and presented the approach as being both a historical and drama-based technique, (CEI Leaflet, 'Why Make a Drama Out of The Past?', October 1995). A sense of common purpose now generally prevails and in spring 1999 The International Museums Theatre Alliance (IMTAL) established a European affiliated branch based in London. IMTAL exists to promote theatre as effective education in museums and other sites and is well established, and influential, in the US and Canada. The creation of this new body offers the opportunity for practitioners to establish a common language, definition and methodology, so obviously currently lacking. This will promote good practice and, by networking, exchange ideas and promote the value of live inter-pretation generally. British delegates have taken part in the bi-annual IMTAL conferences in the US, and for the first time, in 2001, the event, hosted by the European branch, was held in London. This conference provided the opportunity to demonstrate that innovation and ideas do not have to come from across the Atlantic. An example of this process is the use by Colonial Williamsburg of Mark Wallis (Past Pleasures) to train their on-site interpreters and the training delivered by the Museum of the Moving Image Actors Consultancy to staff at Central Park Zoo, New York. These projects and the international conference have certainly have been a milestone in the development of a uniquely British methodology and practice.

For many sites the choice of interpretative style is based on previous experience or personal preference. At least one museum director announced that he chose not to use costumed interpreters because he personally found the approach embar-rassing. At other sites the decision is based on visitor evaluation, the physical nature of the site or the subject in question. At present most museums and other sites choose third-person, costumed guides or demonstrators because staff, or more frequently management, find the concept of first-person role-play challenging. Many sites argue that the interpreters have to know more to be convincing in first person and can never say they don't know the answer to a question. This is an interesting argument that presupposes that other non-first-person interpreters do not have to be as knowledgeable and can say they don't know. Ultimately the selection of the specific technique depends upon the skill of the performer and what information is expected to be conveyed. First person can provide an emotional context to human experience which third person, for example, cannot.

On some sites live interpretation is employed full time, but at many others it is employed during weekend or longer special events. Many of these projects rely upon the use of performers from companies such as Time Travellers or Spectrum Theatre Company who specialise in providing sites with skilled performers able to work with a wide range of audiences. Some sites use their own staff or museum volunteers to stage 'events'. The quality of these 'events' varies greatly and many have 'experience' but little training in the techniques they are using. Distinct from these professionals are the voluntary groups that offer an interpretative service, frequently calling themselves 'living history groups'. Many sites use these groups on a special event basis and sites such as Barley Hall, Sulgrave Manor, Oakwell Hall, Gainsborough Old Hall and others invite groups to perform at weekends and holidays. The quality of these events is variable and they range from the truly appalling (one group was asked to leave a site because of bad language and offensive behaviour) to the sort of enthusiastic event with a large number of participants that professional companies admit to finding difficult to achieve on a regular basis. Whether professional or voluntary, full or part time, the past ten years has seen a quite phenomenal number of experiments with live interpretation, some resulting in innovation and examples of good practice, others convincing curators that if a single event is poor so, too, must all live interpretation be. The role of the Events Department at English Heritage in fostering a coherent standard of what they require from re-enactors and interpreters, and sponsoring of groups that achieved these standards, has had a significant effect in improving the quality of many 'amateur' performers. This process has been linked to a largely military annual showcase 'History in Action' event at Kirby Hall, Northamptonshire that was run up to 2002. In 2003, this event was run at Stoneleigh Park in Warwickshire and, for the first time, the emphasis of the event was social history rather than military.

One area in which live interpretation had no difficulty in becoming established was education. Museums, schools and institutions such as English Heritage and the National Trust quickly established a reputation for using historical role-play with children. This, of course, was not a complete innovation and many teachers and museum educators had experimented with similar Theatre in Education approaches in the past. What was an innovation was not only the diversity of projects, from the Romans to War Time Blitz Evacuation, but also the use of sites to give a unique 'sense of the past' to the participants. This has certainly been the experience of the summertime projects for schools organised at Kentwell Hall for the past 20 years. Because many of these projects have been run by people with a background in Theatre in Education rather than historical interpretation it is not clear to what extent facts about the past are communicated. Ironically, although both English Heritage and the National Trust do organise 'educational' 'living history' sessions, both bodies have a target audience of children under 12 years of age. The National Trust has a long tradition of running Theatre in Education and the National Trust Theatre Project based at Sutton House in Hackney runs annual 'seasons' of presentations using the Trust's buildings as a backdrop (English Heritage Education Service 1995; Fairclough 1994; Woodhead and Tinniswood 1996). These presentations are not usually site specific unlike the approach used at Clarke Hall in Wakefield. This is an example of a site that uses live interpretation methods with young people. Here, a 1680s' house is available in term time for groups of mainly junior school students to experience living in the seventeenth century. The experience the students have is specific to the property and the family that lived there, and is a world away from the 'bed sheets for togas' school of children's projects. What is clear is that these projects have been very good at enthusing young people with an interest in history and there now exists a generation of people who participated in live interpretation projects at an early age and are familiar with the methodology, its benefits and limitations.

Early experiments demonstrated that the average British visitor was more ⌐reticent⌐ than their American counterpart, and if confronted by a costumed interpreter without preparation, would either be deterred from venturing further or be annoyed by the intrusion. Although the Museum of the Moving Image introduced a notice board telling visitors that actors were present, this was only a partial solution and, despite specific training in how to communicate with reticent visitors, many members of the audience were still intimidated by close contact with the actors. For this reason the Orientation Centre is a feature of many of the best 'living history' sites. Here the visitor is welcomed and the approach being used can be explained to them. A sign or small display is insufficient for the public who may as a result be totally unprepared for the site and therefore may find themselves intimidated by interpreters or fail to grasp what the approach offers. Despite the size of the entrance building at Beamish there is no attempt made to explain to the visitor how to interact with the performers. It is interesting to note that similar orientation areas do not feature in more conventional museums although research has shown that fear of the unknown and apprehension as to appropriate behaviour contribute to the decision taken by many of the public not to visit museums. One possible solution to this orientation problem has been suggested by the History Re-enactment Workshop (HRW), a group working at sites all over Britain using a form of first-person interpretation based on the model of Plimoth Plantation. To overcome this problem a group designated 'red T-shirters' (members of the

[handwritten marginal note: inclined to be silent]

company wearing modern clothes, including a red garment bearing a distinctive logo) are deployed to greet the public. Their role is to provide information that could not be presented by role-players because when interpreters are in first person, there is no opportunity to question life in the period after that presented. Red T-shirters are thus able to explain the nature of the interpretative method, give historical context to the presentation and help to facilitate comfortable interaction between interpreters and visitors. Perhaps as the public are more exposed to the technique, and if sites provide orientation centres, this will become less of a problem.

To understand the potential value of live interpretation we must consider the way in which the technique can enhance the visitor experience. Freeman Tilden in *Interpreting our Heritage*, states that interpretation is 'an educational activity which aims to reveal meanings and relationships through the use of original objects, by first hand experience and by illustrative media, rather than simply to communicate factual information' (Tilden 1957: 9). Unlike teaching or lecturing, live interpretation is not a medium intended to simply communicate information, rather it is intended to reveal concepts such as philosophies, religion, emotions and attitudes. As such it is an ideal technique to apply to social history, to extend the scope of the museum, galleries and historic house display. Even critics have been forced to concede that: 'Good Living History is a popular and effective teaching tool because it communicates a relatively wide impression of the past' (Peterson 1989: 28).

Figure 3.2   Aerial reconnaissance with the Royal Flying Corps (courtesy of Mr Norm Reeve)

When the visitor asks questions another crucial advantage of using human inter-preters becomes apparent; flexibility of response. A skilled interpreter will be able to assess the appropriate level of response to each questioner, dealing quite differ-ently with a child, a teenager or an adult. It is also possible to tailor a conversation to focus attention on aspects of the past that may otherwise remain hidden. Importantly, human communication depends upon a whole range of non-verbal components that rely upon there being a human interpreter present to convey. Essentially the visitor can become involved in selecting what interests them, rather than having the choice made by a third party. '[E]ven though museum professionals may savour the well-crafted exhibit labels most Americans [and Britons] prefer to watch and talk with historical interpreters than read labels' making the study of history into 'an active rather than passive pursuit' (Leon and Piatt 1989: 98. It is a first- rather than a second-hand experience, which allows 'visitor participation, either psychological or actual' (Alexander 1987: 200). To ensure that the visitor does not go away with preconceptions reinforced or with new myths fostered it may be necessary to be challenging. Very few museums actively deal with the visitors' preconceptions and this weakness highlights one of the principal strengths of an active live interpretation programme if it is run by curators and interpreters rather than commercial departments.

The ability of other interpretative techniques to involve the visitor, to make them want to know more, is something that is all too rarely achieved, as visitor evalu-ation clearly demonstrates. Yet live interpretation does have a capacity to intrigue visitors, to involve them in a way that other more conventional methods do not. By engaging in a dialogue the visitor may become involved in aspects of the past that are far removed from 'the-heritage-mob-and-Arcadia aspect' of some inter-pretations (Rawnsley 1994). Unfortunately until very recently there has been little research into what and how visitors learn from live interpretation presentations. The research at the Science Museum, *Enlightening or Embarrassing?*, is an early example of this work (Bicknell and Mazda 1993). This study demonstrated that visitors find the experience enriching and that they prefer the approach to captions, video or other technology. Current research funded partly by The Group for Education in Museums and run in co-operation with IMTAL has demonstrated the value of live interpretation to both adults and children.

Despite the analogy with time machines we must remember that the technique offers the opportunity to replicate aspects of the past – not to recreate it. As such we should view live interpretation projects as generalisations about the past. As in any historical account they are based on incomplete evidence. Like any form of museum interpretation what is central to the achievement of high standards is the quality of research and critical judgement applied to the project by those control-ling it. No form of interpretation can promise a return to the past, what it can offer is an interpretation of a period in time; what it might have been like, not what it was like. The past does not have to be sanitised and, despite some doubts about showing the mundane, the low-key approach used in many actually encourages visitors to question interpreters about other aspects of life. This explains the decision taken at many sites to portray servants and other people of a similar status rather than famous or wealthy people. Visitors relate better to performers that they perceive to be of a similar or slightly lower social standing than themselves. The famous or influential figure can be seen as threatening unless the situation is handled very sensitively.

Involvement or interaction with interpreters may result in an emotional response from visitors. In the US a recreated slave auction at Williamsburg led to a sit-in protest by people opposed to the negative portrayal of black people. It could be questioned whether it is right to involve people in this way; certainly there are taboos on many subjects that cannot be dealt with in a direct manner. It is however interesting to note that the inclusion of potentially controversial elements in interpretation came as a response to the criticism that they previously portrayed peaceable kingdoms and ignored conflict. In 2001 the outreach team of the National Army Museum took the step of recreating a Great War medical unit as a way to counter-point the 'bloodless' nature of battle re-enactment. Since then 'the Medicos' have both intrigued and disturbed visitors in equal measure. In 1982 Tony Fyson argued that interpreters should entertain the possibility that the need to know for oneself and understand what happened there, may be a powerful motive for a visit not immediately compatible with a fun day out. If this process was translated into other programmes we might find that future projects may be more industrial, rather than agricultural, and consequently may address social problems and conflicts of the past that are paralleled by the present. It is interesting to note that evidence from the US suggests that people learn more when their emotions are heightened.

A frequently applied criticism of live interpretation is that it is an example of creeping 'Disneyfication', trivialising the past and creating an end of the pier quality of 'edutainment' to museums. For this reason many sites have dedicated time and effort to research, supporting their presentations with strong scholarship, which is translated into their three-dimensional interpretations. To be of any value the three-dimensional view of the past must be based on research and sound judgement, in exactly the same way as any other form of interpretation. Only by doing this can we avoid 'idealising the past and misinterpreting the present' (Leon and Piatt 1989: 83). It appears that many influential institutions see the techniques of live interpretation as fulfilling a specific, if limited role and in common with many other bodies appear to have no concept of the techniques' broader interpretive potential. This has led to accusations from some quarters that some bodies see live interpretation as a form of 'dumbing down' of interpretive provision. It would appear that for many professionals live interpretation is still viewed by some museum professionals as an approach appropriate for children on school trips and 'special events' to promote sites and raise revenue, rather than a valid technique of historical interpretation.

We live in a world in which people are becoming increasingly familiar with high-technology, and multimedia presentations are becoming a feature of many museums.

The buzzword of interactive is applied to many forms of information retrieval in which there is no person-to-person contact. Well before the computer age dawned for most museums Tilden made it clear 'that personal interpretation is the highest and best form of interaction, and the most desirable and best use of the visitor's time'. Despite the very high-tech world in which we live visitors to museums respond well to human contact. They like to talk to other people, and evaluations stress the importance of the human interaction in enhancing visitor experience.

Tilden's second principle is: 'Information, as such is not interpretation. Interpretation is revelation based upon information. But they are entirely different things' (Tilden 1957: 9). For many sites interpretation is simply the presentation of information on text panel, or audio guides. There is no question of revelation at all. Sites using live interpretation have challenged preconceptions and offered the opportunity for the public to become their own investigators of the past; to have an experience that is far removed from the dark ride, the computer screen, audio guide or even well-crafted caption.

All successful live interpreters are well-trained and able communicators who are able to sustain their motivation under the pressure of visitors, or lack of them. Underlying this skill must be a sound historical knowledge and the awareness of the educational impact of their interaction with the visitor. If such training fails then bad 'living history' is certainly worse than poor static displays, graphic panels or computer programmes. If it is successful there can be no doubt that the 'live' form offers far more to the visitor than any other method of interpretation. To achieve this needs good staff training: 'interpretation is an art, which combines many arts, whether the materials presented are scientific, historical or architectural. Any art is in some degrees teachable' (Tilden 1957: 9).

It is the opinion of a growing body of professionals in the UK that live interpretation, in its many forms, can 'bring exhibits to life, is an effective, often powerful, teaching technique, and any museum is wise to consider its purpose and exhibits from this point of view' (Alexander 1987: 20). In Britain this view is put forward in the 1993 HMSO publication *Social History in Museums: A Handbook for Professionals*:

> Living history events . . . bring to museums . . . a sense of dynamism and of movement . . . to create genuine interest in the study of history. Living history has enabled curators to put people back into the past, to explain processes and tackle the complex problem of explaining social networks, rather than unrelated facts.
>
> (Colsell 1993)

The phenomenon of live interpretation is here to stay and the number of sites employing the varied approaches is still expanding. It has been proved that live interpretation has greater influence on public perception of the past than many other interpretative techniques. Although there are still some bad examples of the live interpretation these are increasingly at the battle re-enactment level and not in museums or galleries. That said, if we expect projects to be historically valid and educationally successful they must not remain the province of commercial and public relations departments. We now have the opportunity to exploit the strengths and avoid the pitfalls that have so marred the development and reputation of live interpretation to date. In future, museum and gallery managers will be aware that the varied techniques of live interpretation should be considered as part of a planning process. If the approach is rejected, rather than selected, this decision will be based on sound educational and interpretative principles rather than prejudices or personal bias.

■ ■ ■

Bibliography

Alexander, E. P. (1987) *Museums in Motion*, Nashville: American Association for State and Local History (AASLH)

Anderson, J. (1984) *Time Machines*, Nashville: AASLH

Anderson, J. (1985) *The Living History Source-book*, Nashville: AASLH

Ashmore, A. (1999) 'Turning an Actor into an Interpreter', in M. Maloney and C. Hughes (eds), *Case Studies in Museum, Zoo and Aquarium Theatre*, American Association of Museums, Professional Practice Series

Belcher, B. (1991) *Exhibitions in Museums*, Leicester University Press

Benn, C. (1987) 'Living History Lies and Social History', Toronto: *Museum Quarterly*, 16 (2)

Bicknell, S. and Mazda, X. (1993) *Enlightening or Embarrassing? An Evaluation of Drama in the Science Museum*, London: The Susie Fisher Group

Blatti, J. (ed.) (1987) *Past Meets Present*, Washington: Smithsonian Institution Press

Burcaw, G. E. (1980) 'Can History Be Too Lively?', USA: *Museum Journal*, 80

Carter, W. (1994) 'Reproduction Heroes', *Heritage Today*, 27

Colsell, L. (1993) 'Demonstrations-ethics and Techniques', in D. Fleming, C. Paine and J. Rhodes (eds), *Social History in Museums: A Handbook for Professionals*, London: HMSO

de Boo, I. (1996) *You are Desired to Accompany the Corpse: An Evaluation of Visitor Profile and Visitor Experience*, Birmingham Museum and Art Gallery

Deetz, J. (1981) 'The Link from Object to Person to Concept', in W. Collin, *Museums, Adults and the Humanities*, USA: American Association of Museums

English Heritage Education Service (1995) *Heritage Learning*, London: English Heritage

Fairclough, J. (1994) *A Teacher's Guide to History Through Role Play*, London: English Heritage

Goodacre, B. and Baldwin, G. (2002) *Living the Past*, Middlesex: Middlesex University Press

Hewison, R. (1987) *The Heritage Industry*, London: Methuen

Horsler, V. (2003) *Living the Past*, London: Weidenfeld & Nicholson

Kennon, Kay, W. (1970) *Keep It Alive! Tips on Living History Demonstrations*, Washington, DC: National Park Service

Leon, W. and Piatt, M. (1989) 'Living History Museums', in W. Leon and R. Rosenzweig, *History Museums in the United States: A Critical Assessment*, USA: University of Illinois Press

Leon, W. and Rosenzweig, R. (1989) *History Museums in the United States: A Critical Assessment*, USA: University of Illinois Press

Lowenthal, D. (1985) *The Past is a Foreign Country*, Cambridge: Cambridge University Press

Malcolm-Davies, J. (1990) 'Keeping it Alive', USA: *Museums Journal*, 90 (3): 25–29

Osterud, G. N. (1992/1993) 'Living Living History', USA: *Journal of Museum Education*, 17 (1): 18–19

Peterson, D. (1989) *There is no Living History, There are no Time Machines*, USA: *History News*

Rawnsley, R. (1994) *National Trusts Priorities Today*, letter in the *Daily Telegraph*, 11 August

Robertshaw, A. S. (1990) 'Acts of Imagination', USA: *Museums Journal*, 90 (3): 30–31

Robertshaw, A. S. (1992) 'From Houses into Homes. One Approach to Living History', *The Journal of the Social History Curators Group*, 19: 14–20

Roth, S. F. (1998) *Past into Present, Effective Techniques for First-Person Historical Interpretation*, Chapel Hill, NC: The University of North Carolina Press

Rubenstein, R. (1992) *Evaluation of the Live Interpretation Program*, Toronto: Canadian Museum of Civilisation

Samuel, R. (1994) *Theatres of Memory: Past and Present in Contemporary Culture*, vol. 1, London and New York: Verso

Seaman, B. (1993) 'Not Magic, But Work. Dramatic Interpretation in Museums', unpublished MA thesis, University of Leicester.

Tilden, F. (1957) *Interpreting Our Heritage*, Chapel Hill, NC: The University of North Carolina Press

Woodhead, S. and Tinniswood, A. (1996) *No Longer Dead to Me*, London: The National Trust

Chapter 4

INTERPRETING HISTORIC SCOTLAND

Chris Tabraham

Once upon a time . . .

In the bustling market town of Elgin early in the nineteenth century there dwelt a shoemaker by the name of John Shanks. He was 'a thin, lank, spider-looking being in obsolete costume', observed Lord Cockburn, the distinguished judge, 'with a quiet earnest enthusiasm in his manner – a sort of Old Mortality whose delight it was to labour among the ruins'. John Shanks not only laboured among the ruins of his beloved cathedral, removing 3,000 barrow-loads of rubble (and doubtless much archaeological evidence besides), he also guided visitors around 'his' cathedral, interpreting the place – its architecture, its history – in his own inimitable way. Shanks's labours, both with his spade and his mouth, were rewarded. By the time this 'drouthy cobbler' passed away in 1844 at the ripe old age of 83, the future of the cathedral, abandoned at the Reformation in 1560 and thereafter allowed to fall into ruin, was assured – and this in an age when the town of Elgin itself was casting off its medieval garb and rebuilding anew in stately neo-classical style.

Shanks's epitaph inscribed on his gravestone in the cathedral graveyard, composed by Lord Cockburn, neatly sums up the cobbler's achievements:

> For 17 years he was the keeper and
> the shower of this cathedral
> and while not even the Crown
> was doing anything for its
> preservation he, with his own
> hands, cleared it of many

> thousand cubic yards of rubbish
> disclosing the bases of the
> pillars, collecting the carved
> fragments, & introducing some
> order & propriety

John Shanks would not have realised it of course, but what he was doing among the ruins was not only actively preserving them; he was also carrying out interpretation. He was communicating to visitors his interest in and concern for the monument, for he clearly believed with a passion that the place should be preserved for future generations. His tireless efforts had their desired effect. Not only did he inspire the admiration of the likes of Lord Cockburn, but he was also instrumental in cajoling Robert Reid, the 'King's Architect and Surveyor in Scotland', into preparing a report on works required to secure the ruin from further decline.

In John Shanks's footsteps

Robert Reid had charge at that time of the Scottish Office of Works, the State organisation responsible for Elgin Cathedral. To this day the cathedral remains in State care, just one of an estate of over 300 properties comprising archaeological

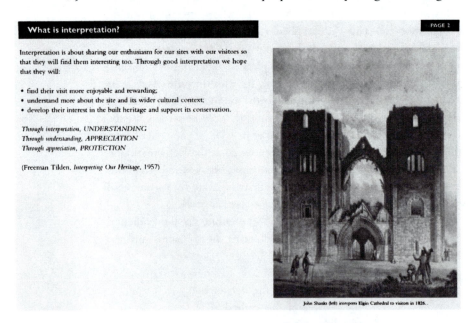

What is interpretation?

PAGE 2

Interpretation is about sharing our enthusiasm for our sites with our visitors so that they will find them interesting too. Through good interpretation we hope that they will:

- find their visit more enjoyable and rewarding;
- understand more about the site and its wider cultural context;
- develop their interest in the built heritage and support its conservation.

Through interpretation, UNDERSTANDING
Through understanding, APPRECIATION
Through appreciation, PROTECTION

(Freeman Tilden, *Interpreting Our Heritage,* 1957)

John Shanks (left) interprets Elgin Cathedral to visitors in 1826.

Figure 4.1 A page from Historic Scotland's *Manual for Site Interpretation at Properties in Care*, depicting John Shanks, the small character on the left with the pointy stick, interpreting Elgin Cathedral to visitors in 1826 (taken from *A Series of Views of Elgin Cathedral*, 1826) (Historic Scotland)

sites and historic buildings of outstanding national importance. While the emphasis historically has been on preservation, the importance of presenting the monuments to visitors has grown, and developed, since Shanks's day.

For a long time the task of interpreting the monuments was left in the hands of the site custodians, the successors to John Shanks. Like him they were generally local 'worthies'. With a lawnmower in one hand and a ticket-machine in the other they would welcome visitors and regale them with their understanding of the monument. It is widely recognised today that the best vehicle for communicating the message is through 'live interpreters' and many good men and women have followed in John Shanks's footsteps.

In the old days, if there was any additional interpretation available to the visitor it was mostly presented in the form of a guidebook. These were invariably written by learned academics, and mostly in a language that only other learned academics could understand. Every discipline has its technical words, or jargon, and architectural history is certainly no exception. Take, for example, this paragraph from an early guidebook to Arbroath Abbey:

> The triforium arcading is of transitional form; each bay consists of a round-headed arch enclosing two pointed open sub-arches. The sub-arches are supported by a sturdy mid-shaft with a moulded capital and base not unlike the mid-shafts of a tribune passage. The semi-circular enclosing arch has moulded capitals. The clearstorey arcading above was similarly fashioned.

We must assume that the author at least knew what they were talking about.

The situation began to change for the better in the inter-war years. It was then that the idea of site museums was developed. There had, of course, been earlier site museums, such as the display of carved stones in a small cottage beside Whithorn Cathedral Priory, set up by the Marquis of Bute towards the close of the nineteenth century. The notion that visitors might like to see artefacts recovered from the site actually on display at the site itself rather appealed. The pioneer was a modest site museum established at Skara Brae, the Stone Age village on Orkney, following on from the major excavations and conservation works carried out in the late 1920s. This initiative and those that came after – including ones at the multi-period settlement of Jarlshof, on Shetland, and the Cistercian abbey of Glenluce in Wigtownshire – have certainly proved their worth over the years.

After the Second World War, another innovation appeared – the introduction of plaques giving positive information. This was a welcome change from earlier notices that had generally incorporated negative, almost threatening information such as:

> This monument is in the care of HM Office of Works.
> IT IS AN OFFENCE TO INJURE OR DEFACE IT

Now the emphasis was on imparting information to aid the visitor's understanding and enjoyment of the site. Perhaps one or two of the plaques might have failed to achieve the objective of imparting nuggets of useful information, such as this one at Jedburgh Abbey:

> This is not part of the medieval church but a post-Reformation intrusion.

The average visitor must have wondered what on earth a 'post-Reformation intrusion' was. Nevertheless the intention was entirely honourable. The move towards providing positive information has continued ever since, with a major initiative conducted in the 1980s, so that today each of our 300-odd properties has some provision. This ranges from a single A3 plaque at our more obscure monuments (and they don't come any more obscure than the enigmatically named 'Wren's Egg' in Wigtownshire) to a combination of interpretative panels, descriptive plaques and exhibitions at the most complex sites.

So much for the past; what about the present?

Interpretation? Why bother?

When Historic Scotland was formed as an executive agency within the Scottish Office in 1991, it set out its stall in a mission statement. That statement, which could have been written by John Shanks himself, declared two aims:

Figure 4.2 A typical interpretation board for one of Historic Scotland's properties in care – the Bridge of Oich beside the Caledonian Canal in the Great Glen (Historic Scotland)

- to safeguard the nation's built heritage;
- to promote its understanding and enjoyment.

The mission statement recognises that the preservation of the built heritage by those charged with the task is not by itself sufficient to secure a future for the past. Hearts and minds have to be won to the cause of conservation. Only by fostering understanding and facilitating enjoyment can we hope to create a better, more informed appreciation of Scotland's built heritage and the wider cultural inheritance among the public at large.

Interpretation is now firmly recognised by Historic Scotland as the key to promoting the educational potential afforded by its estate of properties in care. It is a communication process that seeks not simply to inform but also to provoke a reaction. It has been defined as the art of explaining the significance of a site to the people who visit, with a view to pointing a conservation message.

Historic Scotland has in its care over 300 buildings and monuments for which it has the responsibility to preserve and present to the public. These properties, while by no means the sum of human activity, are nevertheless of individual importance and sufficiently representative of the built heritage in Scotland for them to be regarded as invaluable in helping to achieve our aim of a better informed, more conservation-minded public.

By accepting the challenge posed by interpreting Scotland's leading archaeological sites and historic buildings to our visitors, Historic Scotland has the opportunity to reveal to a large, and growing, number of people why and how a place, building or artefact is important, and to provoke them into thinking about the built heritage and the wider cultural inheritance. This has become even more relevant as Scotland expresses its national identity through the new constitutional arrangements.

Interpretative planning

In 1998 Historic Scotland set down its objectives for site interpretation at its properties in care, and the policies designed to achieve them. A manual and guidance notes were produced at the same time to help those members of staff involved in preserving and presenting sites to visitors. Underpinning everything were the following aims:

- to provide an enjoyable and stimulating experience for the visitor while fully respecting the historic fabric and the setting of the monuments;
- to educate and inform the visitor and so raise their awareness and appreciation of Scotland's built heritage and its cultural and natural contexts;
- to ensure that any interpretative provision supports the sustainable recreational use of the built and natural environments;

- to encourage active support for conservation of the built heritage;
- to promote the work of Historic Scotland as a leading organisation for the preservation and promotion of the built heritage.

It was established that good interpretation is achieved only through good planning. Interpretative planning is the thought process through which we establish:

- what we wish to interpret, and why;
- how we wish to interpret, and where;
- who we wish to communicate with;
- what resources we need to achieve our aim.

The basis for all interpretative provision is therefore the interpretation plan. The plan is a blueprint for action, a clear written statement of our intentions for any given site. Its preparation helps us to find out where we are, where we want to be, and how we are going to get there. Its existence serves to remind us of our aims and objectives for the site.

Each plan follows the standard format. It is divided into two parts. The first part is a succinct, factually based analysis of the site. It focuses on the three essentials – the three Ps:

- know your property;
- know your public;
- know your price.

The first element (Property) is a statement of the site's importance, highlighting unique or unusual features but also stressing any significant areas of concern. The second (Public) is a profile of current visitors, taken from statistics where available, giving numbers, country of origin, and so forth. A separate profile of educational visits is also required. The third element (Price) is a statement of the site's worth, a value judgement of the level of interpretation deemed appropriate given both the property's heritage value and the level of visitor interest.

The second part of the interpretation plan is a more detailed examination of the site and the potential, if any, for interpretation. It identifies and addresses core issues, highlights constraints and proposes possibilities – in that order.

The interpretation plan is, of course, only the beginning of the process, the whole point being not to produce a plan but some interpretation. *The Manual for Site Interpretation at Properties in Care* (1998) produced at the same time as the policy document, therefore serves as a 'step-by-step' guide for staff implementing interpretation. The guidance it contains draws heavily from the excellent *A Sense of Place*, the handbook published by the Tourism and Environment Initiative in 1997. The *Manual* has eight steps to implementing interpretation:

1 Researching the subject

All interpretation should be informed by sound knowledge, including a thorough understanding of the archaeology, architecture and history of the site. A full inventory of artefacts associated with the site is recommended, as well as a visit to the local museum and library, for further information and local 'colour'.

2 Communicating the message

After researching the subject, there will probably be enough material to fill several books. But if we try to tell visitors everything, they will be overwhelmed, or bored – or probably both. Interpretation is about communicating. It is also about communicating more than just information. Information simply gives facts, but interpretation aims to give new insights, ideas and ways of looking at, or appreciating, a place. Interpretation is also about sharing our enthusiasm about our sites so that our audience will find them fascinating too.

Some ground rules are offered as guidance:

- be clear who you are talking to;
- keep it simple and use everyday language;
- use stories and quotations, metaphors and similes that relate to everyday experience;
- think visually – a good graphic says the equivalent of 100 words;
- orientate illustrations to suit the visitor;
- make route directions, instructions and warnings clear;
- test ideas as much as possible;
- make all aspects of the project work together.

3 Selecting the media

There are a number of ways of communicating the message. These include personal interpretation; multi-media; outdoor panels; indoor exhibitions; interactive ('hands on') materials; special guided tours and events; publications and retail products. Each has advantages and disadvantages. However, it is worth remembering that research shows that visitors recall:

- 10 per cent of what they hear;
- 30 per cent of what they read;
- 50 per cent of what they see;
- 90 per cent of what they do.

4 Catering for disabilities

Every effort should be made to make the interpretation accessible to everyone, including the physically disabled, the hard-of-hearing, the blind and partially sighted and those with learning difficulties. A disability audit is recommended, and as well as pointing up the importance of reading Historic Scotland's own *Technical Advice Note 7 – Access to the Built Heritage* (1996), a checklist is offered. This includes the following:

- Make orientation and site accessibility clear at the outset, ensure that the introductory interpretation is accessible to all, and provide a sufficient summary of all the site's main features.
- Ensure that the location of any subsequent interpretation is in the place and at the height accessible to most people. In short, 'lower your sights'.
- Keep things clear. Fussy designs and fancy colours make life very difficult.
- Avoid jargon, and take care to explain specialist terms. Also, bold, relevant headings and clear captions make life so much easier – for everyone.
- Try to use 'hands-on' exhibits, which can help visitors with learning difficulties as well as the blind and partially sighted – and, of course, kids.

5 Catering for children

Interpretation addressed to children (say, up to the age of 12) should ideally require a separate programme and not be a dilution of the presentation to adults. When interpreting for children, most of the points in the catering for disabilities checklist apply.

6 Catering for other languages

The needs of those whose mother tongue is not English in any interpretation should be carefully assessed, and a language audit carried out, using available statistics and taking advice from the site steward. There is a real danger that foreign language supplements to outdoor panels and indoor exhibitions can easily overwhelm the core provision, and suitable alternatives, such as publications and audio-guides should be considered.

7 Respecting the site

Interpretation, however good, cannot be the attraction; that has to be the site itself. Whatever is done in the way of interpretation it should fully respect the site, including:

- the historic fabric;
- non-historic surfaces like grass;
- the setting, including views into and out of the site.

Everything done in the way of interpretation should be fully reversible. It should also be well maintained.

8 Evaluating the interpretation

Evaluating interpretation is important in determining whether we have succeeded in meeting our aims, and if we need to improve things. For the evaluation to be valid, we need to set criteria for performance in advance. It can help to classify objectives into management objectives and interpretative objectives.

Management objectives might include:

* visitor management – e.g. influencing where/what/how people visit;
* financial – e.g. increasing visitor spend.

Interpretative objectives might include:

* Learning – what do we want visitors to know as a result?
* Emotional – what do we want them to feel as a result?
* Behavioural – what do we want them to do as a result?

Interpreting something old – Skara Brae Stone Age village

The first interpretation plan to be produced was for Skara Brae. It was drawn up to help inform Historic Scotland's strategy for dealing with the growing numbers of visitors to this remote site on the west side of Mainland Orkney, and their desire to learn more about its extraordinary story. In 1973 the annual total stood at 16,000; by 1995 this had risen three-fold to almost 53,000; and in 1996, the year the plan was produced, the figure broke the 60,000 barrier for the first time. Yet these 120,000 feet were treading on one of the most fragile archaeological sites in Europe. What were we to do?

The interpretation plan began by acknowledging the site's importance (the 'Know Your Property' element). It stressed two aspects:

* Skara Brae is the best-preserved prehistoric village in northern Europe, inhabited before the Egyptian pyramids were built and Stonehenge was constructed, and as a consequence nowhere else in northern Europe are we able to see such rich evidence of how our remote ancestors actually lived;
* Skara Brae is a very sensitive site, with remarkably fragile physical remains prone to damage and erosion from nature and man, and whatever is done in the way of visitor developments must take fully into account the delicate nature of the remains and the sensitivity of the environment.

The plan thereafter identified the core issues, which included most importantly those of (1) visitor comprehension, (2) the frustration they undoubtedly feel at not being able to walk through the streets and into the houses and (3) visitor pressure on the archaeology. The important role of the village as an educational tool for those learning about remote ancestors was also flagged up.

The most significant point to emerge from the plan was that while we were under an obligation to provide visitors with improved facilities, including better interpretation, this could only realistically be achieved by building a new visitor centre at some distance from the site itself. A purpose-built structure could offer those facilities that today's visitor has come to expect – a friendly reception, toilets, interpretation, food and shop (in no particular order of priority, though the toilets might have the edge after a long coach journey from Inverness and a ferry-crossing over the Pentland Firth) – without impacting on either the archaeology or the setting of the village itself. It was also felt that the provision of quality interpretation off-site might also have the added bonus of reducing, or at least containing, the current visitor pressure on the site in the peak season, by reducing the average amount of dwell-time spent at the village.

Figure 4.3 Part of the interpretative facility in the new visitor centre near Skara Brae. The evidence is presented at two levels, factual and speculative, supported by artefacts, other archaeological evidence, audio-visual, 'hands-on' material and multimedia presentations (Historic Scotland)

The result was that a new visitor centre was built, on a site formerly occupied by farm buildings, a distance of some 800 metres from the village itself. In addition to the visitor centre, the opportunity was taken to build a full-size, wholly accessible replica of one of the Stone Age houses and an accompanying stretch of passageway. This has proved to be one of the highlights for visitors, and goes some way towards answering the feeling of frustration they experience at not being able to wander into the ancient houses themselves.

Arguably the most significant aspect of undertaking research and developing interpretation for Skara Brae was the complete lack of documentary evidence about the village and its inhabitants. What we do know has been gained from detailed archaeological analysis, but much still remains a mystery. The evidence, therefore, was presented at two levels, factual and speculative.

To have presented only aspects of undoubted fact would, it was felt, oversimplify and detract from the significance of the settlement. Indeed, what emerged as most fascinating about Skara Brae was the process of learning about the past through archaeological detective work, and this is what guided the approach to the interpretation.

The exhibition element of the interpretation concentrates on piecing together the archaeological evidence and encouraging visitors to think about how this informs our understanding of the remote past. We used the wonderful array of artefacts recovered from the site alongside other archaeological evidence – such as soil analysis, plant and food remains – to present the best picture of what village life was like 5,000 years ago. A key point that we emphasised is that we are learning all the time about the past, and it may be that a future find may provide fresh insight into Skara Brae.

A good example of our approach concerns diet. We know for a fact that the people at Skara Brae ate an assortment of meats, fish, grains, fruits, nuts and so forth – because we have the direct evidence. We can only guess, however, that they also had milk, cheese, bread – and possibly alcoholic 'beers'. More frustratingly, there are other commonly asked questions for which there is no evidence whatsoever – what did the people look like? what age could they expect to live to? where did they come from? could they write? The two levels of evidence are presented typographically in the exhibition (as they are also in the site guidebook (Clarke and Maguire 1995)) – normal type for things we can confidently say, and *italic* for things we can only guess at.

Invaluable as the new interpretation facility in the visitor centre is proving to be, it plays only a supporting role to the village itself, the prime object of attention. To visit it is a truly amazing experience – no matter what the weather. You really just want to wander about the site, and peep down into the houses and passageways, drift back in time 5,000 years and people the place with your own images and imaginings. Questions aplenty you will have in your mind, but you don't need to seek answers there and then, and so be in danger of dispelling the magic of the place. You can return by way of the visitor centre and take as long as you like to do that. For the visitor centre is there primarily to aid understanding. The village itself is there to be enjoyed.

Interpreting something new – the Arnol Blackhouse

On the west side of the Isle of Lewis, in the Western Isles, is a site which, at first glance, has all the appearance of being just as remote in time as the village at Skara Brae. Yet the blackhouse at No. 42 Arnol was only built in the late nineteenth century and, even more remarkably, was last lived in as recently as 1964.

Unlike Skara Brae, which had been abandoned by its occupants 4,500 years before Historic Scotland took possession, the keys of Arnol Blackhouse were handed over to us on the departure of the outgoing residents. Its interpretation, therefore, presented a quite different challenge to that at Skara Brae. Whereas at the latter we were left only with archaeological evidence, at Arnol Blackhouse we had the full range – archaeological evidence in the form of the house itself, complete with fixtures and fittings (including even the hens); extensive historical documentation for the township and its hinterland; and, of course, and arguably most precious of all, the oral evidence of the residents and villagers themselves.

Until recently, Historic Scotland had only the blackhouse itself in its care, meaning that the dark, smoky interior was perforce cluttered with modern impedimenta,

Figure 4.4 The blackhouse at No. 42 Arnol as it looked in 1966 when acquired by Historic Scotland. The roof has been rethatched, and the cow is probably no more, but other than that it has changed remarkably little since that time (Historic Scotland)

like the telephone and fax machine! Despite this, our stewarding staff performed a splendid job interpreting the place to visitors and imparting something of the way of life in a Hebridean township within living memory. An equally excellent guidebook (Fenton 1978) complemented the provision. But somehow that fax machine continued to irk; an unwelcome guest at the wedding feast.

It was therefore with alacrity and a sense of relief that Historic Scotland took up the offer of acquiring the adjacent 'white house', the successor to the black-house. A 'run-of-the-mill' building by comparison to the blackhouse, it was seen as eminently suited for housing all those facilities expected by today's visitor and

Figure 4.5 The living room (*aig an teine*, 'at the fire') in the Arnol Blackhouse as it looked in 1966. This view, looking towards the bedroom (*uachdar an tighe*), is little changed to this day (Historic Scotland)

required by employment legislation – toilets, reception and shop, interpretation and staff-room – thereby relieving the blackhouse of pretty well all of its modern clutter. The new facility opened to visitors at Easter 1999.

The interpretative philosophy for Arnol was therefore much like that adopted for Skara Brae. By leaving the building more or less as an 'interpretation-free' zone, it would be better able to arouse emotions in visitors and provoke reactions. All the supporting interpretation, for those who wished to avail themselves of it, could be located close by but removed from it. A visit to the blackhouse certainly does provoke reactions, as a leaf through the visitors' book reveals. I estimated that the world was divided equally between those who would have loved to have lived there and those who wouldn't. The reaction to the eye-watering peat-fire was just about the same. Speaking personally, I prefer my central heating, but I do like my bacon smoked!

The interpretation in the 'white house' is quite modest, quite simple, but making full use of the media available. There is archive film from the 1930s and a photographic album of 'stills' giving fascinating glimpses of life in the township, and in the summer shielings – of sowing and reaping, or spinning wool, milking cattle and cutting the peat. There is an interactive architectural model of the blackhouse with its roof cut open at selected points to show how the several spaces were used and also something of the building construction. If a picture can paint a hundred words, then a model can communicate a thousand and more – and what is more, not cost a penny in maintenance *and* never break down.

The 'movie' and model are supported by artefacts from the blackhouse, including a working spinning-wheel for use by the stewards, as well as a modest provision of interpretative panels. Short on text (but more dense than they might have been owing to the fact that everything has to be bi-lingual in the Western Isles) and strong on illustrations, these panels take their cue from the thematic approach encouraged by Sam Ham in his seminal work *Environmental Interpretation* (1992: 33–44). As Ham points out, most folk read the title before anything else; in fact, many people read *only* the title! So we should make sure that the title itself conveys information.

For Arnol the following themed statements were developed:

* people have been building houses in the Hebrides for 8,000 years;
* the blackhouse was built only of local materials;
* Arnol township was originally down by the sea;
* the peat fire was the centre of family life and was never allowed to go out;
* taking advantage of the summer moorland pastures eased the pressure on the grazing around the township.

Nevertheless, no matter how good or bad the interpretation, the star attraction remains the site itself – and in Arnol's case it is that thatched blackhouse with its darkened, thought-provoking interior – and that peat smoke!

One final thought

Prominently displayed on a wall in the 'white house' at Arnol is a quotation taken from Fenton's guidebook to the island blackhouse: 'Change is an inevitable part of life, to be accepted, not deplored.'

In the book itself, the author continues:

> It is important to understand and appreciate the main stages of cultural development. The kind of culture represented by the blackhouse was a very long and basic stage in the history of Highland and Island Scotland, and 42 Arnol will now remain an enduring symbol and reflection of a form of community organisation that in another generation or so will lie quite outside the memory of individuals.

This observation encapsulates for me why it is important that we preserve *and* present our built heritage for present and future generations. Those of us engaged in the process of conserving the past are not against change as such. How can we be when the one thing we constantly learn from looking at the past is that the world moves on? We work to provide a future for the past chiefly because we believe that the past has something important to offer the future.

■ ■ ■

Bibliography

Carter, J. (ed.) *A Sense of Place: an interpretive planning handbook* (Tourism and Environment Initiative, 1997)

Clarke, D. and Maguire, P. *Skara Brae: Northern Europe's best preserved prehistoric village* (Historic Scotland, 1995)

Fenton, A. *The Island Blackhouse* (Historic Scotland, 1978; new edition 2005)

Ham, S. *Environmental Interpretation: a practical guide for people with big ideas and small budgets* (North American Press, 1992)

Tabraham, C. *A Manual for Site Interpretation at Properties in Care* (Historic Scotland, 1998)

Young, V. and Urquhart, D. *Access to the Built Heritage: advice on the provision of access for people with disabilities to historic sites open to the public* (Historic Scotland, 1996)

Chapter 5

HERITAGE INTERPRETATION AND CADW

Peter Humphries

Cadw is a directorate within what is now the Welsh Assembly Government (formerly the Welsh Office). A sister organization to English Heritage and Historic Scotland, it was formed in 1984 and carries out the statutory responsibilities of the Assembly for identifying, protecting, conserving and presenting the ancient monuments and historic buildings of Wales. Currently around 130 monuments come directly within Cadw's care and it is the presentation and interpretation of this group that form the focus of this chapter.

Most of these sites are long ruined and roofless. The bulk of the estate in Wales dates from the Middle Ages, with castles and abbeys predominating; but other periods are plentifully represented too, ranging from neolithic burial chambers and standing stones through to sites of the industrial revolution and later. Most stand in open countryside – small field monuments with open public access and no staff or visitor facilities of any kind; an increasing number are looked after by local key-keepers with varying degrees of visitor provision, while the remainder, around 35 monuments, are staffed throughout all, or part, of the year and attract upwards of one and a quarter million visitors. All of these sites are maintained with public funds and consequently there is a requirement for all to be provided with some level of interpretation as a service to those who visit them, but the style and degree of that interpretation vary inevitably according to the size and condition of the monument.

Cadw's overall interpretative aim is to provide a minimum of one information panel at every site in its care, together with a published account of that site in a guidebook (either singly or as part of a group). Where monuments have covered or enclosed accommodation it may be possible to introduce more comprehensive provision – additional panels, one or more site exhibitions, or an audio tour – but this depends upon the individual circumstances and, to some extent, upon the level of visitor income. Larger projects are normally subject to an investment appraisal, with the initial capital cost of the project balanced against potential additional revenue generation. Examples from both ends of this interpretative spectrum will be discussed below, together with some of the methodology that lies behind them.

Information panels

These form the mainstay of Cadw's site-based interpretation and have twice been recipients of Interpret Britain awards; their production first began in the late 1970s when they were devised to present information for visitors at small isolated field monuments where there was no other provision. When Cadw came into existence late in 1984 it was decided to extend their role to all sites in care other than roofed buildings with furnished interiors and certain small field monuments; thus large castles or abbeys might have a dozen or more, smaller sites perhaps two or three. Usually one panel supplies an introduction to the site – date, purpose, historical background, etc. – and subsequent panels provide specific information about the particular area in which they are located. Generally, the panel will include a plan or graphic of the site; this is always oriented to match the visitor's direction of view and has a 'you are here' locator. As with all of Cadw's site-based interpretation, each information panel is fully bilingual in English and Welsh. Initially, this was regarded as a necessary provision for an organization charged with the preservation and presentation of Wales's architectural heritage; but, since the introduction of the Welsh Language Act in 1993, it is now also a legal requirement for all public sector organizations in Wales. Bilingualism naturally doubles the length of all texts; but this is also a powerful inducement towards brevity and it is a useful discipline. In order to lessen the visual impact of the text different colours and typefaces are used for each language – and it is pleasing to note here that Cadw's panels have been selected as examples of good bilingual practice by the Welsh Language Board and are illustrated in its publication on the subject.

Three sizes of panel are produced, and two kinds of frame system: the panel variants have texts of 85, 150 or 230 words plus brief captions for illustrations; the frames are either freestanding or wall-mounted. On the larger medieval monuments and those with substantial upstanding masonry the wall-mounted variety tends to predominate; first, this is to lessen visual intrusion – a factor of particular significance at sites of outstanding architectural merit – and, second, it avoids potential disturbance to the archaeology. The frames are made up to Cadw's own pattern; they are now very durable and are designed to take replacement panels if required at some future date. They are constructed from galvanized steel and aluminium, and finished in dark brown powder-coat.

The production method and house style of these panels have remained reasonably constant, but both have undergone continuous refinement over the period. Initially, it was decided to employ a system of silk-screening graphics to the underside of clear polycarbonate sheet; a sealing sheet of self-adhesive vinyl was applied over the printed surface and the finished panel then affixed to a frame for positioning on site. This system had two main advantages: it offered good resistance to vandalism and was cheaper to produce than comparable systems such as glass-reinforced polyester (GRP) encapsulation, or laminate production methods; and it could be produced locally, unlike the proprietary systems of the other methods. Local designers and printing companies were sought by competitive tender to carry out the work of production, but the origination of the texts and assembling of other material to be included was done by Cadw's own staff.

Previous refinements have included a change of colour scheme and the inclusion of cibachrome photographic colour prints, which permitted the inclusion of full-colour artwork alongside the silk-screen printing system. Nowadays production methods have changed to embrace modern technology, though the overall design concept has largely been retained. The panels are now designed and output entirely by computer. Any full-colour illustrations to be included are scanned onto disk at high resolution; other graphics, such as plans are usually computer-generated, together with the text. The panel is produced by ink-jet printer at high resolution using light-resistant inks and is bonded to the underside of clear polycarbonate, as before. This system is relatively new and as yet untested for maximum durability, but it does carry a minimum guarantee of ten years in the open air and it is hoped that average life expectancy should comfortably exceed this figure. Not only does this system allow far greater flexibility than hitherto in terms of graphic design, it is also very much cheaper: at around £200, the cost of producing a panel is now one-third of what it was using silk-screen printing.

Reconstruction drawings

There are two main graphic components on information panels: plans and maps (now usually computer-generated) and reconstruction drawings, which at present are still drawn by hand. These drawings are used not just on panels, but in site exhibitions, occasionally in retail items such as postcards and posters, and also extensively in Cadw's guidebook series; they are a great aid to the visitor's understanding of ruined and largely destroyed buildings and one of the mainstays of Cadw's interpretation strategy.

All reconstruction drawings are still commissioned externally. For ancient monuments, work had first begun in this field with the well-known series of 'bird's-eye' views painted by Alan Sorrell during the 1950s and 1960s. Interestingly, at that time these were commissioned for display on site and reproduction on postcards, but they never appeared in the 'blue guides' (the old guidebook series) because they were conjecture and not fact – how views have changed today! The creation of Cadw provided a fresh impetus for interpretative reconstructions and a rolling programme of new drawings was begun. As well as aerial perspectives, a series of more analytical drawings was commissioned: designed to strip away parts of the outer walls in order to illustrate details of the interior arrangements, these might show, for example, the sequence of defences inside a castle gatehouse, or the layout and liturgical arrangements inside a Cistercian abbey church. Sometimes attempts have been made to depict known historical events, or to represent a room interior in use. The intention throughout has been to aid understanding of how buildings would have appeared and of how they were used. In most of these drawings people are shown using the building, not just for the obvious reason that people once lived there, but as a real aid to comprehension – thus, for instance, a cutaway drawing of the extraordinary triple arrowloops at Caernarfon Castle makes immediate sense when several archers are shown firing through them simultaneously. Drawings such as these effectively combine art with architecture, the aesthetic with the technical, and their execution requires the imagination of the artist as well as the accuracy of the draughtsman.

And yet, however much research goes into the production of a reconstruction drawing, it can only ever be a 'best guess'; an attempt, using the fullest and most up-to-date knowledge available at the time, to interpret something that ultimately is unknowable. It was once famously said that 'art is a lie that tells the truth'. Therein lies the dilemma that all practitioners of reconstructions face: people will believe what is presented to them in the name of authority, and it is particularly incumbent upon a public body to take the utmost care over interpretation such as this. Already, as a direct result of more recent research, we have produced second, and sometimes third versions of some of our reconstructions, each one, hopefully, an additional step along the path towards historical accuracy. At Tintern Abbey, for example, detailed analysis of the *ex situ* moulded stonework from the site led to a complete, and somewhat unexpected reappraisal of the form of the cloister arcade and enabled us to attempt a fully-detailed reconstruction of the long-dismembered *pulpitum* screen, dividing nave from presbytery within the abbey church. The very questions asked in the course of preparatory research for a drawing may lead to the overturning of previously accepted supposition, and the process may thus make its own contribution towards a fuller knowledge and understanding of the site.

Guidebooks

Mention was made earlier of Cadw's guidebook series. This, too, has won much praise in the academic and the publishing world and has also been the recipient of an Interpret Britain award. When begun in 1985, the intention was to retain the accuracy and authority of the old 'blue guide' series, but to present information in a broader context and in a more accessible and appealing format. These publications, nevertheless, were still to be guidebooks, in the sense that they were, and still are, written and arranged primarily to guide the reader around the site and to offer a detailed description and interpretation of the features to be seen there. The history and other contextual information may be read either on site or afterwards. Thus the books serve a dual purpose: first as primary interpretation, in tandem with the other material installed at the site; and second both as souvenirs of the visit and, in their own right, as one of the principal published academic authorities for the monument. The early guidebooks were extensively illustrated in monochrome and were designed using the old 'cut-and-paste' method. In large part the success of the series has been due to the improvements in graphics alluded to earlier – all of the reconstruction drawings that we commission are reproduced in the guidebooks as well as the site-based interpretation – but advances in technology and careful use of resources have led to gradual refinements in production methods and design, with a move to the full-colour reproduction of plans, maps and other artwork as well as abundant colour photographs, again specially commissioned for the purpose. These guidebooks, and all the other Cadw publications, are now entirely designed on computer by a contract designer working in our offices alongside Cadw publications staff. It is a formula that has served us well and the steady improvement in quality and output of our publications is testimony to its success.

Audio tours

Returning to site-based interpretation, panel graphics are often used to complement the information presented in another form of on-site interpretation: audio tours. Staffing restrictions make it impossible for Cadw staff to offer personal guided tours, and it has only proved commercially viable for outside groups to operate such a service at the castles of Caernarfon and Conwy, which each receive around 200,000 visitors annually. At several other sites pre-recorded audio tours have been used very successfully to guide visitors around and identify points of particular interest. The system has been in use for well over 15 years with all tours to date being relayed in stereo including commentary, music and various sound effects. At some sites use of the tour is included with the entry price, at others it is a chargeable extra. This is because it was impossible with the older technology (i.e. Walkman-type personal cassette machines) for site staff physically to dispense, take back and reset the equipment if there were more than around 30,000 visitors per annum. A number of companies now operate in this field and most offer a broadly comparable service: production of a recorded tour to satisfy the specifications of the client, together with the supply and maintenance of appropriate equipment to relay it. The chief differences are apparent in the types of equipment on offer – and this has changed substantially over the last few years, with digital random-access equipment now becoming standard. But whatever the advances in technology, tours basically come in two variants: mono and stereo. With the former it is necessary to hold a unit up to the ear, rather like a telephone and usually with similar sound quality; stereo provides much better sound and a more immersive experience, but has the drawback of isolating visitors from others in their group. Despite the need for headphones – always the most vulnerable element in the system – we believe that stereophonic audio offers a better experience to the visitor, and we have recently awarded a new five-year contract to provide and maintain audio tours and equipment at several sites. The new digital units provide full stereophonic reproduction, and have the capacity to provide not only optional layers of information (both audio and text), but to relay tours in several languages, or in differing versions. We are thus now able to offer tours in French and German, as well as English and Welsh and will be reviewing possible additional requirements in due course.

At one site, Plas Mawr in Conwy, a partly furnished Elizabethan house, the self-guiding audio tour is the principal means of piloting visitors around the building (since the guidebook, in this one instance, has not been designed to fulfil this function). Visitors are invited to help themselves to the equipment and return it afterwards. For each area of the house there is a basic description, followed by optional sections dealing with particular aspects of interest – items of furniture and furnishing, plasterwork, activities connected with the room, etc.; there is also a small quiz for younger listeners. Visitors can choose how much of the tour they wish to listen to, according to their particular interests or time available.

Case study 1: Plas Mawr

Plas Mawr was built by Robert Wynn, a then rising member of the Tudor gentry in Wales, between 1576 and 1585; with its distinctive 'crow-step' gables, the house is a prominent landmark at the centre of Conwy town. It was occupied by the Wynn family for little more than 100 years. After Robert Wynn's death in 1598 his descendants became involved in a lengthy dispute over his will which left little money to make changes to the building; by 1683 Plas Mawr had passed down to Robert's great-granddaughter whose new husband already had two major houses in the area and had little need for another. During the eighteenth and nineteenth centuries it was rented out and subdivided and fell gradually into ever greater disrepair. In an attempt to stem this decay the house was offered to the Royal Cambrian Academy of Art in 1887 and became its headquarters for the best part of the following century; but despite sterling work to keep the building from collapse during its custodianship, the burden eventually became too great for the academy and in 1993 it was placed in the guardianship of the State.

Plas Mawr is both a scheduled ancient monument and a grade I listed building, but it is very different to most other sites in the Cadw estate. It was taken into care, first, because it is the finest unaltered town house of the Elizabethan period now surviving in this country – ironically, this is mainly because of the lack of money in earlier centuries to make substantial changes to it – and, second, because its poor condition clearly required the expenditure of a very large amount of money to repair and conserve it. Four hundred years of ageing, weather and neglect had taken a severe toll, and although numerous repairs had been carried out in the past many of them were stop-gap measures that did not cure the underlying problems.

Once the building was in care, a team was appointed within Cadw to see through all the work on the house and to appoint external contractors as necessary. A development plan was drawn up in order to guide the programme of conservation and eventual presentation of the house. This had two principal underlying aims: first, that as much as possible of the historic fabric of the building be retained; and, second, that the modern use of the house and circulation within it should reflect, as far as possible, the original arrangements. Before any work began a detailed measured survey was undertaken to record the structure and condition of the building with the information being recorded digitally for input to computer. Meanwhile, an archaeologist prepared detailed drawings of all the decorative masonry, timberwork and plasterwork. This careful recording and analysis continued throughout the repair of Plas Mawr and was supplemented by full photographic recording; video recordings were made also of progress on the repairs showing each process and illustrating the various stages of the project.

The presentation of the house was to be centred on a date of 1665; this was the date of the only surviving inventory of contents taken after the death of Robert Wynn, grandson of the original builder – and effectively our only information about its early furnishing and use. Unfortunately, the inventory was not overly comprehensive in that it failed to mention most of the smaller chattels and grouped together all the larger items of furniture simply as 'heyrelooms'. No moveable items of furniture original to the house had survived, although there were lengths of fixed benching in the two principal public rooms.

And so a contract was let to a company specializing in the research and recreation of historic interiors; their first task was to undertake a room-by-room survey, using the inventory as a starting point, in order to identify appropriate furniture and furnishings and then to recommend a practical scheme for presenting the interior of the house. Following receipt of this survey and an assessment of the various cost implications, it was decided to refurnish seven rooms in the house completely: six of them were to be based upon the 1665 inventory description; the seventh, up in the attics, would be a late nineteenth-century garret, reflecting the time when the house was subdivided and leased to a variety of tenants. The other rooms in the house (eight of them on the two main floors) were assigned to different purposes. Three interlinked rooms on the first floor were to house an exhibition display about health and hygiene in Tudor and Stuart Britain. Another two interlinked rooms on the ground floor would house a second display about the conservation work on the house, and a third room next to these would demonstrate the various stages of conservation on its plaster and timberwork. The buttery, adjoining the main entrance in the ground-floor hall, was to become the main visitor reception point; and the final remaining room, identified as the bedroom of Robert Wynn and having the most comprehensive assemblage of plasterwork emblems in the whole house, was to be left unfurnished for the time being.

Work on the furnishing and eventual presentation of the house proceeded hand-in-hand with the main conservation process. Appropriate furniture and other items were steadily acquired; these were a combination of original pieces and replicas, for the intention was not to produce traditional historic-house interiors, but to allow visitors full and unfettered access to every part of the furnished rooms.

Detailed consideration was given also to the possibility of colouring the decorative plasterwork emblems and stone fireplaces after their conservation and repair (most of the evidence for this had long disappeared, but some traces of early colouring schemes had been recovered during the conservation process); and, second, to the style, appropriateness and practicality of producing wall hangings and other soft furnishings. Specialist reports were commissioned in both of these areas.

The plasterwork report examined the remaining and comparative evidence for pigmentation. It concluded that there was an overwhelming case for at least partial recolouring and proposed schemes for the hall and the great chamber (the two principal public rooms in the house). It identified appropriate heraldic pigments for these and recommended a methodology of applying the colour over a barrier layer, making the whole process fully reversible and thus satisfying the strict conservation requirements. A separate contract was let to carry out this work.

The report on furnishings examined the question of whether wall hangings were appropriate for a house of this quality at the given date, and of what kind these should be. Hangings had not been specifically referred to in the inventory, but there was mention of Kidderminster stuff (a wool and linen patterned fabric common in British seventeenth-century contexts) in at least one room. After careful assessment of the comparative evidence the report recommended that two rooms in the house should be equipped with hangings: Kidderminster stuff in the principal bed chamber for the lower walls, the bed hangings and the window curtain; and Dornix (another wool and linen mixture) on the lower walls in the great chamber. Dornix is a fabric of more tapestry-like appearance, originating from the low countries and commonly used in houses of the middle rank during the second half of the sixteenth century. Weave diagrams for both fabrics were prepared from fragments of original cloth surviving in the Whitworth Gallery, Manchester and in the museum of Stockholm; the yarns were dyed in the traditional manner in Wales, using vegetable-based dyes and the bolts of cloth were specially woven for the house on a Jacquard loom in Scotland. The hangings were finished with fringes of the same dyes and hung in the rooms in the correct manner on iron tenterhooks inserted into timber battens.

Considerable levels of care and research have gone into creating the historic interiors at Plas Mawr to ensure that they represent what might have been seen there in the middle years of the seventeenth century. This extends to perishable items, too: the kitchen, for example, is kept supplied with fresh herbs and spices and its floor is strewn with rushes and sweet-smelling herbs, while the pantry has salted fish, hams and sides of bacon, in addition to the taxidermist's more permanent contributions of game and fowl. The presentation of the house also comprises the two exhibition displays mentioned earlier. The health and hygiene display includes two computer-based touch-screen interactives: one allows visitors to ask a seventeenth-century physician what is wrong with them (from a list of symptoms displayed); the other is an 'ask the expert' session about cesspits that includes 'talking-head' video. Both of these are run directly from PC hard disk. The conservation display also contains touch-screen video to access information, and here use has been made of material originally produced for conservation and record purposes. The video footage of the conservation work on the house has been edited into a series of short programmes about different aspects of the task – roofs, floors, plasterwork and so on. Into this has been incorporated 'virtual-reality' computer modelling of the house, compiled from the digital survey data, so that diagrammatic 3-D models of the interior structure can be used to supplement and explain the live video footage. The video, which lasts for a total of 25 minutes, has proved so popular with visitors that a retail version has now been produced. Another feature of this exhibition is a one-tenth-scale model of the roof structure and a series of half-scale timber joints, complete with pegs, that can be picked up and taken apart; these are used to help explain some of the conservation work illustrated in the exhibition and video.

The entire conservation and fitting out took some three and a half years and Plas Mawr opened to the public again in May 1997. The total cost of the conservation work was around £3 million, with an additional £300,000 devoted to the presentation of the house – furniture, furnishing and hangings, audio tour, exhibitions and souvenir publication.

Case study 2: Caerphilly Castle

Built by Earl Gilbert de Clare, Caerphilly Castle is a large, impressive and fully developed thirteenth-century concentric fortress. Not only has it the customary double ring of stone curtain walls, towers and gatehouses, but also comprehensive water defences which, on the north and south sides, extend into fully developed lakes. The whole fortified area extends to something over 12 hectares (30 acres), making Caerphilly not only the largest castle in Wales, but one of the largest in Europe. But it is not merely its size that makes a visit to the site memorable; it is also the extensive amount of restoration that has taken place there. This was carried out from 1870 onwards by two successive owners of the castle, the third and fourth marquesses of Bute; during the 1930s, in particular, most of the ruined wall tops and large sections of the towers and gatehouses were systematically rebuilt. Even after the castle was transferred to state care in 1950, that restoration work continued, with the water defences being reflooded in 1958.

When considering ways of presenting the castle to the public, therefore, Caerphilly offered different possibilities to most other ancient monuments: a large site with no shortage of space; comprehensive and highly sophisticated defences; located in an area of dense population; close to major transport routes; but above all, the extent of previous restoration allowed us greater latitude of action than at other sites. It was military considerations that were clearly uppermost in the planning and building of this great fortress, and so it seemed entirely appropriate that warfare should be the theme to adopt in our presentation of the site.

The castle dates almost entirely from the late thirteenth century; it was not greatly used afterwards, and from later in the fifteenth century seems to have been allowed to decay. Thus its main period of use coincided with the era before the adoption of gunpowder, when castle warfare was dominated by the siege engine; indeed it was specifically to protect against these that the castle's great lakes were included in the defensive plan, no doubt following the model of Kenilworth, where Gilbert de Clare had seen similar lakes ward off the effects of Henry III's best engines during the long siege of 1266. Although there is no documentary record of such engines being used at Caerphilly, four large rounded stone balls recovered from one of the drawbridge pits do point to the probability.

Following an option appraisal, it was decided to construct modern examples of these war engines and place them on display at Caerphilly as the first stage of a project to replicate the equipment of medieval war. In order to locate them where they could be operated, however, a compromise had to be made. Clearly they could not be aimed in the direction of a potential enemy outside the castle perimeter. Instead, a location was identified on the south platform, which dams back the waters of the south lake; here, facing westwards along the surface of the lake, there is at least 300 m (330 yards) of clear water, and the reconstructed weapons would be able to propel their missiles without risk.

It was resolved to construct four different sorts of engine, to represent the main types in use during the thirteenth century and illustrate (as we hoped) the three main propulsive forces of torsion, tension and counterpoise. The four were a mangonel (torsion), a ballista (tension, or torsion), a perrier (counterpoise: traction) and a trébuchet (counterpoise: weight). A contract to research and build was tendered and the work was awarded to a company specializing in historical reconstruction. The main criteria were that the engines should conform, as nearly as possible, in construction details, size and materials to those used in the late thirteenth century and should be capable of safe operation. The contract included not only the construction of the engines themselves, but also production of an explanatory video film for display inside the castle, and operation of the engines for public view on agreed days in the summer.

Initially, several months were spent on research to establish the precise details of each engine. Once this was complete, detailed working drawings were made and construction work began. The first engine to be built was a mangonel. This weapon seems to have had its origin in the later Roman Empire and was then known as an onager (meaning wild ass), probably coined from the bucking action of its rear end when operated. It has a heavy ground frame with vertical uprights and cross pieces; through this ground frame passes a horizontal torsion skein into which the base of the throwing arm is anchored. To operate it, the arm is wound down to the horizontal against the pressure of the skein; when released, it flings its projectile forward and upwards. Roman versions of this weapon usually employed a small sling on the end of the arm, but medieval examples seem to have used a spoon-ended arm instead. Huge forces are exerted by the torsion skein on all parts of this engine and, because of this, its timbers need to be massive, making the mangonel heavy and unwieldy. As our later demonstrations were to prove, it is not a very efficient weapon, at least in its normal medieval form, and this no doubt accounts for the relative paucity of descriptions, or illustrations of it in medieval documents.

The second engine was a ballista. This, too, originated in classical antiquity; Greek and Roman versions of this weapon seem to have been operated exclusively by torsion and were employed variously to shoot either large darts or stones, but medieval examples were almost always used to shoot darts, as anti-personnel weapons. From contemporary illustrations and descriptions, it is difficult to be certain how medieval ballistas were normally constructed, but both torsion and tension seem to have been employed. For our version, we had hoped to build a tension-powered weapon (essentially a giant crossbow mounted on a stand), using a composite single bow arm constructed of wood and horn; however, several unsuccessful experiments in constructing such a bow led us, regretfully, to the conclusion that this would be too difficult and costly to achieve, and was likely to be unsafe in operation, and so we decided to produce a torsion-powered weapon instead using two bow arms, each anchored into vertical skeins of rope.

The third engine was the perrier. This class of weapon is the most difficult to identify with precision from the contemporary accounts, because of the variety of names given to it, and seems to have been the most diverse in style. Sometimes referred to as *petraria*, the name simply means 'stone thrower', and denotes a type of weapon derived from the pole sling, with stout wooden trestles supporting a pivoting throwing arm, to one end of which is attached a sling for the projectile and, to the other, traction ropes for the operating crew. It seems to have been of eastern origin, though it had become well-established in the west by the end of the twelfth century. The perrier is the most frequently depicted engine in manuscript illustrations, though it is often not recognized as such by modern commentators. It was thus, in all probability, the most commonly used siege weapon, and this would be supported by our own findings, which confirm that it is relatively easy to construct and has superior adaptability and speed of operation.

The final engine to be constructed was a trébuchet. These weapons comprised the heavy artillery of the pre-gunpowder era and came into common use in the thirteenth century as developments of the perrier. The trébuchet, too, is operated by lever action, but here the motive force is a massive counterweight, rather than human traction. Some accounts of these weapons speak of improbably large dimensions, but they could clearly be of impressive size – even allowing for exaggeration – and were supposedly loaded, on occasion, not only with dead animals, but even human prisoners. We decided to build a machine that was relatively compact, yet which should be capable of reasonable performance. The base frame measures 6.1 × 4.3 m (20 ft × 14 ft 3 in) and the height of the trestles is 4.1 m (13 ft 6 in). The arm is of composite construction and 6.7 m (22 ft) long; a ballast box is suspended on a swivel beneath the arm and contains approximately 2 tonnes of stone and sand; the rope sling is 9.1 m (30 ft) long unlooped. The entire engine weighs approximately 10 tonnes.

All four engines were first tested for safety, and have been operated under test conditions and in front of the public on numerous occasions since their installation at Caerphilly in 1992. All have continued to operate well, though we have had to replace throwing arms on the mangonel (several times) and on the perrier (twice). Of the four engines, the perrier has the greatest speed of operation and was clearly very effective in use. Our perrier is operated by a six-man crew pulling in unison on the ropes at the front end. All the ropes used in this engine, as in the others, are of hardy hemp, a man-made fibre that resembles natural hemp in appearance – a concession made because these engines stand permanently in the open air and need to be capable of continued use. The projectiles are rounded, sea-worn boulders with an optimum weight of around 5 kg (11 lb), and these are consistently hurled for a distance of around 110 m (120 yards). We carried out a test to establish the maximum speed of operation and found that, with six men pulling on the ropes and another loading the sling, up to six shots could be made in the space of one minute. With changes of crew, several such engines could thus keep up a very rapid bombardment in siege conditions. The initial testing of the trébuchet caused us some concern, because it was potentially the most dangerous and destructive of the four reconstructions. However, our calculations proved to have been sound and it has worked perfectly from the outset. The winding down of the arm is a slow and laborious process that requires up to six people: two to turn the winch and four to haul down the throwing arm. The missiles used are also rounded sea-worn boulders, but of around 15 kg (32 lb) in weight, and the entire operation of loading and releasing takes about ten minutes. The range of this engine has been quite consistent, at 120 m (130 yards), and the missiles all tend to land within a closely defined area. With that degree of accuracy and the size of projectiles known to have been used, which were often considerably larger than the Caerphilly examples, bombardment from these engines would undoubtedly have been very destructive, and it is easy to see how they gained their fearsome reputation. That drama is still there today: for modern castle visitors, watching the trébuchet in action is clearly the high point of all our live demonstrations.

The reconstructed siege engines at Caerphilly were never designed to be experimental in the true scientific sense; resources and safety considerations have imposed too many limitations for this. Rather, they were intended to provide for the general public an idea of the likely appearance, size and operation of engines of war in the late thirteenth century and to indicate their potential. It was the first, and is still the most comprehensive, attempt to reproduce all of these weapons in Britain.

As a second stage in the warfare project we have reconstructed a length of overhanging timber fighting gallery (or *hourd*) along one of the wall tops in the castle's inner ward. Such hourds were once relatively common on castle battlements in this country and throughout much of Europe; they allowed the defenders, safe inside, to control the exterior of the curtain wall and thus ward off attempts to scale it or undermine it. No original versions survive, but the beam holes provided to support them are still obvious at many sites in this country and there are numerous documentary references to their erection. The reconstructed stretch at Caerphilly extends for about 25 m (27 yards) and visitors are free to enter it from the main wallwalk. In a tableau, constructed at one end to illustrate its defensive purpose, a crossbowman aims his weapon out though one of the arrowloops while a second defender prepares to drop a heavy boulder through an open floorboard onto an attacker beneath.

Information panels on site at Caerphilly help to interpret both the hourd and the siege engines. Additionally, an illustrated information leaflet about the engines has been produced and an eight-minute video that describes the project and shows each engine being operated can be viewed on demand in the main site exhibition. To date the project at Caerphilly has cost in the region of £100,000. As time and resources permit it is hoped to be able to extend the medieval warfare theme with additional reconstructions and a major exhibition display on the subject, but for now it rests as described.

Cadw is not a large organization and its resources are relatively small compared to other national bodies. The annual budget for site interpretation at monuments in care currently stands at less than £180,000 and there is only a single member of staff to undertake the task, with all production work carried out by contract. The publications budget is slightly less, with three members of staff and a part-time contract designer. Nevertheless, Cadw has achieved much in its 20 years of existence and its reputation in the field of site interpretation and guidebook production has grown steadily. It is to be hoped that the next 20 years will prove even more fruitful.

Chapter 6

CONSTRUCTING PASTS: INTERPRETING THE HISTORIC ENVIRONMENT

Tim Copeland

Introduction

Research into the construction and effectiveness of interpretations at historic sites has rarely tried to explore the underlying nature of the transactions that occur between site, interpreter and visitor. This chapter examines this issue using a constructivist approach and to develop parameters of good practice. It aims to demonstrate that the processes of interpretation are not vastly different from the processes that surround the reception of that interpretation. In both cases it is self-interpretation, or more correctly, construction, since only the individual can interpret the site, albeit within the scaffolding of others' ideas and their own backgrounds. The interpreter(s) construct(s) a view of the site but from the perspective of a wider maturity of experience. In mediating the interpretation to a public, that maturity of experience is often hidden and a more didactic account is presented. This chapter argues that this veiling of experience is neither necessary nor effective and, indeed, in terms of visitor understanding can be counter productive to a more mature appreciation of our knowledge of the past.

Constructivism is interpretation

Constructivism is not a theory about interpretation; it's a theory about knowledge and learning (Brooks and Brooks 1993). Visitors want to understand historic sites and therefore learn at historic locations whether formally or informally, consciously or unconsciously. Learning from a constructivist perspective is understood as a self-regulatory process of resolving inner cognitive conflicts that often become apparent through concrete experiences, collaborative discourse and reflection. This is distinct from a positivist approach that provides only one view of complex issues and presumes that there is a fixed place that the visitor must come to know. It identifies a body of knowledge to be digested and didactic ways of achieving this. It is the role of the interpreter to identify or to engender cognitive conflicts in understanding the past through the tools of concrete experience of the historic site, providing the opportunities for collaborative discourse and allowing reflection.

A constructivist approach simply suggests that we construct our own understandings of the world in which we live. Since the past does not exist any more we have to construct what it might have been like from present evidence. We construct our understandings through reflection upon our interactions with objects and ideas, or in the case we are discussing, with the sites and artefacts from the past and the ideas of others who have already constructed their own understandings and are in a position to share them. This 'expert' status has been gained also through making sense of the evidence for the past through synthesising new experiences and building them into the individual's conceptual framework.

The growth of archaeology has been marked by encounters with objects, ideas and phenomena that didn't make sense to inquirers. The discrepant evidence or perceptions were either interpreted to conform to the prevailing notions about the significance of the past or a new set of ideas were generated to explain more clearly the things that were perceived. Throughout the history of archaeology understandings have been shaped in such a way. Learning has not necessarily been through discovering more, but interpreting it through a different scheme or structure. New knowledge, though of a temporary nature, has been constructed because of the melding of the evidence and the pre-occupations of the perceiver.

Our understanding of the past has grown because inquirers have experienced various aspects of the evidence at different periods of the discipline's development and so more complex understandings have been constructed. Each of these understandings has resulted from the increased complexity of archaeologists' thinking. Each new insight has depended on the cognitive abilities of archaeologists to accommodate discrepant data and perceptions within their growing experience of evidence. An important factor also has been the wider experience of the archaeologist within the general ethos prevailing in society at particular times.

A similar process takes place when visitors encounter historic sites (Copeland 1998 and Copeland 2004). Figure 6.1 attempts to show how a constructivist approach views the processes that take place in the interpreting and experiencing of sites. The past is unseen and unseeable, but the remaining evidence for past actions can be retrieved and examined, though with a number of limitations caused by the nature of the evidence. Archaeological evidence is impersonal and difficult to interpret as well as being fragmentary. Historical evidence is selectively constructed, has precarious survival and biased viewpoints.

The 'expert' interpreter constructs a particularly personal account of the site – how can it be otherwise? The individual internalises information about the evidence that has significance for him or her. That selection is determined by a set of values and previous experience of the evidence. The set of values might be a particular academic viewpoint within archaeology or through personal research and certainly will encompass other aspects of the biography of the person. As the interpreter will have some values about how the evidence should be communicated to an audience there will be a broadly educational theoretical background also. This might

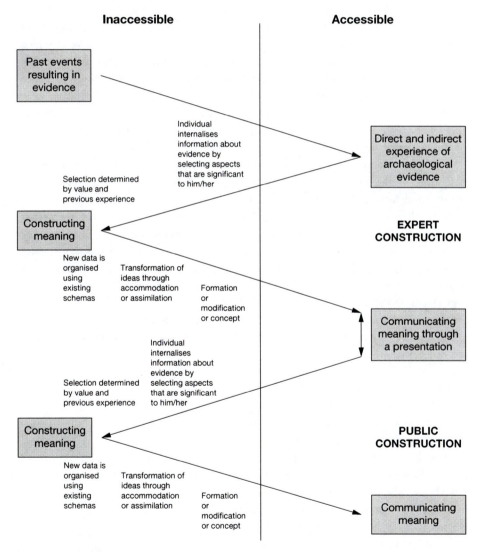

Figure 6.1   Constructions on archaeological sites
Source: Copeland 1998

be the delivery of an academic account or it might be an account aimed at a particular level of non-expert audience. The interpreter uses the selection of evidence
to make a construction that will either involve fitting the evidence into already
available mental schemas (assimilation) or producing new ones to accommodate the
selection (accommodation). A new mental schema is likely to result from cognitive dissonance or cognitive conflict. This occurs when the new evidence does not
fit the interpreter's present experience or when the generally accepted interpretation is viewed through a new viewpoint. Either way a construction is made that is
eventually presented to an audience.

A visitor will treat the interpretation in a similar fashion. It will form the evidence
base for selection from values that are brought to the site from everyday life as
well as education about the past. There will be a process of construction in which
ideas about the site are either assimilated or accommodated. If the interpretation
does not match previously held constructions cognitive conflict is likely to occur
and the visitor will have to accommodate new concepts into their cognitive view
of the site. Successful interpretation will engender these cognitive conflicts and
allow the visitor to develop more complex and clear conceptions of the meaning
of the evidence for the activities that took place at that location in the past.

The type of approach, positivist or constructivist, adopted will depend on the
objectives of the interpretation. Positivistic approaches will generally give ready
constructed facts and a fixed view of the site as it 'was' in the past and require
little of the visitor in understanding the place or the processes that formed it
(Lewthwaite 1988: 86). Getting a deeper understanding of the site will necessarily
encompass going beyond the simple and portraying the complexities of the site and
how constructions about it have been made (Potter 1997: 37). A constructivist
approach needs to be challenging and allow the visitor to make their own meanings (Hein 1998: 155).

Assessment and evaluation of interpretation will indicate whether the interpretation has been successful in meeting its objectives. If it is clear that these objectives
are not being met, the values of the inter-
preter will change and another cycle of
construction will take place.

A flow chart of site interaction using a
positivist model shows that the main flow
of information is from the evidence to the
interpreter, whether actually present, or
in the form of 'deferred' presence in a
guidebook, and then to the visitor who is
expected to internalise the interpretation
(Figure 6.2). Light (1988) suggests that such
clear objectives are needed to determine
what a visitor is expected to achieve on
a visit.

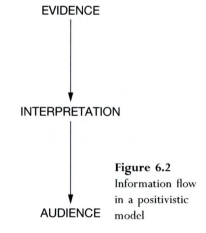

Figure 6.2
Information flow
in a positivistic
model

However, using the constructivist perspective, the model of transactions, on site becomes much more complex (Figure 6.3). The interpreter and interpretation becomes tangential to the site itself and the audience. The surviving evidence for the site influences the interpreter in that it circumscribes what can be known about the location, the 'site' presented is a selection from significant aspects for the interpreter and the value these hold within the previous experience of the interpreter. The interpretation is designed for audiences and they should determine its form so that their needs can be met. The interpretations are therefore able to empower the audience to make their own constructions from the evidence. While the audience experiences the site through engagement with it, it will be constructed in terms of what they see as significant in terms of relevance to their experience and the wider world. The site will have many meanings for them, and there is the possibility of numerous pasts being constructed. Visiting a monument is a cultural negotiation between the terms laid out in presentation and the visitors' own pattern of interaction (James 1986: 51).

Table 6.1 further develops these ideas and offers a contrast between positivist and constructivist approaches to interpretation. The positivist approach can be, and is, mediated through state of the art information technology, interactive figures, smells and sounds. However, the tasks' demands on the audience to construct their own understanding of the site are very limited even though the media through which this takes place appears to be challenging. Constructivist interpretation seeks to engage visitors with evidence and to help them understand it through providing problem solving approaches that enable them to construct their own meaning. It can use 'low-tech' activities as it is the 'message' not the 'medium' that is fundamental to understanding, but it can also use 'high tech' as a means to challenge not just give information.

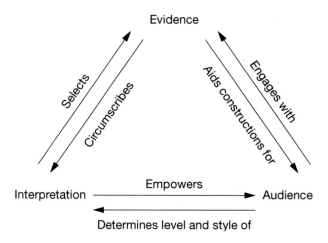

Figure 6.3 Information flow in a constructivist model

Table 6.1 Constructions on archaeological sites

Positivistic interpretation	Constructivist interpretation
The site is presented part to whole with emphasis on locational and factual knowledge.	The site is presented whole to part with emphasis on concepts of chronology, change, evidence and interpretation.
Sites rely heavily on guiding and intermediary technology such as audio-visual techniques.	Sites rely heavily on the use of evidence.
Visitors are viewed as consumers of knowledge.	Visitors are viewed as thinkers with present conceptions and emerging ideas about the past.
Interpretation is didactic.	Interpretation mediates the historic environment for visitors.
Strict adherence to set-out routes and explanations is highly valued.	Visitor exploration is highly valued.
Interpretation strategies are aimed at the individual.	Interpretation strategies are aimed to encourage discourse.
Assessment and evaluation seeks the correct response to validate success of strategies.	Assessment and evaluation seeks to discover visitor perspectives and improve interpretation.

In a constructivist setting interpreters must invite visitors to experience the site, empower them to ask their own questions and seek their own answers, and challenge them to understand the complexities of the evidence for the past in a particular location. Interpretation should be structured in ways that allow the construction of knowledge and become settings for visitors to be invited to search for understanding, appreciate the uncertainties and undertake enquiries as far as their present knowledge and the scaffolding of new ideas allows them.

Implications and strategies

If a constructivist approach is accepted by interpreters as having more validity for making meaning from the evidence of the past than a positivist approach, then this must be transposed into practical strategies to help audiences engage with the evidence of sites and to incorporate it into their present knowledge.

The site is presented whole to part with emphasis on 'big' concepts of chronology, change, evidence, interpretation

Structuring experience around primary concepts is a critical dimension of constructivist approaches (Brooks and Brooks 1993: 46). When designing interpretation, activity and information should be structured around conceptual clusters of problems, questions and discrepant situations. Many visitors become engaged when problems and ideas are presented holistically rather than in separate isolated parts. Making sense of the parts once the whole has been seen is often more effective than trying to build the whole from the parts. Many visitors never manage to see all the parts of the site to make a whole as they become disengaged over time and attempts to 'linearise' sites quickly stifle the understanding process. This has implications for initial interpretation on sites. There need to be panoramic views of the site and guided routes that enable the visitor to get an image of the whole site.

Constructivist approaches also work with 'big' concepts such as evidence types, change, chronology and interpretation. Rather than presenting facts in a linear pattern, the visitor is made aware of the emphasis on these 'big' concepts, so that it is easier for them to reflect, analyse, compare and contrast what they are seeing. Facts are still important in providing detail but they can be assimilated into a broad framework and they become more relevant for visitors. The use of broad concepts can also provide multiple entry points for visitors and invite participation irrespective of individual backgrounds and interests. The implication of this is that the evidence selected by the interpreter needs to reflect these concepts and the concepts must form the main structure of the interpretation. There need to be presentations that outline the concepts being used. Exhibitions, which are often situated at the end of the tour, need to be at the beginning where they would be more valuable in raising relevance issues of these concepts.

Some sites are particularly amenable to the concepts of either physical change through decay or weathering, or through human agencies and the advance of technology. Castles are a good example of where these large concepts can be introduced and used throughout a visitor experience. Many country houses have well delineated demarcations between the domestic and high status areas that can be constructed through evidence.

The use of big concepts allows the visitor to gain incremental knowledge of the evidence of the past in the landscape. It helps to ensure that visitors do not see every heritage venue as a special and unique case separate from the evidence of all the other sites that they have seen, but as part of a wider historic environment existing all around them.

Sites rely heavily on the use of evidence

A constructivist approach prefers, where possible, to use primary sources along with manipulative and interactive materials. Because interpretation can be abstract, a constructivist approach endeavours to present the real-world possibilities of the site to visitors. In many ways this is interpretation without 'interpreting', and the skill of the expert lies not in presenting information to the visitor but in identifying the most appropriate evidence and suggesting the types of questions that can be asked of it. Presenting ready synthesised information that relies on the authority of others can stifle enquiry. Sites make the problems and solutions immediately relevant – they can be investigated readily. Using a single example of evidence and identifying characteristics and meaning can be seen as 'specialisation'. Using many examples of similar types of evidence, carefully selected by the interpreter, can lead to 'generalisations' around the identified 'big' concept.

In choosing to work through evidence it is necessary not to overcomplicate the interpretation by drowning visitors in many examples of a particular concept. The examples that are identified need to show the characteristics to be focused on and be similar enough to allow generalisation. While it is possible to detect similarities between two examples of evidence, it usually takes three of more for the visitor to see the 'sameness' between evidence and the generalised meaning from them. Manipulative and interactive materials can act as a catalyst in this process, but should not be the starting point or the only experience of an aspect of the site offered to the visitor.

Visitors are viewed as thinkers with present conceptions and emerging ideas about the past

Visitors bring with them their own conceptions of the past to sites. The idea of 'emerging' means that these conceptions can be developed. An important requirement in helping visitors make meaning at sites is to ascertain what constructions they are bringing to the location. This may appear daunting, but because people have similar personal and social backgrounds they tend to produce constructions that are not widely varying, but they may do it in different ways. Constructivist sites need to take great care in the provision of activities that match the present conceptions of visitors through research into their experience and values. It will be important that some elements of these experiences and values are incorporated in the designed activities as visitors will use their present pre-occupations as a base from which to construct new ideas. It will always be important to work from and with the familiar as well as using the 'strange' and new. Clearly, careful evaluation of audience preconceptions is as valuable as post-site experience in designing an interpretation.

Interpretation mediates the historic environment for visitors

Effective constructivist interpretation mediates the present experience of visitors with a new and complex historic environment. Interpretation is at the interface of the individual and the evidence and provides the scaffolding to enable the visitors to make their own constructions. The onus should be on the visitor to do the thinking and sites need to value risk-taking by visitors through asking questions and to engender relevance through creating cognitive conflict.

One of the criticisms that might be aimed at a constructivist approach to sites is that it subordinates the information about the site to the needs of the visitor and that it will only be effective if the visitor has a pre-existing interest in the site.

While one of the main planks of constructivist thought is posing problems of emerging relevance to visitors, however, this does not mean that all visitors have to have a pre-existing interest in a site. The relevance of an aspect of the site can emerge through interpreter mediation; relevance can be created and stipulated.

To reach the audience and allow them to make constructions about the site for themselves involves identifying or engendering cognitive conflicts in understanding the past through the tools of concrete experience of the historic site, providing the opportunities for collaborative discourse and allowing reflection. Cognitive conflicts arise when present experience does not match that being presented. Problem solving situations engender cognitive conflict and therefore the emergence of relevance.

While visitors are acknowledged as intelligent by their presence at a site and the nature of the language used and visual formats employed in interpretation, this does not mean that they are viewed as thinkers. Thinking is an active process and many sites treat the transaction of knowledge as passive. Problem solving is a useful way of making visitors active as they see the relevance of an activity.

An effective problem-solving situation involves:

1   creating cognitive conflict or dissonance through a question or enquiry;
2   making use of the evidence of the site;
3   requiring the visitor to make a testable prediction;
4   being complex enough to have a number of approaches at a number of levels;
5   gaining from group discourse.

Asking questions of the visitor based on big ideas is a useful structure.

The problems to be solved should mix the unusual and commonplace and in comparison of the types of evidence analysis, synthesis and evaluation are encouraged.

At Rochester Castle the problem was 'What will happen to the wall in the future?' (Copeland forthcoming). Visitors brought with them the idea that the walls were 'real' and unaltered if weathered and had not suffered remedial intervention. Visitors liked the idea of permanence and a link with the medieval past. The interpretation used two vehicles. One was the image of a person inside the wall and the question 'What is it like to be a wall?'. Through the anthropomorphised figure, the effects of wind, rain, sun and humans were demonstrated. The second motif was a series of visual constructions of scaffolding around this section of wall throughout recorded history. The visitor was asked to examine the wall and to find the evidence of rebuilding. They were encouraged to discuss their observations after individual perusal. For audiences of children an elevation drawing was used so that the individual changes could be identified and recognised. Evaluation suggested that the visitors were able to understand the processes of weathering and human action on the walls and that this disturbed them, though, on reflection, it made the site more complex and meaningful as well as giving consideration to the future of the site. This was followed up with visual interpretations of Rochester without its castle and the question asked 'What would you miss if the castle did collapse?'. Evaluation showed that this was a significant issue for visitors and one that had not been thought about before. It highlighted the importance and fragility of the historic environment.

It was crucial for the interpretation to avoid making the problem too simple by giving more information than was necessary. Often it is the over-simplification of sites that confuses the visitor. Here the visitor had to construct their own meanings through using familiar categories and touch and sight, and making connections that they were competent to make and which might have been difficult if the exotic and new had been used.

Visitor exploration is highly valued

Since at many sites the construction of new knowledge is not so highly prized as the requirement to show what has been prepared for the visitor, routes around the location are often circumscribed, though the need for managing people and health and safety are crucial considerations. If new constructions are to be made then ease of access, ability to orient oneself to the site, and available time are important factors for consideration. Three-dimensional maps of the site are invaluable in the first respect as they reinforce the 'place' concept as well as allowing positioning within the site. The Cadw series of guides uses the central pages of the guidebook to show a realistic aerial view of the site that fulfils this requirement well. If the linear route is dispensed with, and the 'big concepts' used as a structure, then it should be possible for visitors to explore more widely. Comfort is also important in that it can extend visitor 'stay' times if there is somewhere to rest that is familiar. Comfortable places to rest or reflect also help visitors to seek relevance in what they see or have been introduced to and give them the opportunity to think through their point of view. Such modern features may alter the site, but if sites are not seen and made meaning of, why are we keeping them?

Interpretation strategies are aimed to encourage discourse

The process of construction does not take place in a vacuum. It is much easier to seek assimilation or accommodation of concepts when they can be verbalised and thought through out loud (Hein 1998: 172). One fundamental way for visitors to change or reinforce conceptions is through social discourse. Having the opportunity to present one's own ideas, as well as being permitted to hear and reflect on the ideas of others, is an enabling experience that reinforces self-determination and ownership. The benefits of discussion with others, particularly peers, facilitates the meaning-making process. Visitor to visitor dialogue is the foundation upon which co-operative meaning-making is structured. When constructed meanings are shared through social interaction, including shared views or shared affective experience often 'cognitive dissonance' is engendered as previous experience is tested against new ideas. This dialogue can lead to further construction and reconstruction of meanings from the physical evidence.

Many sites and historic settings structurally discourage co-operation and discourse and therefore the possibility of higher order responses. At other times it is the provision of 'expert' testimony about the site that inhibits dialogue. Often it is the non-negotiability of the ideas about the site that leads to visitors giving their own opinions in whispered asides.

Interpretation strategies rarely bring together non-educational parties in pairs or other groups. It is not the normal practice to encourage visitors to share their experiences except in a self-congratulatory manner through a visitors book or through evaluation of what has been provided. English Heritage Education Service produced 'family packs' which required work in pairs or small groups around the site and then the meeting up to share perspectives. These had a successful formula and with increasingly challenging material might make for a useful template for other sites. Clearly, fostering social interaction is easier in guided groups than in non-guided situations. However, if the ethos of the site is constructivist and these principles become overt and a 'selling' point, not 'see the past' but 'make the past', this habit can be engendered. Signage needs to be thought through so that discussion cues can be seen at particular points and through the provision of incongruous situations to provoke cognitive dissonance and encourage discussion.

Assessment and evaluation seeks to discover visitor perspectives and improve interpretation

Assessment of a constructivist approach needs to be concerned with process as well as being product oriented. It recognises the development of constructions over time and responds with understanding to the individuality and diversity of meaning-making. Clearly, the aims of such an approach to interpretation are not only concerned with the acquisition of knowledge about the site, and there- fore multiple choice questions to discover if the visitor has read and internalised the contents of the signage, display boards or the contents of the guide's dialogue are inappropriate in this context. Assessment of visitor experience should examine meaning-making in the context of the transactional relationship between the evidence, interpretation and audience.

Constructivist assessment has three main aims each of which reinforces the concept of individual experience and difference that is a cornerstone of construc- tivist approaches:

1   monitoring meaning-making development in terms of knowledge, experience and expertise;
2   identify difficulties in using evidence;
3   provide insight into interpretation and intervention strategies.

It is important to listen to visitor responses as much can be revealed by the way visitors talk to each other or to the 'expert'. The way visitors use language can help to assess the nature of their understanding and constructions and can help the interpreter to refine, extend and modify his/her ideas. Observing visitors engaging with evidence through 'shadowing' or 'chasing' can enable the effectiveness of chosen examples of evidence to be evaluated.

More formal techniques can be used in focused sample assessment and evaluation: discussions in groups, the writing of simple logs during the visit, using 'word-stems' to frame and scaffold responses: 'I expected to see . . . I learned that . . . the most surprising thing . . . The greatest insight was . . .', getting visitors to annotate drawings of evidence with their conceptions of what they see, and drawing concept maps, are all ways of eliciting visitor responses that respect individuality and difference.

Assessments such as these enable the interpreter to re-focus visitor activity through careful evaluation of the objectives of the interpretation and to undertake another cycle of construction themselves.

Conclusion

Using a constructivist approach inevitably makes the processes of interpretation more challenging, but not necessarily more complex. A constructivist approach might appear to devalue the knowledge of the expert in asking them to be an expert without communicating their academic expertise, and might engender resistance from more traditional visitors and employers. However, a constructivist approach actually increases the status of the interpreter and the site. It requires not only familiarity with the historical or archaeological parameters of the site, but with the processes that are used in meaning-making, identifying what is of relevance and instigating relevance, understanding the wider context of the visitor's background, producing situations where visitors learn through their own enquiry, and adapting words and images to those the visitor brings with them.

The outcomes of using a constructivist approach are more varied than those of a simple positivist approach. They will give value to the historic environment, allow visitors an insight into the 'secret garden' of the expert and enable value to be given to other sites that may be seen. The visitor will not be in the situation of disparate specialising every time they visit a site but be able to make more complex generalisations about the past and its complexity. The development of a constructivist approach to the historic environment offers a route out of the anodyne landscape of the heritage presentation.

■　■　■

References

Brooks, J. G. and Brooks, M. 1993. *In Search of Understanding: The Case for Constructivist Classrooms*. Alexandria, Virginia: Association for Supervision and Curriculum Development.

Copeland, T. 1998. Constructing History: All *Our* Yesterdays. In *Teaching the Primary Curriculum for Constructive Learning*, Littledyke, M. and Huxford, L. (eds), 119–130. London: David Fulton.

Copeland, T. 2004. Presenting Archaeology to the Public: Constructing Insights On-site. In *Public Archaeology*, Schadla-Hall, T. and Merriman, N. (eds). London: Routledge.

Copeland, T. (forthcoming). Interpreting and Presenting Recent Interventions at Historic Sites. Conference Paper: *Heritage Presentation and Interpretation in Europe*. Bournemouth University.

Hein, G. E. 1998. *Learning in Museums*. London: Routledge.

James, N. 1986. Leaving it to the Experts. In *The Management and Presentation of Field Monuments*, Hughes, M. and Rowley, L. (eds), 47–57. Oxford: Oxford University Department of External Studies.

Lewthwaite, J. 1988. Living in Interesting Times: Archaeology as Society's Mirror. In *Extracting Meaning from the Past*, Bintliff, J. (ed.), 86–98. Oxford: Oxbow Books.

Light, D. 1988. Problems Encountered with Evaluating the Educational Effectiveness of Interpretation. *Swansea Geographer* 25, 79–87.

Potter, B. P. Jr 1997. The Archaeological Site as an Interpretive Environment. In *Presenting Archaeology to the Public: Digging for Truths*, Jameson, J. H. (ed.), 35–43. Walnut Creek, California: Altamira Press.

Chapter 7

THE NATIONAL TRUST

Ruth Taylor

> It is the capacity to inspire which
> remains our most important contribution
> (Reynolds, 2004)

The Trust has come a long way since it was founded in 1895 when the three visionaries Octavia Hill, Canon Hardwicke Rawnsley and Robert Hunter campaigned to protect places of historic interest and natural beauty for the benefit of the nation. The words of the Duke of Westminster in 1895: 'Mark my words Miss Hill, this is going to be a very big thing' (Waterson, 2003) have indeed come to life.

The Trust is now the largest conservation charity in Europe. In 2004 the Trust had 3.1 million members, 43,000 volunteers, and cared for over 240 historic properties, including 49 industrial monuments and mills, 19 castles, 49 churches and chapels, 160 gardens, 73 landscape/deer parks, over 250,000 hectares of countryside and over 600 miles of coastline. Eighty per cent of the UK population live within 20 miles of a National Trust property. The Trust welcomes over 50 million visitors per annum to its coastal and countryside properties and over 13 million to its pay for entry properties; in addition these properties provide the biggest out of school classroom in the country with over 500,000 educational visits each year supporting curriculum topics from history and citizenship to creative arts. The importance of access continues to permeate all areas of the Trust's work. Over 100 years after its foundation, the Trust is engaged in a continuing process of maintaining relevance to the nation and in continuing to fulfil the vision laid out by its founders. The properties of the National Trust, with their beauty and history, contribute significantly to the health and well-being of the nation – learning in the fullest sense of the word. They offer a source of inspiration and provide life-enhancing experiences to people of all ages. Interpretation has an important role to play in this area.

The way the Trust has developed with emphasis on differing perspectives through an ever changing world has been a strong influence on its approach to learning and interpretation. In 1895 the three founders of the National Trust cared deeply about the need to protect beautiful historic places from being swept away by the processes of industrialisation in Victorian England.

> Octavia Hill was a devoted follower of Ruskin, a housing campaigner and passionate about the conditions in which people lived and brought up their children. She wanted open spaces, fresh air and nature to be available for everyone, however limited their means. She would take her tenants from poverty stricken inner London on outings to the countryside, to pick flowers, picnic and have the chance to fill their lungs with fresh country air.
>
> (Reynolds, 2004)

Sir Robert Hunter was Solicitor to the Post Office, a highly effective administrator and an authority on the legal status of common land. Canon Hardwicke Rawnsley was a campaigner for a number of good causes especially for the protection of the Lake District.

The founders wanted everyone to be the beneficiaries of their passion and for people's lives to be enhanced by the chance to enjoy the places their organisation would acquire. By 1894 they had won influential support from people such as the Duke of Westminster, Professor Huxley and James Bryce MP, and were ready to launch their new organisation – which they called 'The National Trust for Historic Sites and Natural Scenery'. The function of the proposed company was to be 'the acquisition and holding of properties to which common rights are attached; . . . and the maintenance and management of any buildings associated with them as places of resort for recreation and instruction'. Although education is not mentioned in the functions, 'instruction' suggests that the purpose was there. The Trust's founding Act, passed in 1907, again does not contain any reference to education although it did contain the phrase enabling the Trust to hold properties 'in perpetuity for the benefit of the nation'. This is now translated into the 'for ever for everyone' slogan. In 1895, within a few weeks of being registered under the Companies Act, the National Trust was given its first property. Fanny Talbot presented the Trust with five acres of gorse-covered cliff top at Dinas Oleu, overlooking Cardigan Bay in Wales. Shortly after this came Wicken Fen, Alfriston Clergy House and Long Credon Court House in Buckinghamshire. These and other acquisitions, often supported by public appeals, did more than establish the organisation. There were also many iconic places with important cultural associations – Coleridge's cottage at Nether Stowey, the stone circle at Castlerigg in Cumbria and the Old Post Office at Tintagel.

A strong social purpose was evident from the start, summed up by Octavia Hill when describing the Trust's purchase of Brandelhow Park, lying below Catbells Fell in the Lake District in 1902:

> It commands views of Skiddaw in one direction and Borrowdale in the other, from its slope you can see the whole space of the lake set with its islands, it has crag, and meadow and wood, on it the sun shines, over it the wind blows, it will be preserved in its present loveliness and it belongs to you all and to every landless man, woman and child in England.
>
> (Waterson, 1994: 45)

The appeal for Brandelhow brought many moving testimonies. One donor from Sheffield enclosed a contribution of 2s 6d and wrote, 'All my life I have longed to see the Lakes. I shall never see them now, but I should like to help keep them for others' (Waterson, 1994).

Looking back it is clear that the Trust was slow to embrace learning in its widest sense. A National Trust summer school at Attingham Park on Great Houses was inaugurated in 1953, but the Trust's Solicitor raised questions about the legitimacy of the use of Trust funds for purposes not specifically spelled out in its Acts of Parliament. Fortunately he was reassured. There are many reasons why the importance of education and interpretation were not understood as the Trust was developing. One was the sheer magnitude of the Trust's responsibilities. At a time of high levels of acquisition, the repair and conservation of the places was felt to be more important than enabling public access. However, as the membership numbers rose in the 1970s, members visited Trust properties in greater numbers and demanded more from their visit. The Trust was slow in meeting these demands and the tensions led to strong criticisms of the Trust at an EGM in 1967. This led to changes, with committees being set up and recommendations made. Many of the changes made were regarding the way the Trust interacted with the public. These sowed the seeds of a new approach with much greater priority given to informing visitors about the properties and their history.

A radical new approach was used at Quarry Bank Mill under the leadership of David Sekers. The mill was restored as a working museum with the noisy, clattering cotton milling machinery actually making cloth and former mill workers explaining the processes involved. The Apprentice's house was restored to show what conditions were like for children living and working at the mill. Visitors could appreciate the workings of a mill and children could experience what life was like as an apprentice.

Erddig near Wrexham was restored to show the affection the Yorke family had for their servants, with visitors entering through the kitchens to see the portraits of the servants – unheard of at that time! At Sudbury the Trust created the Museum of Childhood associated with Sudbury Hall. This provided innovative exhibitions for children including a mock Victorian chimney, up which small children could climb.

These innovations were so successful that a Panel for Youth was established in 1973. Some truly exciting programmes were launched at this time. In 1977 the Young National Trust Theatre was established. This was a theatre-in-education company working with schools to explore social and moral issues at Trust properties through drama. Also the schools guardianship scheme was set up. In this scheme a school establishes a long-term relationship with a Trust property, rather than a one-off visit, and the children engage with the property in a sustainable long-term programme, getting involved in the conservation and maintenance of the site through activities such as tree planting, path clearing and surveying the plants and animals.

There was also a new trend in the acquisitions the Trust made in the 1980s and 1990s with houses such as Mr Straw's and Paul McCartney's house driving a new, more people-focused approach to interpretation.

In 2004 the Trust launched its new Learning Vision supporting the National Trust Strategic Plan objective of 'Putting education and life-long learning at the heart of everything we do' (see p. 101).

The Trust has recently (2004) conducted a review of the way it interprets its properties, chaired by Simon Murray, Territory Director North, recognising that interpretation is never static and, indeed, is a fast developing specialist subject. As well as looking at best practice within the Trust a consultant was employed to review current best practice in Britain and to review academic writing and thinking on the subject from around the world. This has heralded a great sea change in approach.

The Trust's interpretation philosophy

Simon Murray (2004) writes:

> Not so long ago access meant simply opening our doors to visitors. Interpretation meant guidebooks written by art historians. Now we realise that visitors come from a whole range of backgrounds and want a whole range of experiences. They may want to hear stories about Kings and Queens or architects and painters. On the other hand, they may want stories about servants or tenants. They may want to know where the plants in the garden come from or what insects and fungi are found on the ancient oaks in the park. They may simply want to hear the sound of running water from the cascade or the organ in the Music Room.

Indeed we have found through undertaking market research that only 7 per cent of our visitors come wanting to learn something but a massive 73 per cent go away

The Vision for Learning commits the Trust to:

- Becoming an organisation dedicated to learning and to creating opportunities for life-changing experiences for those with whom we engage both internally and externally.
- Ensuring our properties become spaces where visitors can experience inspiration, relaxation, enjoyment and enrichment.
- Enabling visitors and new users to experience and share a sense of discovery by engaging with formal or informal learning experiences at National Trust properties.
- Valuing learning for its own sake and the equality of opportunity it brings in all the work we undertake.

Our aims include:

Meeting the needs of our current core audiences

Learning is seen as a two-way process with importance placed on the National Trust providing ways for people to learn that are appropriate to them. This will be done by:

- Evaluating our work with schools and developing a sharper focus for future formal education programmes.
- Ensuring there is a range of choices at properties to suit the different learning needs of our visitors.
- Improving the formal and informal learning opportunities offered to older audiences.

Reaching out to new audiences

Our strength will be to use our diverse properties as venues and catalysts for learning, enabling new audiences to participate and develop their skills. We will:

- Expand the Trust's work with young people (13–25).
- Enable inclusive and participative access to our properties.
- Actively seek to establish sustained relationships with new or excluded user groups.

Developing a culture of learning for all staff and volunteers

Through examination of both our successes and failures, the Trust will become a learning organisation that encourages experimentation, innovation and observation. We will:

- Encourage an ethos among staff and volunteers that views learning as vital to the Trust's work.
- Offer learning opportunities for staff and volunteers.

having learnt something. Our aim should be to enable people to take what experience they want from the visit and that it contributes to enriching their lives. This
means moving away from a didactic approach and instead understanding our visitors and listening to their needs. However, this interaction between the Trust and
its audience does not mean a rejection of traditional narrative but, rather, emphasises that there is no one objective narrative, more a number of subjective ones.
The philosophy that underpins our approach to interpretation is one that understands who our visitors are and offers them a range of experiences so that every
visitor leaves feeling that they have enjoyed themselves and enriched their lives
either consciously or subconsciously, unlocking the doors to inspiration and knowledge. *Interpretation is all about exploring the meanings of places and collections with
people, whether it be a landscape, building, object or idea. It strives to help people find
their own meaning and values and make sense of the world around them.*

Summary of interpretive philosophy

- Our interpretation aims to be *aspirational*, striving to enhance people's lives
  and deliver real benefits. A benefit could be leaving a property, having taken
  part in an activity, inspired to try something new or leaving with a deeper
  understanding of some aspect of history, culture or conservation, for example.
  Aspirational interpretation should be broad and not exclusive, everyone at a
  property can be involved in interpretation and their encounters with visitors
  should reveal the values of the Trust.
- Interpretation must *resonate* with people's lives. Learning is a life-long activity
  but scholars and toddlers, for instance, learn in a different way. So we need
  to layer interpretation to suit the different needs. We know that people need
  to be actively engaged in learning and that interpretation is a two-way communication process, just telling people facts may not enthuse and enrich their
  understanding. Resonance is about making connections. Themes based around
  customs such as eating, sleeping and building a home are ones that everyone
  can recognise and relate to.
- Interpretation needs to be *bespoke* to the property. The themes and stories
  are rooted in the place. These may be based on the Statement of Significance
  for the property which will have been prepared by listening to people and
  gaining their views. Significance is multi-layered and may be particular to
  individuals.

Interpretation process

The process of interpreting the property takes place through the management planning process. As part of the property management plan a learning plan is written.
Each property management plan has a Statement of Significance that expresses the

'spirit of place' and summarises, at the time of writing, the key features and attributes that are considered to be the most significant and which the Trust should seek to conserve. Views on significance are actively gathered through a dialogue with the many communities who have an active interest in the property. Significance can be about historical features but it might also cover social or cultural records associated with the place, such as folklore. There might be particular aesthetic responses such as peace and tranquillity or the intimacy or the wildness of a place. This Statement of Significance forms the basis of discussion on the themes for interpretation. Research on the existing and potential audiences is carried out for the learning plan and the possible themes and stories are tested out on these audiences. Once the themes and stories are clear and the target audiences have been identified, the appropriate media for interpretation can be chosen to suit the particular property, story and audiences. Pre-testing, piloting and evaluation are all important parts of writing and realising a property learning plan.

Interpretation is never static. In the same way that caring for our historic environment embraces a changing process, ideas of what is historically significant are constantly changing. Millions of visitors each year seek inspiration in the special places the Trust cares for. There is a never ending dialogue as each generation discovers fresh meaning and value by interacting with the properties. Interpretation needs to be aware of the different ways people discover meaning and value from the Trust's properties. The uniqueness of the Trust lies in the rich variety of natural, cultural, scientific and historical connections the properties possess. For example, Wordsworth House, the childhood home of William Wordsworth demonstrates a cultural connection through Wordsworth's writing but a visitor can also see the natural world that inspired his writing. Patterson's Spade Mill, Belfast, reveals the significance of rural skills. Visitors can see spades of every shape and size used in Ireland for purposes from turf cutting to shovelling. The story of technology is revealed by places such as Orford Ness where the first radar trials were carried out or at Lacock Abbey where the processes used in producing the first photograph through the negative positive process were invented by Fox Talbot. The silver collection at Dunham Massey would, at first sight, be of aesthetic interest but there is a revealing human story behind the pieces. The finest pieces were crafted by Huguenot silversmiths, banished from France for their Protestant beliefs. They were given asylum and employed by the Earl of Warrington because of his strong religious and political beliefs. Southwell Workhouse reveals the harshness of the nineteenth-century poor laws.

It is all too easy to assume that the Trust has been limited in its approaches to interpretation, and has done little beyond the provision of guidebooks, on-site panels, and the role of the room steward at houses and the warden at coast and countryside sites. In fact, the Trust has a track record of innovative interpretation work. Across the properties there are examples of many inspirational interpretive programmes and techniques, although there is a long way to go needing investment of time and resource.

Case studies

Mrs Garnett at Kedleston Hall

Kedleston Hall in Derbyshire was built between 1759 and 1765. The State Rooms by Robert Adam remain largely untouched and are a major attraction of the house. The East Midlands region has trialled an interpretive approach involving a welcome to the house by Mrs Garnett, the housekeeper. It was the duty of the real Mrs Garnett to greet and show around the house the eighteenth-century visitors who came to admire the house of Lord Scarsdale. In costume and in role, the present-day Mrs Garnett offers an introductory talk for visitors, stressing that Kedleston was built as a show house, placing it in its historical context and offering glimpses into the domestic life of the house and the role and conditions of the servants. Tours take place at intervals, and visitors are given the opportunity to join as they wish, or to use more traditional approaches such as the guidebook, or merely to wander and soak up the atmosphere.

Tyntesfield

Tyntesfield is one of the last great Victorian country estates to survive intact. With its pinnacles and turrets, red and black roofs and magnificent Gothic chapel set against a backdrop of hanging woods, parkland and gardens it is a magical place. Four generations of Gibbs family lived there, increasingly quietly until it was put up for sale and acquired by the National Trust in July 2002 after a hugely successful public appeal and a £17.5 million grant from the National Heritage Memorial Fund.

An unusual approach has been taken by the Trust in opening up Tyntesfield to the public. Instead of closing the place for ten years while essential conservation work is carried out, the property has embraced public access from the start. The Tyntesfield project aims to use every possible aspect of their work as an opportunity for learning and personal development, involving a wide cross-section of people from work experience students and apprentices to youth and community groups and back to work schemes. Projects have already included 30 young people from the Prince's Trust and AMBER foundation in a community drama project and local school placements assisting with administration, conservation and gardening. The first guided tours began within ten weeks of the Trust acquiring the property and by the end of 2003 Tyntesfield had welcomed over 28,000 visitors.

Repair work at Ightham Mote

Another example of conservation in action is the repair work taking place at Ightham Mote. This property is a superb moated manor house, nestling in a sunken valley, dating from 1330. It is undergoing the largest conservation project undertaken by the National Trust on a house of this age and fragility. The programme of conservation and repair work began in 1988 and is now nearing completion. The property has remained open while work is under way and access to a viewing platform and interpretation panels illustrate the work in progress. Free introductory talks are offered and an exhibition 'conservation in action' explains the work taking place. The repair work was the subject of a 'Time Team' television programme that illustrated the historic techniques still being used for restoration, such as the on-site manufacture of lime mortar.

The Untold Story at Sutton House

The Untold Story is an innovative project that uses contemporary performing and creative arts to explore the relevance of built and natural heritage sites to people who might not normally be found sipping tea in a National Trust restaurant. The project is a three-year pilot supported by the Heritage Lottery Fund that enables the Trust to work in partnership with youth and community groups to reach new audiences. Supported by a team of specialist community drama workers and artists, the participants explore Trust properties, as well as their own imaginations, and produce an interpretation in the form of a performance or exhibition.

At Sutton House 12 young people (between the ages of 11 and 15 years) from Hackney Quest worked with a visual artist, drama worker and sound artist to explore their interpretations of the house over a period of ten weeks. They used visual techniques to help understand the history of the house and their connections to the place. Large pieces of paper were covered with their footprints, on one side of the footprint they wrote stories about their lives, on the other side stories connected with Sutton House. They developed a story about a man trapped in the linenfold panels of the parlour telling the story of events through history he had witnessed. This was visualised by the artist and acted out in their final performance of their work. This was so successful that it has now been incorporated into the Sutton House Discovery Days as a live interpretation event.

Birmingham back to backs

Birmingham's last surviving court of back to backs has been restored by the Birmingham Conservation Trust and the National Trust. The story of the site is told through the experiences of the people who lived and worked there. Visitors move through four different periods from 1840 to 1977. The design of each interior reflects the varied cultures, religions and professions of the families who made their homes there. Community consultation has taken place through a local advisory group of people from many different cultures, some of whom remember what life was like living in such conditions. The project team realise that a visit to the back to backs may bring back poignant memories to some visitors so have built in a section of the exhibition to share such thoughts.

Challenges for interpretation

There is a growing interest by visitors in how and why we do things, in addition to exploring the heritage assets themselves. People are interested in the reasons behind 'on the ground' management decisions and the various strategic policies of the Trust. Interpretation can be used to explain why and how we do things and promote a dialogue with visitors about their own values and views. Where the cracks appear (often literally) and remedial or essential management work is undertaken, an opportunity arises to make the conservation activity itself the subject of interpretation. Ongoing work highlights the influence of processes and of cause and effect, countering the view that properties are frozen in time and preserved forever. Interpreting the work while it is in progress is a challenge in balancing access, conservation and health and safety.

Increasingly we need to communicate the environmental principles that underpin our work and recognise the Trust's role in integrated land management and conservation. The Trust properties are subject to a range of processes acting upon them and from which they are not immune. Interpretation of such processes in lively and relevant ways will help our visitors to understand our objectives and the dynamic nature of conservation.

A large part of our success in delivering interpretation that provides inspiration from the scholar to the toddler will rest on our ability to create interpretative programmes that provide opportunities for discovery, enjoyment and learning at different levels and with different layers. The Trust now runs the widest range of events for families of any heritage provider.

By any measure, the Trust has been an enormously successful organisation, unique in its portfolio of properties and in its range of management objectives. To continue to be successful the Trust needs to continue to maintain relevance and provide benefit to people, while still ensuring the long-term conservation of its heritage assets. We have set interpretation within the wider concept of access, both physical and intellectual, and linked it with our wide-ranging education programme. However, we recognise that barriers do exist for some audiences and we need to work hard at identifying and overcoming these. This will involve an increasing use of audit and research techniques, an audience-focused rather than object-centred approach, and a team approach to interpretive planning, supporting an ability to balance aesthetic and specialist values with an improved and rewarding visitor experience.

We have a range of interpretive techniques in our toolkit, many of which have been trialled and used successfully at Trust properties. The decision regarding which techniques to use will depend on the themes and stories, the nature of the property, the audience segments and the purpose of the interpretation. A visit to a property should appeal to all the senses. This is possible in some places with fires lit, food laid out, and rooms presented as if their occupants have just left the second before the visitor has entered. Music playing in rooms ahead on the visitor route can create a sense of expectation and anticipation, making a house seem lived in. Where possible we want to extend this approach. Houses have become peopled as a result of Living History activities. Handling collections have been assembled and, increasingly, demonstrators and artists can be found at various turns, using the properties as an inspiration for their work, and for those visiting. The 'have a go' philosophy is growing as visitors try their hand at tapestry work, paint a view in a garden or help build a dry-stone wall. The open-space properties have seen similar developments with walks, demonstrations, a range of integrated print and panel approaches, information and visitor facilities and a growing informal and formal programme of learning activities.

In engaging with our visitors, we put great store on the personal approach and one-to-one contact through staff and volunteers. While labour-intensive, this approach can often provide the most effective educational and interpretational experiences. This is a key area for us to build on through the use of both first- and third- person interpretation. A key part of our work in this area will be realised through a more proactive approach to interpretation from staff and volunteers enabled through training. Reminiscence workshops have also provided opportunities to hear first hand from people who worked at properties or who lived on estates. The key to all these activities is the power of real stories and real people. We know from research that visitors are interested in the social history of houses, and the stories of those who built, lived and worked in them.

What is specific to the Trust's experience?

Can we therefore identify any interpretation issues that are, perhaps, specific to the Trust's situation? The holistic nature of the Trust's work, while offering enormous opportunities for interpretation, also brings with it particular challenges. Unlike single site institutions or single purpose organisations, the diversity of the Trust's work can create particular challenges for interpretation due to the number and variety of potential messages across properties, and national versus regional and local interest. Interpretation has to be bespoke – no one blueprint for properties will work and would, indeed, be far from desirable.

The recognition of each property's particular qualities is important, and we must use it to inform interpretation and education activity, but not to let its uniqueness become a barrier to undertaking these visitor-focused activities. Curatorial and presentational decisions, while meeting the standards of the specialist, must also reflect the needs and interests of present and future visitors.

The digital opportunity

The heritage community is currently coming to terms with the impact that information technology is having upon how people access and use information. Investment is currently high but our knowledge of how people learn from these systems is lagging behind. The technology offers rapid access to large amounts of information; it offers choice and non-sequential routes that offer new approaches other than a flowing narrative or a fixed route. Information technology has provided a management tool that the Trust has already embraced and we will need to do the same in the area of access. The technology in itself is non-threatening; what is daunting is the sheer potential it offers, the resource required to use it effectively and the scale of the Trust's as yet untapped potential.

CD-ROMs and computer interactives have been used in many exhibitions and the Trust has a comprehensive website with property-specific information, collections information, and a learning section with interactive games and a site for young children – Trusty.

At the time of writing the Trust is embarked on a major process of digitisation of its picture library and of its inventory systems. A prime purpose of this digitisation is to enhance and create new kinds of access to the Trust assets. The key to effective use of digital technologies will be to apply them to the kinds of information and content to which they are suited, to focus on multi-use of digital resources rather than on particular delivery systems and to integrate them into other learning activities.

The future

The principles underpinning the interpretation philosophy inform our work as we progress informal and formal learning across the Trust. Through consultation, evaluation and research, we need to continue to understand our visitors better; their needs and interests, the ways in which they learn, and what makes a good visit for them. In particular we need to be proactive in addressing attitudinal and external cultural barriers.

In addition the Trust will need to:

* realise the potential that interpretation holds to unlock the stories of our conservation work;
* continue to develop a strategic approach to interpretation and learning as part of physical and intellectual access, creating activities based on learning, inspiration and enjoyment;
* have a true two-way communication process that engages with people and helps them to their own understandings of, and connections with, places, objects, ideas and processes;
* build layers that reflect the complexity of the places we look after and are able to appeal to all levels from scholar to toddler;
* build on the value the Trust places on its staff and volunteers and on the importance of face-to-face contact;
* develop minimum standards of service and quality while reflecting the individual and unique qualities of properties;
* build partnerships, to listen and learn from others and to contribute our own experiences for others to learn from;
* build on visitors' interest in the stories of the people who shaped the properties we care for on their behalf. Through these stories, we will be able to communicate other areas of interest;
* communicate our conservation purposes and the impact of various processes that act upon our properties, and how people are an integral part of such processes;

- build multidisciplinary approaches to interpretation by using team approaches to projects, linking a range of staff and people with different skills and knowledge and include within the teams a 'champion' for interpretation.

Unlocking the powerful stories that lie within every one of our properties is the challenge for interpretation.

■ ■ ■

Bibliography

Gaze, J. (1988) *Figures in a Landscape*, London: Barrie and Jenkins in association with the National Trust

Murray, S. (2004) *Interpretation in the National Trust, the Work of the Interpretation Review Group*. Management Board paper (unpublished)

Newby, H. (1995) *The National Trust, the Next Hundred Years*, London: The National Trust

Reynolds, F. (2004) Purcell lecture (unpublished) Britain's Biggest Classroom

Waterson, M. (1994) *The National Trust, the Next Hundred Years*, London: The National Trust and BBC Books

Waterson, M. (2003) *Our Story. For Ever, for Everyone*, London: The National Trust

Other sources

National Trust (1997) *Visiting Historic Properties, Improving the Visitor's Experience*

National Trust (1998) *Education Vision Paper 1998–2001*

National Trust (1999) *Curatorship in the National Trust*

Russell, D. (1995) *Linking People and Place – A Consultation Report*, London: The National Trust

Tinniswood, A. and Woodhead, S. (1996) *No Longer Dead to Me*, London: The National Trust

Waterson, M. (2004) *The Trust's Contribution to Cultural Heritage: an update*. Management board paper

Chapter 8

INTERPRETING INDUSTRIAL HERITAGE

Jon Price

Top-down, or bottom-up, organisation of interpretation

What industrial heritage is, and what we think we are doing when we interpret industrial heritage depends on who we are and where we live. I shall define industry in its old sense of productive activity. It can be primary (extractive) such as mining, quarrying, fishing, farming or forestry; secondary (transformational) such as metal-working, carpentry, milling, spinning or weaving; or tertiary (service) such as transport, catering, banking or security. Of these only transport (limited to boats), and security (limited to state security forces) are dealt with elsewhere in this volume.

Organisations carrying out the work of interpreting industrial heritage can be corporate entities with policies, overt or not, which produces 'official' interpretation; or groups of individuals with varying degrees of organisation, with a shared agenda, which produces 'community led' interpretation. Official organisations can include museums and sites that are in effect independently run by close groups of individuals, such as Beamish and other open-air museums in Britain; and community-led organisations can include apparently official organisations, such as La Mine Bleu and other eco-museums in France; but the basic distinction between the two categories remains clear.

Official, top-down, heritage interpretation will always take a different line to community-led, bottom-up, heritage interpretation. Official interpretation is concerned with the development of the visitor, and concepts of historical validity. It has a general didactic intent, and is concerned to place its subjects in context in a perceived social and historical continuum. An example of this approach can be seen in this quote concerning the China Coal Museum, in Shanxi Province:

> The exhibition was designed to put on display different development periods of China's coal mining industry and achievement it has obtained. Visitors are able to have a view of the distribution of China's coal, reserve, transporting and sales, and the blueprint of China's coal mining through illustrations. Also on display are some pictures about top Chinese leaders inspecting coal mines, such as of late Chairman Mao Zedong, Zhou Enlai, Liu Shaoqi, Deng Xiaoping, and President Jiang Zemin, Premier Zhu Rongji. Simulant coal mines in the museum help visitor learn the vicissitude of coal mining from the ancient time to today.
>
> (*Peoples Daily*, English edition, 16 September 2000)

This approach is seen in every national science and industry museum throughout the world, and at many smaller 'official' museums. Historical development, technical information, and appearances by dignitaries all feature somewhere in the displays of all these museums.

Community-led interpretation, on the other hand is concerned with the validation of recent experience. Its didactic intent is to explain the behaviour and activity of preceding generations to present generations, and it places its subjects in a polarised context of 'then' and 'now'.

> Recently, heritage tourism has found a niche in Johnstown . . . The Open-Hearth Project, started in June of 1990, employs the use of former steel workers and coal miners to give tours of the mines and mills as part of the 'Path of Progress.' . . . Tourists can be assured that the tours will be good – their guides are not there for the pay. Rather, they are there to share the history of the town they have grown to love. Their own blood, sweat, and tears have mingled with the very soil on which the town rests. They are, in a sense, the stuff Johnstown is made of.
>
> ('Johnstown Takes Lickin', Keeps Kickin'', Jody Mihelic, *Zine 375*, Issue 1, Fall 1996)

This divergence of approach will also tend to produce different definitions of industrial heritage. Community-led interpretation of industrial heritage, because it is driven by a desire to validate personal experience, tends to deal directly with the detail of processes, whether strictly industrial work place processes, or ancillary related domestic processes. Official interpretation, because of its concern with appearing to be historically valid, and with placing its subject within a historical continuum, tends to deal with the broader context of the industrial activity, and places the activity and its context in juxtaposition with examples of comparable activity from elsewhere.

Naturally no organisation or approach will conform exactly to this model, but the behaviour of organisations can be compared with it. In many cases both approaches will be found operating together, and this is particularly clear where official organisations are supported by active 'friends' organisations: the official organisation will promote and support top-down models of interpretation, while the friends will promote and support community-led models. This can easily be observed where the official organisation is responsible for text- and AV-based interpretation, which puts things in their context; while friends or volunteers (docents) are largely responsible for live interpretation, which focuses on individual experience and processes. This is not to say that text panels and AV will always be contextual, or that official organisations will always shun live interpretation, merely that there is a tendency for this to be the case.

A sensible interpretation manager will therefore consider the methods they choose to employ to interpret industrial heritage, not only in the light of visitor response, but also with regard to the underlying organisation and philosophy of the heritage organisation by which they are employed. This is not a prescription, but an explanation of why some proposals will be received more favourably than others.

Industrial heritage can be interpreted in many ways. They are all valid, so long as the organisation understands what it is doing, and does not believe that they are doing it the right way or the only way.

- You can interpret through the location of industrial activity, and usually this happens where the interpretive site is a vehicle, factory or mill, or where the locus of activity is reconstructed for the purpose of the interpretation.
- You can interpret through the machinery of industrial activity, either in conjunction with location, or as a stand-alone artefact. This latter is more common in museum interpretation.
- You can interpret through visitor participation in activity. There are limits to this kind of experiential interpretation in the context of skill-based and hazardous industrial activity. In the case of the outputs of industrial processes it is often considered that the sale of the end product to a visitor can be a form of experiential interpretation.
- You can interpret through a display of skill, though this is limited by the availability of skilled operatives.
- You can interpret through placing your site in a broader context through trails and discovery routes. This requires co-operation with other sites and agencies, and a political acceptance of the role your site plays in the broader agendas of tourism and economic development.

A place for everything, and everything in its place: interpreting through location

At simple levels of industrial organisation activities tend to take place in and around the homes of those involved in the activities. At this level, with low levels of mechanisation, and with processes carried out with hand tools it is difficult to distinguish between industrial and non-industrial heritage. In the Western and Northern world this phase of industry took place several hundred years ago. This mitigates against community approaches to this type of industrial heritage and presents a particular interpretive problem: hand processes and home-working are ideal subjects for live interpretation, but because there is a tendency for these sites to be treated as archaeology and operated by official organisations there is generally little live interpretation carried out. Instead the interpretation of hand processes and home working tends to take place in a neutral constructed or reconstructed environment where modern craft workers revive and demonstrate old methods.

From their first origins in Skansen, Sweden, open-air museums, such as Old Sturbridge Village, Massachusetts, US; the Hungarian Open Air Museum; the Zuiderzee Museum, The Netherlands; and the Weald and Downland Open Air Museum, England; tended to be set up by urban (bourgeois) 'folk-life' enthusiasts to memorialise an imagined idealised social environment that was perceived to be rapidly disappearing, or had already disappeared. As a result the reconstructed environments of open-air museums are frequently used for this kind of craft-revival. Because this is craft-revival there is heavy emphasis on the industrial processes, although because the processes take place in a constructed environment, which is largely unrelated to that process, the interpretation of the environment overshadows the interpretation of the industrial activity. Unconsciously these organisations project a cosy view of cheerful families of hand workers, dancing on the village green, being god-fearing in chapel or church, and engaging fully in healthy participatory democracy, which fails to address the unremitting nature of life for those engaged in this type of production.

Where industrial activity takes place more formally in specialised structures, locations, landscapes or vehicles, interpretation will tend to focus more on the experience of industrial activity, and less on the broader landscape. The most extreme form of this is in mining. Whether interpretation takes place in a real coal mine, as at Big Pit Mining Museum, Wales; a reconstruction within old workings as at Kilhope Lead Mining Museum, England; or in a completely constructed 'underground experience', such as the coal mine reconstruction *Into the Thick* at the Black Country Living Museum, England; or the uranium mine reconstruction at *Section 26* at the New Mexico Mining Museum, US; the exclusion of light, and the ritual donning of protective headgear and miners' lamps, brings the danger that the experiential aspect of the interpretation will outweigh all other considerations. Where the transition from real to interpreted world is less drastic the interpretation can be more developed, and this is especially the case on ships where people lived as well as worked, such as the trawler *Arctic Corsair* moored in Hull, England.

Satanic mills: interpreting time and motion

For a range of practical and psychological reasons there is a strong emphasis on process in the interpretation of industry. At its best the process can be used to interpret the human aspects of the industry, at its worst it simply becomes a method of mesmerising visitors for a few minutes.

This is particularly the case where the process being interpreted involves circular motion. The intention is often explained as a desire to explain how the machine works, but all machines work simply by converting circular motion into other circular motion or into linear motion. The cutaway steam locomotive grinding its wheels round without progressing along the track, as at the National Railway Museum, England; the waterwheel thundering round without powering a machine, as at Otterburn Mill, England; the winding engine rocking backwards and forwards without raising the miner's cage, as at Beamish, the North of England Open Air Museum; these are all examples of the interpretation of process through mesmerisation.

Where the process is a linear activity there is a clear outcome and end to each stage of the industrial process. At its most straightforward is the process of manufacture by hand: the chain maker at the Black Country Living Museum or the potter at Old Sturbridge Village can be seen changing something from its basic state into a finished product. This can only take place where the process of production (iron bar to chain link, lump of clay to turned pot) is short, a process such as boat building involving creating a product over several days or weeks is too slow for a visitor to see outcomes. This renders the interpretation of process straightforward as objects are visibly transmuted by the interpreter or demonstrator from one state to another, accompanied by a commentary on the process.

Less straightforward is the interpretation of larger scale, more hazardous linear processes. In the case of the steel rolling mill at Blists Hill Victorian Town, in England, the process is sufficiently hazardous that visitors must stand well beyond the reach of the interpreter/demonstrators' voices. In any case the interpreter/demonstrators do not wish to be distracted as they throw long snakes of red-hot steel through the rollers. The result is that the interpretation becomes more of a display of skill and much of the interpretive intent is lost.

The physical sensations of a process can be seductive to the extent that the process itself is sidelined and the machinery and its sounds becomes a show in itself. This is often the case in the interpretation of the textile industry. Machines that ran almost continuously in factories are set to run continuously in the same factories for visitors, but nothing is produced and the spinning bobbins are empty. No single site is more prone to this than any other, but an example is the Bradford Industrial Museum in England. At its most extreme this seduction by sensation results in the process becoming a display of fireworks, which occurs without apparent human intervention. This is the case at Magna in England – which is admittedly a Science Centre, not a Heritage Centre – where a blast furnace has been turned into a multi-media sound and light rock and roll show lasting 12 minutes.

Where the process to be interpreted is transportation there are a number of dangers for interpreters. Visitors are often encouraged to ride on the transportation involved, as an experience. To be honest one train-ride is very much like another train-ride, any difference is down to location (up a steep slope, over a bridge) rather than any industrial heritage considerations. The reason for this is that the visitors are inside the exhibit looking out, whereas any interpretation of the process requires observation of the vehicles from the outside. In some cases visitors are encouraged to ride in or on vehicles or routes that were never intended to carry passengers. A further danger for interpreters is the question of authenticity of vehicles. Where original vehicles exist, or replicas have been made or purchased, then it can reasonably be said that this is interpretation of the heritage of the transport system. In some cases vehicles are used that have no connection with the transport system, but which happened to be commercially available. If the vehicle was manufactured locally for another market then it can be used to interpret the manufacture of vehicles, but not the local transport system heritage.

An example of a site that encompasses all these transport faults is Beamish. The museum runs a tramway with vehicles representative of transport systems in the region, however it also regularly runs a tram which, although manufactured locally, was made for the Lisbon system in Portugal, and worked there until sold in the 1970s. The vehicle has been modified and repainted to look like a tram that might have run in the North of England. Other examples of this vehicle run on railway preservation society lines as far from Lisbon as the Whitehouse Waterfront, in Alaska. Beamish also runs a line simulating steam traction during the first decades of the nineteenth century. The invented wagons have been created to allow visitors to ride in them as though this was a passenger railway, something that never occurred in reality as the locomotive depicted was a colliery locomotive and the load hauled should be coal. In both of these cases the transport is fulfilling a leisure experience function, and not a heritage interpretation function.

Buying favours: interpreting through participation and product

Participation in simple processes is a staple of interpretation on industrial sites. Visitors are encouraged or assisted in the performance of single manual tasks such as splitting slate, hand-grinding grain or spinning wool with a drop spindle. The function of this activity is to bring the visitor into closer contact with the materials (wool, stone, grain), and with the interpreters. The high level of skill required to achieve any of these craft activities, necessitating long periods of training to achieve a high quality of output means that the value of such participation in bringing visitors to an understanding of the process is often minimal.

In some cases this interpretive process is operated as a commercial transaction with the visitor paying to 'have a go'. At the Jorvick Viking Centre in England, visitors can pay a costumed interpreter who lets them make their own replica Viking coin. The process involves no particular interpretation of minting in a proto-monetary economy, and the coins are struck from aluminium blanks, rather than silver. The visitor gains three things from the interaction: proximity to a costumed interpreter for a short time, appreciation of the weight of the coiner's hammer and a souvenir of their visit.

The approach of interpretation through participation in a process reaches its abstract culmination in the exchange of money. This is often seen as adding interpretive value to the commercial transactions that normally take place at the end of a site visit, as it is considered that changing money from current to historic currency is part of a site's interpretive process. Initially this takes place as a form of added value for a standard commercial transaction, as at Llechwedd Slate Cavern, Wales, but in the case of reconstructed banks (such as at Beamish or Blists Hill) the visitor is engaged in the process of comparing current currency with past currency, and it is the handling or ownership of coinage that is the focus for the interpretation. In these cases the interpreters working in the exhibits are responsible for adding interpretive value to the process, and whether they do this or not depends on their training and competence, and on the attitudes of the employing organisation.

It is possible to interpret an industry primarily through its products, without merely selling them, and a good example of this is the Matakohi Kauri Museum, New Zealand. The museum interprets the industry of logging Kauri trees. The Kauri is an extremely large and ancient tree and the industry produced hardwood, and as an incidental product Kauri Gum, a type of bog amber. Although the museum is a community-driven museum, and hence deals with the lives of people in the recent past, it also focuses heavily on the output of those people. The uses to which the timber was put, including the construction of ocean-going yachts are interpreted in detail, as are the displays of carved Kauri Gum created by the loggers and their families.

People heritage: interpreting through skill

In the end, no matter what aspects or methods are used to interpret industrial heritage it is necessary to come back to the people involved. The reason for this is basic to all interpretation, of any topic: in order for interpretation to be successful it must have meaning to the visitor, in other words it must make a connection with something in the experience and understanding of the visitor. The easiest way to do this is to put people into the picture. The criticism of visitor participation in craft activity is that it does not address the levels of skill achieved by skilled industrial workers. The only way this can be made visible is where skilled workers are employed to demonstrate their skills.

Depending on the skill in question such an interpretation can be a straightforward process interpretation, or it can be an entertainment or show in the full sense of the word. Process interpretation will often take place in original buildings, and this is particularly the case where large machinery is involved, so at Bradford Industrial Museum, England, and Helmshore Textile Museum, England, retired textile workers operate the machines for visitors.

At a more developed level the show requires the full panoply of entertainment with grandstand seating, and amplified commentary. This can be seen at the Farm Show, at Rainbow Springs and the Sheep Show at the Agrodome, in Rotorua, New Zealand; and at the display of horsemanship at the Plains Museum at Bugacpuszta, Hungary. In both these cases the performance includes a display and explanation of the agricultural live-stock, a description of the life and work cycles of the workers in the industry and a display of skill. At Rotorua this involves shearing sheep, and at Bugacpuszta riding horses. The Rotorua shows are purely commercial, while the Bugacpuszta show is insti-tutional, but both require real competence and ability on the part of the demonstra-tors. This means that the content of both shows celebrates and conveys the importance of current, or recent past activity of a group of workers.

Interpretation in a broader context: industrial heritage meets the world outside

All industrial activity takes place in a physical and socio-economic environment, and the interpretation of industry must acknowledge and work with that. While the open-air museum approach may be thought to address this issue, it is clear from visiting these sites that any kind of reconstructed environment tends to encourage a hermetically sealed view of the world, and a dolls house approach to the displays and interpretation. The best interpretations of industry, whether community led or official, accept the place of industry in its wider context, and take account of the socio-economic changes that have led to the industry becoming industrial heritage.

At its simplest level this means integrating museum-based, reconstructed, and preserved site interpretation within a landscape, and a good example of this is the range of sites around Telford, England, which are managed by the Ironbridge Gorge Museum Trust. The sites lie within the Ironbridge Gorge World Heritage Site. The sites include interpretation located on site or in buildings, such as the Iron Bridge Tollhouse next to the Iron Bridge itself; interpretation dealing with the products of industry, such as the Jackfield Tile Museum, and the Coalport China Museum; and a reconstructed open-air site, Blists Hill Victorian Town, where interpretation of process, product, skill and social environment takes place through a variety of live interpretation methods.

Although Ironbridge has some connection with current industrial activity, through the Coalport China Museum, the site is largely an interpretation of long-gone industry. The organisation is an official organisation with little real community involvement; indeed, the activities of the trust have led to some tension with local community interests as it has a conservation ethos that can conflict with the require-ments of a living community.

At Waihi in New Zealand there is a much closer linkage between industrial heritage and current industrial activity. The Waihi Gold Mining Museum is a community-driven museum. It focuses on the lives and skills of miners and their families in the relatively recent past. Many of its exhibits are working models or illustrations of industrial activity created by workers in the industry. It links to the outside world through descriptions, and 'then and now' illustrations of sites in the vicinity. An example of this is the Cornish Pumphouse, which is illustrated by models and photographs in the museum, but can be seen as a preserved monument close to the town centre. Mining is still a significant industry for the town, in the shape of the Martha Gold and Silver Mine. The mine is a very big hole in the ground, and visitors who walk beyond the Cornish Pumphouse reach a viewing platform from which they can look down into the hole and watch the large earth-moving equipment in action. There are on-site interpretation panels, and the company website has sections dealing with the history of the mine.

There are also broader approaches to contextualising industrial interpretation, in which individual sites benefit from involvement in broader initiatives. In South West Pennsylvania, US, a heritage trail called *The Path of Progress* has been created. The initial impetus behind the trail is clearly economic regeneration through tourism. The area was one of the earliest industrial areas in the US and had large concentrations of coal mining and iron and steel manufacture. During the 1970s and 1980s the majority of this industry was shut down. The *Path of Progress* brings together a range of commercial and public sites, and has encouraged and enabled a variety of community responses to these events and the wider history of the area.

The family-owned Seldom Seen Mine, typical of the small mining operations in the area converted directly from industrial activity to tourist operation in 1963, and is now part of the trail. The largest single heritage site on the trail is Johnstown. Here, the closure of the large Bethlehem Steel Works destroyed the town's economy. An early attempt to set up a heritage centre foundered through lack of support, but in 2001 the Johnstown Area Heritage Association opened a Heritage Discovery Centre, which focuses on the lives of the people who came to the area to work in the iron and steel industry. According to its own statement of intent the association 'operates as a clearinghouse and catalyst for community revitalization efforts based on cultural tourism and preservation of the built environment'. The Association runs a restored steelworker's house, and other museums relating aspects of the area's history. Participation in the *Path of Progress* trail has clear benefits, in terms of visitor routing, both for commercial sites such as the Seldom Seen Mine, and for community organisations such as the Johnstown Area Heritage Association.

In Europe those areas characterised by heavy industry, such as the North East of England and the Rhineland, underwent a similar process of plant closure and economic decline to that experienced in the US. Some areas, such as the North East of England have seen little co-ordinated activity in the industrial heritage area. Other areas, such as Blaenavon in Wales, and the Ruhregebiet in Germany, have begun to develop approaches to stimulate growth. The North Rhine-Westphalia Route of Industrial Heritage has been sufficiently successful to be taken as a model by the INTERREG programme of the European Union. This led, in 1999, to the creation of the European Route of Industrial Heritage, with the government of North Rhine-Westphalia as the main organiser. The plan is to define a series of anchor points, key industrial heritage sites such as the Voeklingen Iron Works, a World Heritage Site in Germany or the Blaenavon World Heritage Site in Wales, which will be promoted as highlights of the routes. Beneath this layer it is planned to create regional sub-networks comprising themed routes of other sites within a particular region. The benefit for participating sites will be not only the direction of visitors, but also assistance from within the INTERREG programme to develop their site facilities.

Exploring industrial heritage interpretation to develop a better understanding

The basic principles of interpretation expounded by Freeman Tilden, and elaborated by Sam Ham have remained constant, because they are based on the principles of communication. They are based on good theory tested against solid practice. There is no magic or secret method. The examples given in this chapter are not meant to be the best examples, or the only examples of good interpretation of industrial heritage. They are simply the ones that have stuck in my mind. There are hundreds of thousands of industrial heritage sites around the world. New sites open, and old sites close or change every year. The best way to develop and improve your interpretive practice is to visit sites on a regular basis. Be critical in your approach. Try to work out why a particular approach was used, what the constraints were, what works and what doesn't work.

■ ■ ■

References

You can discover the theories of Tilden and Ham and the practical application of those theories from their books:

Ham, Sam (1992). *Environmental Interpretation, A Practical Guide*, Golden, Colorado: North American Press

Tilden, Freeman (1957). *Interpreting Our Heritage*, University of North Carolina Press (first edition, republished in a variety of places many times since)

Useful websites

The best way to find out more about most of the sites and projects mentioned here is to go online. The web addresses were correct in September 2005:

Open-air museums

Beamish: www.beamishmuseum.co.uk/
Black Country Living Museum: www.bclm.co.uk/
Skansen: www.skansen.se
Sturbridge Village: www.osv.org
Weald and Downland Open Air Museum: www.wealddown.co.uk
Zuiderzee Museum: www.zuiderzeemuseum.nl/

Mining

Big Pit: www.nmgw.ac.uk/bigpit/
Llechwedd Slate Cavern: www.llechwedd-slate-caverns.co.uk/
New Mexico Mining Museum: www.grants.org/mining/mining.htm
Martha Gold and Silver Mine: www.marthamine.co.nz/
Seldom Seen Mine: www.seldomseenmine.com/
Waihi Gold Mining Museum: www.waihimuseum.co.nz/

Agricultural skills

Agrodome: www.agrodome.co.nz
Bugacpuszta: www.welcome.to/bugacpuszta
Rainbow Springs: www.rainbownz.co.nz/

Broader heritage initiatives

Blaenavon (World Heritage Site): www.world-heritage-blaenavon.org.uk/
European Route of Industrial Heritage: www.erih.de/
Ironbridge Gorge Trust: www.ironbridge.org.uk/
Johnstown Area Heritage Association: www.jaha.org/
Path of Progress: www.sphpc.org/

Other sites

Arctic Corsair: www.arctic-corsair.co.uk
Bradford Industrial museum: www.bradford.gov.uk/tourism/museums/indust_museum.
    htm
Jorvik Viking Centre: www.jorvik-viking-centre.co.uk/
Magna: www.visitmagna.co.uk/
Matakohi Kauri Museum: www.kauri-museum.com/
National Railway Museum (UK): www.nrm.org.uk
Otterburn Mill: www.otterburnmill.co.uk

Chapter 9

PUBLIC ART: ITS ROLE AS A MEDIUM FOR INTERPRETATION

Carol Parr

Introduction

The challenge of designing innovative, provocative and effective interpretation has led many practitioners of heritage, environmental and countryside management to look to the arts for inspiration. Under the current regime of National Lottery funding and European Regional Development Fund grants, opportunities to include arts projects in environmental improvement, cultural development, heritage interpretation and tourism marketing programmes have never been greater. The inclusion of what is termed 'public art' in these programmes can satisfy a range of funding criteria such as encouraging community involvement and stimulating cultural awareness. By bringing art out of the gallery and into public spaces it is intended to make it accessible to all, supporting equal opportunity policies and making art part of our everyday lives.

In the words of Freeman Tilden, 'Interpretation is an art', and to be successful it should provoke, stimulate, reveal and relate to its audience (Tilden, F. 1977). Public art has the capacity to achieve all of these. It has the power to relate to a wide audience by removing the obstacles of traditional learning techniques and opening doors to a range of learning styles. It can engage with our emotions, encourage us to become more aware of our surroundings and even change our attitudes. But how many public art projects achieve their full potential?

This chapter describes the multi-functional nature of public art, traces its historical development and by looking at case studies, seeks to identify some of the issues, benefits and pitfalls of its use as a conveyor of interpretive messages.

What is 'public art'?

The term 'public art' cannot be simply defined and is used to describe a massive array of art features and processes. Any artwork located within a public place, outside of a gallery is generally described as public art. This can include three-dimensional sculpture or two-dimensional mural painting, paving or mosaic. It may be sited in an urban environment or the wider landscape. It may be a permanent fixture, ephemeral feature or event linked to performance art. It may be created by the community or provided for the benefit of the community by any number of organisations with differing agendas.

The materials used can be equally diverse, ranging from stone, wood, glass, resins, fibreglass and metals to less permanent materials such as fabric, flowers and paper, or even living materials like willow, to create a growing and evolving feature.

Using the definition of 'art in a public place' can therefore be very broad ranging. The notion that true 'public' art should represent the aspirations or beliefs of the people within whose community it is sited, or relate to those people who share its space, introduces the concept of public art as socially engaging. It becomes a medium through which the messages of its creators or commissioners are communicated to its viewers, who are in turn encouraged to think and react.

An alternative definition provided by the Public Art Forum (the national association for public art) suggests that public art is not actually an artform, but a principle. It is a principle of improving the changing environment through the arts, utilising the arts to assist those involved in increasing quality in the environment (Cox, L. 1996).

Functions and benefits

Claims as to the functions and benefits of public art are as diverse as its definitions. While the methods employed in its design and construction, and the objectives of its commissioners and creators have been subject to cultural, political and economic changes, its fundamental role as a communicator has remained throughout history.

Current claims for public art include the following:

- creating a richer visual environment;
- enhancing enjoyment and appreciation of the environment;
- improving conditions for economic regeneration;
- encouraging increased use of open spaces and thereby reducing levels of vandalism;
- raising heritage and cultural awareness;
- developing tourism potential;
- re-inforcing regional identity and stressing the importance of place;

- improving community spirit and generating a sense of pride of place;
- identifying and celebrating local distinctiveness;
- humanising the urban environment;
- creating employment opportunities for artists, craftspeople, fabricators, manufacturers, suppliers and transporters;
- expressing corporate identity;
- increasing the value of land and property.

An ancient tradition

Regardless of which definitions are adopted or which benefits are claimed, art in its many guises has been used through the centuries as a means of communication. It could be said that public art has its roots in the cave painting and rock carving of prehistoric man. Archaeologists remain uncertain as to the meaning of such 'art' and what messages it was intended to convey. Recent speculations about cave paintings in France and Spain suggest that their artists may have been inspired by hallucinogenic drugs as much as by the environment in which they lived. In Kilmartin, mid-Argyll elaborate Neolithic symbols such as cup-and-ring markings, spirals, parallel grooves and stars have been painstakingly carved into rock outcrops, standing stones and cist slabs (RCAHMS 1999). The time and effort required to create such markings, and their presence on stone circles and monuments suggests an esteemed spiritual or religious significance. Other unsubstantiated suggestions for more practical application include rock maps or identification markers for sources of metallic ores (Burgess, C. 1980). Such is the intrigue surrounding these features that a five-year research project, launched in 1999 will catalogue all British prehistoric rock art in the hope of finding the key to unlocking the messages left by our ancestors.

One of the longest continuous artistic traditions is to be found in Australia. Rock engravings and paintings dating back 50 millennia remain central to Aboriginal life, performing political, utilitarian, social and instructional purposes, with an inherent connection to religious belief. Aboriginal art produced for the public domain has different levels of interpretation relating to the ritual knowledge of the artist and viewer. It reveals 'outside' stories, which are open to everyone, and 'inside' stories, which are restricted to those of appropriate ritual standing (Carvana, W. 1993).

Myth and legend have played a significant role in the way we interpret ancient art features. Take for example chalk hill figures. We can merely speculate at the reasons for their creation as tradition and information have been lost over generations. Recent debate has challenged the origin and age of some of these figures but there is still a popular belief that the Cerne Abbas Giant of Dorset was associated with Hercules or considered to be a powerful fertility symbol, in some minds as efficacious today as to the ancient culture to which he was believed to have been a guardian. Less easily understood is the Long Man of Wilmington in Sussex. Some consider him to represent a doorkeeper, guarding the way between the worlds. Others believe him to be a solar cult figure, while others refer to him as a surveyor, one of the first to chart ley lines (Matthews, J. and Stead, M.J. 1997).

Throughout history art has been utilised as an expressive and public display of cultural unity, ritual and religion. The Celtic tribes that dominated much of Europe between 2000 BC and the second century AD, are best known for their artistic tradition. Most of our knowledge of Celtic culture has been deciphered from the work of their artists, who held important positions within their society. The artist's ability to capture and represent the soul of the natural world played a crucial role in holding that society together (Sandison, D. 1998). Some traditions dating back to pre-Roman Celtic society are still celebrated today. Between April and September communities of Derbyshire and the Peak District maintain the ancient tradition of well dressing. Intricate and detailed picture boards, painstakingly created from natural materials adorn springs and wells. They depict local wildlife, produce, buildings, people or biblical scenes, an interesting subject for a tradition with its roots in more pagan celebration.

From the seventh century the spread of Christianity was profoundly influential. Richly decorated stone crosses fulfilled an instructive role while serving as parish boundary markers and memorials. Detailed biblical scenes, such as those on the Ruthwell Cross, near Dumfries were used to interpret a new religion to a largely illiterate society.

Public art's role in the assertion of authoritarian leadership was introduced to Britain by the expanding Roman Empire. New technology, materials and skills in sculpture and monumental inscriptions presented the ruling classes with a powerful medium for the declaration of authority. Stone and bronze statues of the Emperor and Roman gods were erected in public places. In more recent times this function has been demonstrated most forcefully in Stalin's Soviet Union, where sculpture was employed to represent importance through gigantism (Causey, A. 1998).

Sculptured monuments and statues remained one of the most common forms of public art for centuries. They embellished architecture, enhanced townscapes and became features of landscaped parks and gardens. They continue to commemorate national and local heroes and signify pride in industrial, social and technological achievement.

Following the Second World War however, attitudes towards memorial sculpture began to change. Rebuilding programmes in Britain presented new opportunities to treat open spaces as extensions of galleries and bring art into the public domain. This move was demonstrated by the significant manner in which sculpture featured as public art at the Festival of Britain in 1951. The construction of Harlow new town in the 1950s, with its planned collection of outdoor sculpture and art, signified a new role for public art as a central feature of urban development.

The vogue for art at this time was Modernism. With its tendency to focus on the artistic expression and attitude of its creator, its value as 'public' art, addressing

Figure 9.1   Universal links to human rights, Amnesty International Irish Section, Dublin, 1995

itself to the masses, was sometimes limited. Association with activism became more prominent, a role that public art has maintained and demonstrated through sculpture, mural painting and even graffiti. In the centre of Dublin, Amnesty International clearly presents its message through public art in the form of a giant ball of chains enclosing a constantly burning flame. Surrounding the ball is the inscription: 'The candle burns not for us but for all those whom we failed to rescue from prison who were tortured, who were kidnapped, who disappeared. That is what this candle is for.'

Major players in public art

Following the creation of the Arts Council in 1954, Government support of the arts largely focused on fine arts and entertainment. February 1965 however marked a turning point. The government white paper, 'Policy for the Arts: the First Steps' referred to the arts developing a new image in the life of the community and overcoming the drabness and uniformity of much of the social furniture inherited from the industrial revolution (Baldry, H. 1981). One of the main directives was for local authorities to embrace the arts as an integral part of new building plans, for which financial support was to be available via the Arts Council. This placed local authorities very much at the forefront of the development of public art, a position that they have largely maintained. In 1967 the Arts Council revised its Charter adopting a philosophy of co-operation with Local Authorities and a more even geographical spread of support, with the aim of increasing accessibility of the arts to the public.

The mood of the 1960s manifested itself in the work of community artists. Acting as enablers, they engaged communities in expressing their local agenda through art. Carnivals, mural painting and community gardens were an outlet for this mass participation with art acting as a tool for drawing the community together and a medium for communicating to outsiders the attributes that created their sense of place. This activity continued through the 1970s with many examples of large-scale mural works in deprived areas, one of the most prolific being the Greenwich Mural Workshop (Selwood, S. 1995).

The Arts Council saw community arts as recreating a sense of community, encouraging communication and consultation, bolstering self-confidence and generally enriching people's lives (Baldry, H. 1981). Being non-income generating, demand for funding was high. Under pressure from campaigners, the Arts Council set up a Community Arts Committee in 1965/66, but stressed the importance of local authorities providing financial support to such initiatives and devolved their own responsibility to the Regional Arts Associations.

There are now nine regional offices funded by Arts Council England. Their aim is to increase access to the arts for all sectors of society and strengthen the arts economy by stimulating and channelling Lottery funds, Percent for Art initiatives, European Regional Development Funds and other capital investments. They provide professional training, advice, information and a campaigning voice. They act as a catalyst within strategic planning and partnership projects.

During the 1980s' unemployment crisis, arts funding looked towards the private sector for support. The Association for Business Sponsorship of the Arts (ABSA), established in 1979, began to play an active role in securing business support, often in partnership with local authorities. Initiatives such as the 'Pairing Scheme' were introduced, whereby additional government grant funding was offered to art organisations that received sponsorship from private businesses.

The 1980s were something of a boom time for public art, with the public sector very much at the helm. Between 1984 and 1988, 124 local authorities in England, Scotland and Wales commissioned 433 works (Selwood, S. 1995). Much of this activity was a direct result of Government policy for inner city re-development and urban programme initiatives. The establishment of Urban Development Corporations in 1981, Action for Cities in 1988 and City Challenge in 1991 put arts on the agenda for planners and developers. Public art was recognised as playing a role in the economic regeneration of deprived inner city areas and derelict industrial regions, a stimulus for tourism, catalyst for urban renewal and providing employ-ment and training. Many local authorities began to employ Arts Officers and adopt a more strategic approach to the planning and implementation of schemes.

Re-development projects were encouraged to demonstrate partnerships and community consultation. This has become a criterion for funding applications to sources such as the National Lottery, European Union grants for assisted areas, the Civic Trust, National Heritage Memorial Fund and English Heritage. The role of the Arts Officer in networking, providing a forum for discussion and drawing the many threads of potential public art projects together is crucial considering the number of interested parties, opportunities and pitfalls. In a single local authority alone there may be need for consultation with officers of Planning, Tourism, Economic Development, Education, Leisure, Cultural Services and Social Services Departments.

The 1980s also saw the establishment of Rural Development Areas. The arts were regarded as appropriate media to interpret the environment and countryside and the very process of developing arts projects was seen as reaffirming community bonds and expressing local distinctiveness.

Figure 9.2 Cleveland Way 'New Milestones' project (courtesy of Cleveland County Council Photography Archive)

The charity, Common Ground, have been one of the major influences in this field, initiating a number of projects aimed at encouraging people to identify what is special about their neighbourhood, to celebrate that distinctiveness and share it with others through writing, sculpture, photography, painting and events. One such initiative is the New Milestones project, which uses sculpture to express how people feel about the landscape in which they live. In the former county of Cleveland, a New Milestones feature was accomplished through a partnership of Common Ground, regional and local arts agencies, local authorities, parish councils, British Steel and the artist, Richard Farrington. Three steel sculptures were sited along a spectacular section of the Cleveland Way as it passes along the North Yorkshire and Cleveland Heritage Coast. The themes of the pieces reflects what local people feel is distinctive about the locality. Steel was used to represent the region's industrial heritage. The sculptures themselves soon became a feature within the landscape they represented and are used to promote the Cleveland Way and coastline as a heritage tourism resource.

Another of Common Ground's long-running initiatives is the Parish Maps project. This aims to bring people together to chart the things they value in their locality. The resulting map, whether it be a publicly displayed painting, tapestry, mosaic or mural is a value laden statement made by and for a community. One of the project's objectives is to encourage communities to take action and some control over shaping the future of their place (Common Ground, 1996). This was demonstrated at Thirsk in North Yorkshire where a 24-foot textile map was used to represent local opinion in a planning dispute.

The Countryside Agency's support of public art as a medium for interpreting the countryside increased in the 1990s. Sculpture was introduced as interpretive way-marking and presented the opportunity to create distinctive gates, stiles and steps along newly developed regional routes, such as the Teesdale Way. These 'Marking the Ways' projects, and similar 'Bailiwick' markers around Community Forests, encourage cross-boundary co-operation between local authorities, partnership approaches to funding, support for artist residencies and community consultation.

A similar approach has been taken by Forest Enterprise. In a move to encourage greater recreational use of their commercial forestry, sculpture projects, such as those at Grizedale and the Forest of Dean, have been developed in the hope that new visitors will be attracted to what for some, could be a bland, monotonous environment.

One of the major influences on the development of public art into the new millennium was the Department for Culture, Media and Sport's 'New Cultural Framework'. In January 1999, the Government Department announced that an extra £290 million would be available to the cultural sector between 1999 and 2002, with a significant proportion to support the role of arts as a medium for facilitating social regeneration. 1999 also saw a move towards greater delegation of power to the Regional Arts Boards in a bid to ensure a more even geographical spread of support and resources.

The urban setting

The urban environment has provided the setting for public art in the form of memorial sculpture and commemorative art for many decades. Major re-development
schemes of the 1980s and 1990s, to remove the decay and dereliction of redun-
dant heavy industry and manufacturing from the landscape provided the opportunity
and inspiration for a new wave of urban public art as represented by Middlesbrough's
'Teessaurus Park'. Overlooking what is today an open, landscaped parkland stretching down to the River Tees, stand a group of life size steel dinosaurs. Their feet
are firmly rooted in the foundations of Teesside's glory days, in a location that was
once filled with the smoke, sweat and toil of daily life in the former Ironmasters
District. Many similar representations of local heritage mark urban development
regions across the country.

   One of the most significant influences on urban public art has been 'Percent For
Art', launched in Britain by the Arts Council in 1988. Local authorities, Urban
Development Corporations, private developers and government departments are
encouraged to adopt a policy whereby a small percentage (normally 1 per cent)
of the capital cost of new buildings and environmental improvement schemes is
committed to the commissioning of artists and craftspeople to produce public art
to enhance the scheme. An important consideration is that the artist should work
as part of the project team, rather than as a contractor, thereby producing work
that is an integral element of the project, not just an additional feature.

The Birmingham experience

Birmingham's Centenary Square was one of the first 'Percent for Art' schemes to
be implemented by a local authority and became the largest public art scheme in
the UK between 1987 and 1991. A 'City Centre Strategy' to improve Birmingham's
image as an international centre for business and tourism included proposals for
the construction of the International Convention Centre (ICC) overlooking a pedes-
trianised Centenary Square that would become the focal point of this new, safe and
stimulating city centre environment.

   One per cent of the originally estimated capital cost of building the ICC was
committed to works of art, which amounted to around £800,000. Two pieces were
commissioned, Raymond Mason's 'Forward' and Ron Haselden's 'Birdlife'. Other
works, such as Tess Jaray's paving and street furniture and Tom Lomax's 'Spirit of
Enterprise' fountain, were funded through the City Council's Planning Department.

   The brief for the artworks was fairly open so as not to impede artistic expression and style. Materials were to be selected by the artists and siting options
considered as the project developed. The project team expected the works to represent the significance of the city, be intellectually accessible and relevant to the
people who use Centenary Square. Despite these aspirations, public consultation

was low on the agenda. The City Council regarded its Councillors as representing the 'public'. It was considered difficult to define a 'public' who might be consulted for a place where the community is more transient that resident. An exhibition of maquettes of the proposed works was however publicly displayed during the application for planning permission.

Projects such as Centenary Square inevitably attract media attention. This was especially the case following the installation of 'Forward', which appeared overnight, a result of engineering requirements. Some people interpreted this to represent the City's embarrassment while others criticised the use of fibreglass in its construction as being wholly unrepresentative of the city's manufacturing heritage. One of the most common media angles was the expenditure of public money on art at the expense of struggling core services. References were also made to the lack of public consultation. While 'Forward' intended to represent the city, its citizens and its advance in time, it was produced according to the artist's own terms of reference rather than in consultation with the people of Birmingham. Public opinion polls conducted by the local media found that 76 per cent of respondents were in favour of the removal of 'Forward' to an alternative location, while others felt that the art was drawing people into the city centre and was something to be proud of (Selwood, S. 1995).

The requirement of evaluation to assess the impact of the project, its success in attracting business tourism and interpreting Birmingham's culture and heritage was not built into the brief, but has since been the subject of City Council reviews and reports. Observation of people being drawn to the art works and taking photographs suggests that their social impact is high. Images of the public art are used to represent Birmingham in tourism and economic development brochures.

The City of Sunderland approach

The issue of public consultation is a key element in Sunderland's public art programme, established in response to public fears that regeneration of the area would not reflect its history and culture and would result in the loss of local character. A £70 million re-development of the city included a 7-year programme of artist residencies to work with local people, creating public art for public spaces around the city. Managed by a partnership of the City of Sunderland and Northern Arts, the project commenced in 1993 with funding assistance from the National Lottery and European Regional Development Fund. In the words of the City of Sunderland Chief Executive:

> Sunderland is a new and vibrant city, with a strong cultural identity of its own. We firmly believe that public works of art are an integral part of Sunderland's development; raising awareness of the city's past, present and future, stimulating debate and educational projects.

> (City of Sunderland 1998)

The most ambitious project was 'Ambit' by Alison Wilding. The floating structure of 24 stainless steel cylinders with underwater lighting, held together by sprung
joints in a form reflecting the outline of a ship, was located in the River Wear at
Austin's pontoon in 1999. The pontoon was previously used to raise ships out of
the water for repair, a popular sight for local people during the Wear's shipbuilding
era. 'Ambit's' designer worked together with marine engineers, planners, lighting

Figure 9.3   'Shadows in Another Light', St Peter's Riverside Project, Sunderland

experts and structural engineers to create an ever-changing form that moves with the pull of the tides emitting a glowing image deep into the river.

Throughout the period of 'Ambit's' development, local schools and community groups took part in arts and sculpture projects inspired by the city's public art strategy. Community projects focused on the processes involved in designing, creating and siting public art in an attempt to encourage and empower people with the knowledge to play a more active role in decision-making and development of the public art programme. For example, members of youth clubs designed and constructed their own temporary sculpture works and schools related National Curriculum requirements to projects around sculpture and public art.

Overlooking the site of 'Ambit' is the St Peter's Riverside sculpture trail which forms part of the Coast to Coast cycle route. Developed over six years, the artists have worked with local people to create a series of art works that reflect their memories and concerns about this rapidly changing environment. Tactile images and text in the form of notepad pages around the base of 'Shadows in Another Light' communicate this cultural heritage in a memorable way. A touch of humour in the messages helps the visitor to connect with the characters involved in the project. As a result of consultation, an independent 'St Peter's Sculpture Support Group' was established to oversee the future development and management of the project. The aim of the group was to provide a mechanism by which local people could continue to influence and contribute to the changing riverside.

The wider landscape

While public art in the urban environment grew from the move to use open spaces as an extension of the gallery and a desire to bring art within reach of more people, the introduction of art into countryside settings has stronger links with country-side management and imaginative interpretive planning. Commissioning of art is bound up with objectives for encouraging greater participation in countryside recreation and increasing people's awareness and understanding of countryside and environmental issues.

These core policies of the Countryside Agency are also paralleled by a need to conserve and enhance the beauty of the countryside. Adding 'alien' structures in the form of artworks can easily detract from the natural beauty of landscapes. To successfully 'fit' art within the context of the natural, living landscape requires careful selection of materials, shape, colour and site. Art should be creative intervention, not intrusive imposition. It has the capacity to sensitise people to the landscape, helping them to discover for themselves the attributes that make a landscape special. It can grant a perception of what is hidden from view, either in the physical sense of unseen wildlife or historical sense of revealing clues to the past.

Figure 9.4   'Wild Boar Clearing', Sally Matthews, 1987–89, Grizedale Forest, Cumbria

Forest art

Grizedale Forest in Cumbria represents one of the longest running and best known major 'art in the landscape' projects. Since 1977, nearly 200 sculptures have been created within the forest by artists who have gone on to acclaim national and international reputations. Employed on residencies, the artists have worked on site, taking their inspiration and materials from the forest itself, creating works that are an organic part of their environment, maturing and decaying with the cycle of nature.

While many people visit Grizedale to see the sculptures, the experience is very far removed from that encountered at a sculpture park or contrived countryside sculpture trail. The lack of formal interpretation, or even precise location guides, encourages visitors to explore the forest, often stumbling upon the sculptures unexpectedly in a small clearing or viewed on a distant horizon. This element of search and discovery encourages people to see multitudes of sculptural forms in the rocks, trees and earth that make up the forest's fabric. When a sculpture is encountered, it stands alone as sole communicator, where the viewer and the viewed must establish their own dialogue and understanding.

Along tracks and trails

The use of art to enhance countryside trails is now widespread. Pieces act as punctuation marks, encouraging passers-by to stop and think about the landscape through which they travel, or perhaps rest at a uniquely crafted seat or shelter directing them to look at a particular aspect of the view. The River Parrett Trail through Dorset and Somerset has many such features. Students of a local agricultural college worked with an artist in residence to design and construct distinctive stiles and bridges. Living willow sculpture celebrates this as the heart of English basket-making country. Memory boxes sited along the route contain carvings depicting aspects of the trail that are important to local people and sculpted way-markers are created from local materials.

Discreet plaques act as clues along the way. Walkers are encouraged to take rubbings, collect clues and find out more about the wildlife, people and heritage of the River Parrett valley. An information pack, visitor centre exhibition, web site and collection of music and stories have also been compiled as part of the trail project.

This 50-mile trail, largely funded through the European Life Fund and supported by four district councils, was created under the banner of cultural tourism. Through careful development and management, the trail seeks to establish sustainable tourism to support the economy within this environmentally fragile area. The objectives for its creation were very much concerned with involving and benefiting all of the communities within its locality. It aims to improve access to the countryside, be a vehicle for people to better understand and celebrate their heritage and increase social activity. The latter is achieved through school educational projects, craft workshops, guided walks, talks and other events for locals and visitors alike. While the subject of the events varies, they all follow a celebratory or discovery theme and intend to help people to express their feelings and values of the landscape around them.

Issues and conclusions

The examples described in this chapter are intended to raise a number of issues regarding the value and appropriateness of employing public art as a medium for interpretation. At a time when opportunities for securing funding are high, there is a danger that under-planned projects and over use will eventually lead to a degradation of meaning. How long before we expect to find every country park, forest or urban square littered with works of art that largely go unnoticed because the element of uniqueness or surprise has been taken away?

If there is to be a relationship between the art and the public, the process of identifying and consulting those people can be as important as creating the art itself. Without such consultation and involvement there is a danger that commissioned public art will not reflect on its location and community, but become a monument to its commissioners or the private indulgence of its creator. The process of involving local people also has an important role to play in the long-term maintenance and further development of public art projects. Spin-off activities, such as the River Parrett Trail's events programme are keeping the project alive.

Some public art, such as the Cleveland New Milestones project, begs the question — are the pieces really interpreting the landscape and heritage or do they need interpreting themselves to uncover their hidden messages? The most usual form of this extra level of interpretation is a leaflet available from a nearby Tourist Information Centre, but how long before the leaflets are out of print and unavailable? Some feel that interpreting public art reduces its status; that it should stand alone and speak for itself. Introducing interpretation doesn't necessarily mean adding a panel or printing a guide. The St Peter's Riverside project included specific interpretive messages as an integral part of the public art project, introduced at the design stage to become part of the art itself.

If public art is intended to be interpretive, raising environmental, heritage or cultural awareness, there should be some mechanism for evaluating how successfully it achieves those aims. The fact that people visit a place to see the art, doesn't necessarily mean that they have been provoked or stimulated by it. In New Zealand, a research project at a park on Mangere Mountain, Auckland, revealed that visitors' reactions to sculptures designed as aids to interpreting the complex history of the park, ranged from fascination to frustration and disinterest. Some visitors failed to notice some of the sculptures, few realised that the artworks were attempting to interpret the site, while others were encouraged to seek further information for themselves (Burns, L. 1999).

While evaluation plays an important role in planning and implementing the use of other interpretive media, it appears to be assigned a minor role in the development of public art programmes. An interpretive panel may be tried and tested before it is finally produced and installed to reduce the risk of wasting money on what is considered an expensive interpretive medium. Some feel that art is unquantifiable. It is based on aesthetic judgement, meaning many different things to different people. If this is true, against whose standards can art be evaluated? Would evaluation counter the very essence of art and integrity of the artist? Public opinion regarding Birmingham's Centenary Square tended to have a symbiotic relationship with media coverage. In such cases there is a danger that a critic's description and interpretation of an artwork may be adopted as 'the' interpretation, preventing people from expressing their own reactions and feelings.

Using public art as a medium for interpretation can be expensive and risky. If successful it can be one of the most memorable, provocative and enlightening experiences. In failure, it can represent an intrusive object of ridicule and embarrassment.

Reducing risk – the role of public art policies and strategies

Reducing the level of risk is the role of strategic planning. In 1990, Public Art Forum research showed that only 6 per cent of local authorities in England, Scotland and Wales had public art policies. By 1993, according to University of Winchester research, this had risen to 42 per cent in England and Wales (Selwood, S. 1995). The rise in National Lottery and European funding of public art has increased the demand for clearly defined strategies, policies and objectives that must be submitted with funding applications.

Developing a Public Art Strategy will reduce risk by:

- defining the purpose of a project;
- identifying the target audiences;
- describing the desired outcomes;
- making a commitment to future management.

The definition of clear objectives provides the framework against which outcomes can be evaluated and the success of the project assessed. Objectives can be many and varied as demonstrated by the case studies. They may, for example, relate to economic regeneration, tourism development, raising environmental awareness or celebrating cultural heritage.

The statement of strategic objectives should then lead to the development of a more detailed project brief. This will specify the role of individuals within the project team and act as the mechanism for selecting the right artist. If community consultation is to be undertaken, selecting the right person can be critical. A good understanding and dialogue between client and artist will allow the artist flexibility to be creative and inventive, helping the project to evolve. The Arts Council of England recommends that the brief should include the following:

- detailed description of the project's aim, context, budget and timetable;
- description of the role of the artist and criteria for selection process;
- details of the project team, their roles and responsibilities;
- description of site, conditions and planning permissions required;
- degree of community participation;
- specification of materials (availability, environmental concerns);
- historical, social or other contextual detail;
- any constraints on the project;
- maintenance and durability requirements;
- artist's copyright position and clarification of ownership of work;
- documentation required.

(Adams, E. 1997)

If the project requires the involvement of many different organisations, it may be appropriate to appoint a co-ordinator or project manager who understands the needs of all concerned. Within local authorities this is usually the Arts Officer, or equivalent, who will identify and apply for funding, select the artist(s), market and promote the project, liaise with the community, identify training needs, draw up contracts and generally keep the project moving in line with the stated objectives.

Many public art projects are instigated by a highly motivated individual. Without the involvement of a mediator, such projects can have a very one-sided agenda.

If well planned and executed, public art can be a very powerful medium for interpretation. Its visual nature allows it to convey messages that words cannot. It has the capacity to engage with its audience in a very personal, and even spiritual way. The question as to whether it can stand alone as communicator of precise messages, without the inclusion of explanatory information, or helpful clues to its meaning, will depend upon the complexity of the messages to be conveyed. This may not be a medium that can successfully achieve all interpretive aims and objectives, but it can play an inimitable part within a wider interpretive portfolio.

While the development and implementation of a detailed brief can take some of the risk out of utilising public art, the importance of interpretive planning must not be overlooked. If the interpretive planning procedure is followed, public art will only become part of an interpretive programme if it is the most appropriate medium to convey the messages to the target audience, in a manner that is suitable to location, budget and management capability.

■ ■ ■

Bibliography

Adams, E. 1997 *Public Art: people, projects, process.* Sunderland: AN Publications.

Adams, E. 1999 'Whispering or shouting – just what is public art?' in *Interpretation, A Journal of Heritage and Environmental Interpretation* Vol. 3 (3) April 1999: SIBH.

Arts Council of Great Britain, 1991 *Percent for Art: a review.* Sunderland: AN Publications.

Baldry, H. 1981 *The Case For The Arts.* London: Martin Secker & Warburg Ltd.

Binks, G. (Ed.) 1999 'A common language' in *Interpretation, A Journal of Heritage and Environmental Interpretation* Vol. 3 (3) April 1999: SIBH.

Burgess, C. 1980 *The Age of Stonehenge.* London, Toronto and Melbourne: J.M. Dent & Sons Ltd.

Burns, L. 1999 'Clues in the ground' in *Interpretation, A Journal of Heritage and Environmental Interpretation* Vol. 3 (3) April 1999: SIBH.

Carter, J. 1990 'A tale of two forests' in *Interpretation, The Bulletin of the Centre for Environmental Interpretation* October 1990; Manchester: SIBH.

Carter, J. 1999 'Where does this adventure go to?' in *Interpretation, A Journal of Heritage and Environmental Interpretation* Vol. 3 (3) April 1999: SIBH.

Carter, J. and Masters, D. 1998 'Arts and the natural heritage'. *Scottish Natural Heritage Review* No. 109.

Carvana, W. 1993 *Aboriginal Art.* London, New York: Thames & Hudson.

Causey, A. 1998 *Sculpture Since 1945.* Oxford, New York: Oxford University Press.

Clifford, S. and King, A. 1990 'Nature and her most worthy interpreter, ART' in *Interpretation, The Bulletin of the Centre for Environmental Interpretation* October 1990; Manchester: SIBH.

Clough, R. 1997 'Archaeology in the Kilmartin Valley' in *Institute of Field Archaeologists Yearbook & Directory of Members, 1997*; Reading: IFA.

Department for Culture, Media and Sport, 1998 *A New Cultural Framework.*

Ford, B. (Ed.) 1988 *The Cambridge Guide to the Arts in Britain, Volume 1 — Prehistoric, Roman and Early Medieval.* Cambridge: Cambridge University Press.

Ford, B. (Ed.) 1988 *The Cambridge Guide to the Arts in Britain, Volume 3 — The Middle Ages.* Cambridge: Cambridge University Press..

Grant, B. and Harris, P. (Ed.) 1996 *Natural Order. Visual arts and crafts in Grizedale Forest Park.* Cumbria: The Grizedale Society.

Hillier, D. 1990 '. . . On the ground' in *Interpretation, The Bulletin of the Centre for Environmental Interpretation* October 1990; Manchester: SIBH.

Jones, S. (Ed.) 1992 *Art In Public: what, why and how?* Sunderland: AN Publications.

Lacy, S. (Ed.) 1995 *Mapping the Terrain, New Genre Public Art.* Seattle, WA: Bay Press.

Longworth, I.H. 1985 *Prehistoric Britain.* London: British Museum Publications Ltd.

Matthews, J. and Stead, M.J. 1997 *Landscapes of Legend. A photographic journey through the secret heart of Britain.* London: Blandford.

Matthews, S. 1994 *With Animals.* Tyne and Wear: Pedalling Arts Ltd.

Milner, P. 1999 'Art in its rightful place' in *Interpretation, A Journal of Heritage and Environmental Interpretation* Vol. 3 (3) April 1999: SIBH.

RCAHMS 1999 *Kilmartin, Prehistoric & Early Historic Monuments. An inventory of the monuments extracted from Argyll, Volume 6.* Edinburgh: RCAHMS.

Sandison, D. 1998 *The Art of The Celts.* London: Hamlyn.

Selwood, S. 1995 *The Benefits of Public Art. The polemics of permanent art in public places.* London: Policy Studies Institute.

The Parrett Trail Partners, 1997 *The River Parrett Trail . . . Following a river from source to mouth.* South Somerset District Council: The Parrett Trail Partnership.

Tilden, F. 1977 *Interpreting Our Heritage.* Chapel Hill: University of North Carolina Press.

The following unpublished documents were also used as a source of information:

City of Sunderland, Education and Community Services 1998 'publicart.sunderland.com'. City of Sunderland.

Cleveland Arts, *Percent for Art* (leaflet).

Common Ground, 1996 *Parish Maps* (leaflet).

Cox, L. 1996 Public Art Forum opening statement to the National Heritage Select Committee.

Middlesbrough Borough Council 1995 *Public Art Strategy.*

Skelton and Brotton Parish Councils. *Skelton & Brotton New Milestones* (leaflet).

Chapter 10

'JESSIE'S CATS' AND OTHER STORIES:
PRESENTING AND INTERPRETING
RECENT TROUBLES

John Schofield

Every Friday after work Jessie would collect a standing order of
minced meat from her butcher in Hanover Street. She bought the
mince specially to feed the cats in our area. Come rain or sunshine,
Jessie turned up every Friday afternoon in the lane behind our
house. Here she would stand on tiptoe to reach onto the high wall
where all the neighbourhood's cats were gathered.

The cats loved her. They turned up in different shapes and sizes,
colours and temperaments. Some of them were rough and ugly,
but when Jessie fed them, they all behaved like sweet, adorable
kittens . . . One Friday afternoon, Jessie, the 'fairy godmother of
the cats', failed to arrive. The hours passed and the cats waited
and waited. They all lingered, clearly hoping that she was merely
delayed.

But Jessie never turned up to feed them . . .

[. . .]

After [the forced removals under the Group Areas Act, 1966],
rumours started going around that Jessie had [returned to the area
and] been seen feeding the cats. Some of the people who were still
living in District Six swore that one could on a Friday afternoon
sometimes catch a glimpse of a silhouette standing up on tiptoe to
feed the cats on the wall.

Many Friday afternoons around five we looked out for the silhouette. We never saw it. It made us sad, because even today, many
years after the service lane and all the houses in Tyne and Godfrey
Streets have been demolished, some people still say that Jessie and
her cats can sometimes be seen on that spot on a Friday afternoon.

(Fortune 1996: 70, 94–5)

Introduction

'Jessie's Cats' is one of many stories that gives depth – in the sense of human experience and memory – to the now deserted and scrub covered townscape of District Six, an area of Cape Town from which people were suddenly and forcibly removed under the Group Areas Act on account of their race or colour (Hall 1998, 2000 Ch. 7, 2001; Malan and Soudien 2002; Malan and van Heyningen 2001). Yet, 30–40 years after the first removals, much of the character of the District and of its former community remains, and with some prior knowledge of South Africa's recent past, this character *is* tangible as sense of place (e.g. Bell 1997) and local identity. Of course, not everyone can or will experience this character in the same way: for insiders, such as former residents, memory will be the dominant factor; while outsiders will require more background to the events of the late 1960s and 1970s, and an awareness of the way of life of the District's former inhabitants, for the place to 'come alive' to anything like the same degree. This means that, for most visitors to Cape Town, interpretation is a necessary precursor to any site visit, and here the District Six Museum plays an important role, telling the story of the removals and acting as an outlet for the numerous accounts and histories of the area that are now being told.

This chapter follows on from one in a related publication in this series (Schofield 1999). It looks specifically at approaches to presenting and interpreting troubled pasts, primarily through the events of the apartheid era in South Africa, and explores how a combination of material culture, engaging museum displays, photographs and the use of narrative – preferably in the first person – is necessary if these events are to be presented as they really were, and not as some fabrication of some truth,[1] nor as a diluted, sanitised or unbalanced interpretation of past events (cf. Geiryn 1998 and Linenthal 1995). The treatment of recent military and civil conflicts could easily be made rather cool and dispassionate to avoid controversy; it is argued here that in cases like District Six, engaging (or 'hot') interpretation is a necessity, with reconciliation an achievable objective (after Uzzell 1989; Ballantyne and Uzzell 1993; Uzzell and Ballantyne 1998). It should be stressed that, in presenting this case study, the intention is only to give a particular spin to a story already well represented in the literature. For example, much has been written about the District's archaeology and architecture (Hall 1998; Malan and van Heyningen 2001; Fransen 1996), its social (e.g. Fortune 1996) and political history (Jeppie and Soudien 1990), its presentation as heritage (Ballantyne and Uzzell 1993) and its future (Malan and Soudien 2002). This chapter will use these sources, combined with personal experience as a first time European visitor, to highlight the significance of the place, and the way it is remembered and presented, promoting it as an example of best practice for interpreting monuments and sites of conflict, injustice and atrocity. Some further examples of this same approach to heritage interpretation are also given.

'You are now in Fairyland': interpreting recent events in District Six

A brief history

In the words of a Museum brochure:

> District Six was an area of Cape Town at the foot of Table Mountain, near to the harbour and the city bowl. [It] was a cosmopolitan area. Priests, teachers, school children, prostitutes, families, politicians, midwives, gangsters, fishermen, pimps, merchants and artisans lived in the area. They came from all over the world and the different corners of South Africa and together created a rich mix of different cultures. They also introduced into South Africa a strong political tradition. The area was a seedbed of ideas and activities. Most of the people who lived in District Six were working class. They wanted to live close to the city, harbour and factories where they worked. Rich with memory, it was a place which has made a great contribution to the history and culture of Cape Town, and indeed to South Africa. As a result of the apartheid legislation only the memories of District Six remain.

What happened to District Six under the apartheid regime is well documented (Hall 1998). Having been declared a whites only area under Proclamation 43 of the Group Areas Act (1966), virtually the entire District was physically erased from the map. Some 62,000 people had previously occupied the area according to government figures, which also indicated that three-quarters of these were tenants, and all but 1,000 were classified as 'coloured' (i.e. of mixed descent) in the terms of the Population Registration Act. By 1978 some coloured families were still resident in the District which, by this time, had become a rallying point for opposition to the forced removals that were taking place throughout South Africa. By 1984 the removals were complete. All that remained was the scar, separating Cape Town from its suburbs (Figure 10.1): South Africa's Hiroshima, as one commentator described it; alternatively, 'the preserve of South Africa and all of humanity' (Nagra pers. comm.). In 1986 BP (Southern Africa) announced its intention to rebuild District Six as South Africa's first open residential area, once again attempting to impose policies on communities without consultation. BP's proposal further focused an already strong opposition and stimulated the formation of the Hands off District Six Campaign (HODS), an alliance of organisations and former residents that campaigned for the abolition of the Group Areas Act prior to any redevelopment. Abolition of the Act has since happened and in August 1997 a Land Court ruling gave the area back to former residents.

District Six today is an eloquent symbol of the policy of racial segregation that dominates South Africa's recent history, and of the sense of community that the apartheid regime attempted to destroy (Figure 10.2). District Six was once heterogeneous and cohesive; there was no residential segregation between classes; and there

Figure 10.1   General view of Cape Town from the north-west – the edge of District Six can be seen to the left (with permission from the District Six Museum)

existed a level of tolerance among people that could accommodate a range of religious and political beliefs (le Grange 1996: 8). This state of affairs was unacceptable to the apartheid regime. The District is now empty, 44 hectares of scrub which effectively hides the drama of the natural red earth, which 'bled' at the time of the removals (Figure 10.3), but which does at least protect a rich and significant archaeological record documenting the history of the District's occupation and ultimately its clearance (Hall 1998). Furthermore, there remains a strong District Six community on the Cape Flats, and the plan now is to rebuild the District, returning some former residents alongside first time occupants (this is discussed further below).

The District Six Museum

> In 1989 ex-residents of District Six envisaged a museum to commemorate the area and honour the people who fought against the forced removals and Group Areas Act. On 10 December 1994, the District Six Museum opened with its first exhibition 'Streets – Retracing the Past'. The museum provides a space for the community to come together and share their experiences and retrace their memories. The District Six Museum is a reminder that forced removals must never happen again.
>
> (Museum brochure, undated)

Figure 10.2 'You are now in Fairyland' (photographer unknown) (with permission from the District Six Museum)

The Museum is more than just a display. For a start it acts as the focus of a now dispersed community, and for this reason its location in the old Methodist Church on the edge of the District is particularly apposite. It was this church, for example, also called 'the freedom church', that took a stand against the injustices of the Group Areas Act and other apartheid legislation. It now serves as a meeting place, an educational resource and a point of contact. The Museum also has an important political role in the District's redevelopment, as well as acting as a conduit for narratives and personal accounts (publishing some of its own works and selling others), oral history, sound archives and artefacts, such as those from archaeological excavations undertaken by the University of Cape Town in recent years. It was also closely involved in a public sculpture project in 1997, designed in part to reclaim the district for its former residents.

The Museum is interactive. Former residents are encouraged to sign a cloth, which is later embroidered.[2] Much of the ground floor is taken up with a map of the District, prior to the clearances, with the road names marked on. Here former residents sign their names and number the houses where they once lived (Figure 10.4). The Museum also houses a huge photographic archive. When this was first

Figure 10.3   Bulldozers at work in District Six (photograph: Pastor Stan Abrahams) (with permission from the District Six Museum)

shown publicly, it led to a celebration of life among former residents; singing, arguing and debating. And among the museum staff are former residents who will discuss the District with visitors, adding colour to an already engaging interpretive experience. What the Museum does not overtly do, however, is to show the horror of the removals. As many visitors have remarked, the power of the Museum lies in the fact that it has a celebratory air about it. There are no 'in your face bulldozers'; rather people are remembering themselves as a community, in a Museum that is essentially a homely place.

The District Six Museum currently receives comparatively few visitors; only around 50 overseas tourists a day visit for example, mostly arranged through tour operators. Fewer still visit the District itself, probably because of concerns about personal security,[3] even though the engaging and interactive interpretation that the Museum provides prepares visitors well for touring the District. To facilitate this, a leaflet has been produced by the Museum which provides a guided tour by Pastor Stan Abrahams, a former resident. One of the 30 points on the tour gives an impression of the whole:

> Parkers was a corner shop which dealt in 'cash and credit'. Amongst other things one could buy bread, paraffin for the primus stove and fish oil for frying fish. On hot Friday evenings, my brothers and I would push our way through the adults who were buying their weekly provisions to get to the soda fountain counter where we would spend our week's pocket money on bulls-eyes, almond rock or a koeksister.

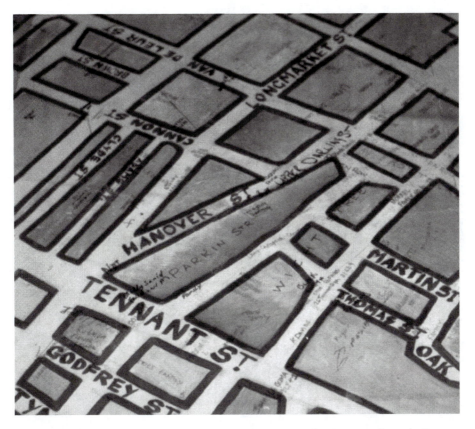

Figure 10.4   The street plan in the District Six Museum (with permission from the District Six Museum)

The tour takes in: the existing churches and mosques; the one terrace of cottages that survived the clearance and which today gives an impression of the District's original appearance (Figure 10.5); the cobbled streets, in many ways the centre of District life; and the foundations of front steps from which people all over the District watched the passing scene.

To summarise then (after Hall 1998), between 1966 and the present,

> the raw scar of District Six was encrusted with a variety of meanings. For its former residents, it was marked ground, the geography of dispossession and dispersal. For the apartheid government it stood for white entitlement and the principle of separate development. For reformist business and municipal interest, the land was an opportunity for investment and economic development.

It remains now to consider the future of the District, and specifically the role the physical remains and sense of place must play in presenting and interpreting its troubled past.

Figure 10.5 Terrace of cottages, prior to its removal (with permission from the District Six Museum)

The future

Proposals to redevelop District Six have been under discussion for some years. It is a controversial matter and one that the local community will have to resolve with politicians and city planners if a mutually acceptable solution is to be found. From a conservation perspective, it is important that the character of the District, and at least some of its physical remains, are retained to work alongside the Museum in interpreting the past, for three main reasons.

First, for the sense of belonging such areas provide for their former inhabitants. The Museum at District Six for example has served to galvanise a community that was scattered among the townships in the years following the passing of the Group Areas Act, while the 44 hectares of empty ground (excepting the churches and mosques that remain) has, throughout the apartheid years and beyond, acted as a daily reminder of the removals, to Capetonians and visitors alike.

Second is the 'lessons from history' argument, that the social injustice of the forced removals must be kept in the past. There is also the hope that lessons from South Africa will eventually attain wider geographical and geopolitical significance and influence.

Third, that increasingly people want to know about the recent past, and in particular about the momentous events of the twentieth century. What happened in South Africa under the apartheid regime constitutes a major episode in recent world history, and District Six tells that story arguably better than anywhere else (but see p. 155 for reference to Robben Island).

What is finally agreed will need to be sustainable in the long term, and for this reason alone the strategic location of the vacant land, the size of the area and the increasing need for affordable inner-city housing suggest that a significant amount of development will be necessary, and this is perhaps appropriate in the circumstances. Rehousing those forcibly removed sounds attractive, but not all individuals removed can (or perhaps even want to) return, and new developments such as the Technikon – built originally for white students only – can't simply be removed. But as le Grange (1996: 15) has sensibly argued, District Six can still be used as a model for how to address the wrong-doings of the past and as a way by which to heal a divided city. Of course this would require the participation of the affected community and the concerted political will of government to deal sensitively with the planning and implementation of a reconstruction programme. Three specific aspects of this 'model' can be identified.

First, it is important that the future development of the District draws upon the urban planning traditions of its past. For example: the fine-grained street network; the mixed land-use development; a mix of housing types to ensure social heterogeneity; the street as community space; and the population density that shaped the area and which can be reinterpreted and adapted to serve contemporary requirements (after le Grange 1996). The surviving churches and mosques could serve as foci within a redesigned District Six, with one of them housing the Museum.

Second, views and vistas will be important, particularly for former residents revisiting the District. To this end le Grange (1996) produced designs to retain as open space an area either side of the sloping and cobbled Horsley Street which uses mounds of rubble to obscure the foreground, yet showing glimpses of the city, a view that residents would have had.[4] This area also includes the site of one of the three excavations undertaken in the District by the University of Cape Town; artefacts from these excavations could remain on view at the Museum.

Third, places specifically of memory should be (and in fact are being) considered, to serve for example as areas for quiet reflection and play. In 1993, the District Six Museum Foundation called a public meeting to get sanction from the community to set aside land in District Six for such 'memorial parks'. This remains on the agenda at the time of writing and would be important for many reasons, such as allowing easy access to the District for those who cannot or choose not to return as residents. As we have seen, the front steps of houses, from which residents 'watched the passing scene', survive in some areas, along with original cobbling. In terms of presenting and remembering past events, these steps and cobbling are arguably the most meaningful of all material remains surviving within the District and would be an important component of such 'memorial parks'.

In summary, District Six is an evocative and an important place, both for former residents and visitors. For those who understand its significance its atmosphere is tangible, obviously so for former residents but for visitors too. What happens to the District matters to all these people, but most significantly of course it matters to the future generations who will visit and interpret it. For those future visitors the steps, the cobbles and the bare red earth may be the most powerfully symbolic of all its material remains, and for that reason alone the arguments for their retention are compelling. District Six is not however unique in these terms and a few examples follow where comparison with aspects of presentation and interpretation at District Six demonstrates and confirms the strengths of this approach.

'Don't forget us': other troubled pasts

Wartime monuments in England

English Heritage has, since 1994, been undertaking a national review of England's recent monuments of war, developing the sound understanding necessary to secure their future management (English Heritage 1998). As a result of this work some sites – examples of the typical and commonplace as well as the rare – will be afforded statutory protection through scheduling, some will be listed, while others will be managed locally through the development control process (Schofield 1999: 182). Many of these sites are accessible to a public who are increasingly aware of and interested in the fabric of war: popular books, television programmes and museums have ensured that. And an approach to interpretation and presentation that engages the visitor and which is 'in keeping' with the site's original function, is now fairly typical. Orford Ness, for example, a Cold War experimental site on the Suffolk coast, is presented to visitors through a 'philosophy of non-intervention'. An extract from the guide book explains that this philosophy 'stems from a need to protect the features and geomorphological value . . . as well as its aura of mystery'. It goes on: 'The main structures of the buildings and their impact on the landscape should survive for many years; and their symbolic value will thus be maintained for future generations.'

Orford Ness is thus presented in a way that is compatible with its role in experimentation and atomic weapons testing. Similarly, Cold War control bunkers, such as that advertised on road signs for miles around as 'The Secret Bunker' at Mistley, Essex, are typically presented as cold, grey structures from which visitors depart feeling suitably chilled. At Mistley the monotony and silence of empty corridors and bare rooms, mostly underground, is broken by three cinemas, each showing public information films of the time. In this atmosphere the '3 minute warning' is a dramatic interruption.

Preserving such sites serves several purposes, one of which is the opportunity they provide for exploring, experiencing, interpreting and deconstructing the recent and contemporary pasts. The statutory protection of Second World War anti-aircraft gunsites is an example of this. Over 2,000 heavy anti-aircraft gunsites were built in England between 1939 and 1945, their distribution confined mainly to the east and south coasts, and around cities and industrial centres: the areas or places most vulnerable to attack (Dobinson 2001). From studying modern aerial photographs of known sites it has now been established how few of these sites survive (Anderton and Schofield 1999), and how rare are those examples where the layout of the site – with its gun emplacements and control building and the domestic sites – provides a visual impression of scale and function. Plans and photographs are one thing, but for visitors wanting to appreciate the site's layout, the spacing of buildings, and their configuration and alignment, and even to experience the 'ghosts of place' (Bell 1997), the survival of structural remains including the original road layout are necessary, ideally in an environment virtually unchanged since 1945. Although some examples of incomplete gunsites will be protected (in view of their overall rarity as a monument class), complete examples that enable interpretation are a priority.

Unfortunately the urgency with which these sites must be protected, and the speed of the national review of which this example forms a part (the Monuments Protection Programme (MPP) – see English Heritage 2000 for further details) means that information from those serving on these sites cannot easily be included in our site assessments, or in the resulting documentation, unless already available in local records or in published form. The value of such testimony as a source of information is recognised however. At Brixham in Torbay, for example, an emergency coast battery survives well, with its gun emplacements and associated buildings. Some of these are now protected through listing and scheduling, and the site has a conservation area designation. But what really gives this site colour is the fact that several of those who served on the battery live locally and 'keep an eye' on the place. An interpretation booklet and panels have been provided, lectures are given locally about the site and, most impressively, veterans approach visitors to the battery with the offer of guided tours.

Blitz experiences

Wartime monuments enable Second World War and Cold War sites to be experienced by a public who are increasingly knowledgeable of, and interested in, the material culture of these recent historical events.[5] But as with District Six and Oradour (below), engaging museum displays have a complementary and significant role. The experience of the Blitz, brought to life to varying degrees by the Blitz Experience at the Imperial War Museum, and another at the London at War Museum, both in London (and critically reviewed by Noakes 1997), for example provides a focus for exploring landscapes of the Blitz in contemporary London (Holmes 1997). To take the latter first, the display at the London at War Museum encourages the visitor to understand the Blitz by 'experiencing it'; to share the wartime experience, to 'see it, feel it, breathe it . . . be part of those momentous days'. As Noakes describes it (1997: 96–7):

> Descending in a rickety lift, the visitor emerges into a reconstruction of a
> tube shelter, where she or he can sit on original bales of wartime blankets,

to watch a collage of wartime newsreels . . . Emerging from the Tube shelter, the visitor next walks along a corridor lined with photos of London during the Blitz and newspaper headlines of the time. At the end of this corridor the visitor can choose to enter an Anderson shelter, where she or he can listen to recorded sounds of an air raid, look at an exhibition, or pass on to the centrepiece of the museum, the 'Blitz Experience'.

The Imperial War Museum's 'Blitz Experience' is rather different:

Visitors are ushered into it by a guide, entering through a small dark doorway to find themselves in a reconstruction of a London brick-built shelter. The shelterers are urged on into the shelter by the taped voice of George, a local air-raid warden. As the shelter fills more voices appear on the tape, all with strong London accents. Some talk about their day whilst others complain of lack of sleep. As the bombs begin to fall, George leads them in a hearty rendition of 'Roll Out the Barrel'. As the bombs get closer George's daughter Val becomes hysterical, her screams gradually drowning out the singing. A bomb drops uncomfortably close and the shelter reverberates. Everything goes quiet.

The shelterers are then helped outside by the museum guide, whose flashlight plays around the devastated street that they are now standing in. In front of them lies an upturned pram, its front wheel still spinning . . . As the shelterers leave blitzed London to become museum visitors once more, their last experience of the Blitz is George's fading voice saying 'Don't forget us'.

(Noakes 1997: 95–6)

There are common factors here. Both experiences involve damage to property not people. Emerging from the experience at the London at War Museum, what may at first be thought to be bodies are, on closer inspection, mannequins from a bombed shop, though the initial impression may be deliberate. Also, both experiences are of large communal shelters, even though these accommodated only a small percentage of London's population. As Noakes puts it (1997): the experiences represent a sanitized version of a minority experience presented as a majority experience, and the display at the London at War Museum bears little resemblance to the Tube shelter recalled by a former shelterer in Calder's *The People's War* (1969: 183) who described a place where, 'the stench was frightful, urine and excrement mixed with strong carbolic, sweat and dirty, unwashed humanity'. Yet despite obvious limitations in telling the typical Blitz experience precisely as it was, these are engaging displays. There are personal accounts to be read, photographs to be seen, and – not too far away from either Museum – bombsites to be visited, such as the ruined churches of St Mary Aldermanbury, St Dunstan-in-the-East and Christ Church.

Wartime atrocities

Sites of wartime atrocities, and notably Holocaust sites, present particular problems for presenting and interpreting past events, and Gilbert's recent *Holocaust Journey* (1998), in which he describes being accompanied by MA students studying the Holocaust, outlines some of these difficulties as well as demonstrating the effects an engaging display can have on its visitors. Their visit to the lakeside villa, where on 20 January 1942 Reinhard Heydrich introduced the 'Final Solution' to ministerial bureaucrats is described thus:

> In what is believed to have been the actual room in which the Wannsee Conference took place, with its tall windows looking out over the patio and lawn down to the lake, there is a stillness. We walk into the room, through it, round it and then out of it, as if it must not be disturbed. It is as if the voices of those who spoke here, and the heads of those who nodded their agreement here, must not be alerted to our presence. One feels a palpable sense of the presence of evil.
>
> (Gilbert 1998: 47)

Gilbert goes on to describe how his students were 'deeply affected by the visit to the Wannsee', how the meeting had been so clinical, and how the interpretation of events now presented this in a direct and unencumbered way. As one student put it: 'You don't get lost. You don't get bogged down. It's all depicted in a nutshell. Very comprehensive. It is a credit to the authorities that they have decided on this place – of all places – to have this mind-boggling exhibition' (ibid.: 50).

Another stop on their 'journey' was Prague, where they visited the Orthodox Cathedral Church of St Cyril and St Methodius, where Heydrich's assassins were trapped and killed in June 1942. Although not explicitly a Holocaust site, the interpretation of events provided for visitors is worth recounting:

> We enter the crypt . . . There is an exhibition provided by the Imperial War Museum in London, as well as a film. The story is tragic; [after their betrayal] the trapped men [Czechs, trained in Britain] barricaded themselves in the crypt and tried to dig their way through the brickwork into the sewers. The hole they dug penetrated six feet into the brickwork but they could get no further. The Germans pumped water into the crypt. When this failed they pumped in smoke. Finally they burst in. The men refused to surrender and were killed in the crypt. The hole they were digging is preserved as a memorial; it is a shattering site.
>
> The film starts. It is a dramatic reconstruction, and it is a strange sensation to be standing in the room which is being portrayed in the film. After the silence and sombre nature of the crypt, however, the noise of guns firing is jarring. Most of us drift out before the end. There is something unreal, but also unnerving, about the reconstruction.
>
> (Ibid.: 64)

Gilbert gives many other examples and tracing his students' reactions to how the past is presented at the Wannsee, and particularly at sites like Auschwitz and Belzec, provides an interesting dimension to the 'journey'. The particular point that it is his 'readings' of contemporary accounts that most influences their reaction, is noteworthy in the context of the other examples presented here. As Gilbert said about the effect of his 'readings' at the death camp of Sobibor (1998: 251): 'It is difficult [to read the passages I have prepared]. Even words written by survivors seem to intrude on the awfulness of the place. And yet, without these words, the awfulness is somehow diminished.'

Contemporary photographs are a particularly powerful medium in interpreting atrocities of the Holocaust. At Auschwitz-Birkenau, photographs set up on two small exhibition boards form part of a collection known as the *Auschwitz Album*. These include the only known photographs of people arriving at Birkenau, 'waiting, bewildered and uncertain, before being taken to their deaths' (Gilbert 1998: 160–1). Gilbert tells the story of this collection, including the circumstances of its discovery:

> The photographs had been taken on a single day (quite illegally), probably by SS Second-Lieutenant Bernhard Walter, Director of the Identification Service at Auschwitz . . . The pictures were put in an album with neatly inscribed introductory captions, the first of which read: Resettlement of the Jews from Hungary. Several months later, it would seem that a guard at Auschwitz named Heinz (his surname is unknown) sent the album to a guard at Nordhausen, perhaps his girlfriend, and probably someone who had earlier served with him at Auschwitz. He inscribed the album: 'As a remembrance of your dear, unforgettable, faithful, Heinz'.
>
> [. . .]
>
> The album was found in Nordhausen concentration camp on the day of liberation in May 1945 by eighteen year-old Lili Jacob . . . who had earlier been deported to Auschwitz from the Beregszasz ghetto. She fainted when she found the album: for among the 193 photographs was one of the rabbi, Rabbi Weiss, who had married her parents. On continuing to look through the album, Lili Jacob found photographs of two of her five brothers, eleven year-old Zril and nine year-old Zeilek. They had both been gassed shortly after the picture was taken, as had her parents, her other three brothers, her grandparents, and her aunt Taba and her five children (who also appear in the album).
>
> (Gilbert 1998)

As Gilbert states (ibid.: 161), these are terrible pictures, since we know the fate of those standing about, sitting with their bundles or walking along the fence. But they only record a single day out of more than 800 on which deportees arrived here at one camp of the many that existed. Standing there today, looking at the photographs, and looking around, one can almost match up the trees with those in the photographs, giving an immediacy that only an *in situ* presentation could achieve.

Finally here, at Oradour-sur-Glane in western France a company from Das Reich armoured division killed 642 people on 10 June 1944, among them 244 women and 193 children and babies. Most were locked into the church, which was then burnt down. Every year half a million people now visit the town, where burnt-out houses, cars and public buildings have been maintained as they were left in 1944 (Uzzell 1989), following the decision not to rebuild the village but rather construct a new settlement on the outskirts. Until a few years ago a tour guide, related to one of those killed, took visitors around the town, explaining in detail the events that took place there (Uzzell and Ballantyne 1998: 156); tourists also visited the small museum, where personal effects can be viewed. On 9 July 1999 Jacques Chirac opened a vast £6 million underground war crimes centre – Le Centre de la Memoire – in the village. The discrete architecture – a 10,000 sq ft crypt whose low entrance will be through a giant mirror reflecting the rural valley overlooked by Oradour – underlines (in the words of those responsible) 'the contrast between the gentleness of the valley and the sombre aspect of the ruins'. More significantly, the new centre now provides the interpretive context for atrocities conducted over a longer period embracing much of the twentieth century, in a place where the impact of a single such event can still be experienced by visitors. In this sense the co-location of Le Centre de la Memoire and the burnt out remains at Oradour will convey a powerful message to visitors as memory of the atrocity fades.

Robben Island

Returning to South Africa, another significant monument to past troubles, and specifically to the apartheid era, is Robben Island, whose international importance is reflected in its World Heritage Site status. This was the place where, after serving as a convict station, farm and leper hospital, and after fortification during the Second World War, it became known the world over as a place of brutality, harshness and a symbol of human rights abuses under the apartheid regime. Famously Nelson Mandela was imprisoned on the island for 27 years (Clark 2002; Smith 1997).

Here the 'experience' of visiting the island – now the Robben Island Museum – is engaging and emotionally charged; the story is told as it was and importantly by those who were there. The focus of the visit is, not surprisingly, the prison, in which photography is forbidden, and where the tour guides are one-time political prisoners, some of whom were held on the island and whose tour is – inevitably – an intensely personal account, if not of Robben Island then of the experience of political prisoners elsewhere in South Africa. And it isn't just the prison buildings that convey this experience. A visit to the island also includes the quarries where prisoners laboured, and suffered eye damage from the sun's reflection off the limestone; and the cells where some prisoners – like Robert Sobukwe – were kept in solitary confinement over many years. This insight into the island's landscape beyond the confines of the prison, its obvious remoteness, and particularly sharing the tantalising glimpses prisoners had of Table Mountain, give a clear impression of a further perhaps more obvious dimension of the apartheid era, telling another part of the same story that is presented so effectively in District Six.[6]

Tourjeman Post Museum, Jerusalem

Finally, and to contrast with the success of presenting and interpreting the past at District Six and Oradour among other places, is Jerusalem, and a programme for the renewal of the Tourjeman Post Museum following the peace process of the early 1990s. Here the difficulties of dealing with recent or ongoing troubles are exemplified, demonstrating that, despite the best of intentions, some situations will be too hot to handle, for the moment at least.[7]

In what was originally a museum devoted to Israeli heroism, the intention was to establish a 'museum of co-existence', an establishment where the narratives of the city's Palestinian and Jewish parts could be set out together, side by side (Ben-Ze'ev and Ben-Ari 1996). Within Jerusalem the division between the Arabs and the Jews characterises the city. These two national groups are spatially divided, and are separated in terms of education and employment, and it was this separation that eventually led to the project's failure. As Ben-Ze'ev and Ben-Ari state (ibid.):

> [it was in the] negotiations, struggles and discussions that the predicaments of creating the museum emerged in their full force. We emphasise that despite the expectation that a museum of 'co-existence' could be established, in retrospect this was but an illusion. Politics imposed itself to forestall such an opportunity.

Conclusion

The examples used in this chapter cover a range of topics, social conditions, political contexts and – of course – spatial and temporal diversity. The common thread however has been the presentation and interpretation of past troubles in a particular way and with the emphasis on human experience and its material manifestations. This is partly demand-led. There is considerable interest in the recent past, just as there is fascination with conflict, military especially, but also civil unrest and social injustice. It is true, there needs to be a cooling off period before such things are presented as heritage, but that need not necessarily be long. It is interesting to note that in Berlin for example, where the Wall was seen as a symbol of division in a once united city, it has taken only ten years, from the Wall's demolition and a recognition after the initial destructive phase of the need to preserve short sections, for a debate to start about its 'reconstruction' in some areas. So the point is not so much about when, but what and how, and it is on these issues that this chapter has laid emphasis.

To summarise some key points from the examples quoted, they have emphasised the need for (re)presentations of the past to be:

Accurate: Displays should aim to tell the story as it was, and not some sanitised or diluted version or fabrication of the truth; stories can of course be tailored for younger visitors, and some sensitive information can be effectively hidden in the more technical guidebooks or 'top-shelf' display facilities, if that is considered appropriate. On occasion, controversy – either about what happened or the implications of certain events or actions – will prevent a consensus of opinion, and in such cases displays may never materialise. This proved to be the case with the now well documented disagreements over the Smithsonian's display about Hiroshima (see Gieryn 1998; Perkins 1999; and Linenthal 1995 for example).

Facilitating: As we have seen,

> sense of place is not a given, and therefore cannot necessarily be passed on only by interpretation. It is created by individuals, and the aim of displays should be to give people the means to develop their own appreciation of significance. Interpretation . . . should facilitate . . . [There is also a need for] sense of place to be 'owned' and to grow out of individual experience, needs and perceptions . . . The sense of discovery is vital. Residents and visitors – and scholars and interpreters – should jointly participate and share their perceptions.
>
> (Fairclough pers. comm.)

Engaging: Presenting troubled pasts will be most effectively achieved by emphasising human experience. This can be achieved in different ways and here we have seen several: the value of written accounts, through 'Jessie's Cats' for example; the use as guides of former prisoners at Robben Island and former residents at Oradour-sur-Glane and District Six; audio-visual techniques to tell the story of Heydrich's assassins, and the simple and uncomplicated use of photographs at Auschwitz-Birkenau; the direct involvement of veterans in managing Brixham Battery; and the use of fictional characters, represented by Val and her growing hysteria in the underground shelter in the Imperial War Museum's 'Blitz Experience'. Another notable approach is for museum visitors to take on the identity of contemporary characters. This has proved to be both popular and successful at the In Flanders Fields Museum, Ypres, and the Holocaust Museum at Washington DC.

Respectful of past events: It is important that the correct balance is struck between providing a tourist 'attraction' and preserving the character of the place one is presenting to visitors. Plans to develop Auschwitz-Birkenau are an example:

proposals include enlarging the parking area, building a small by-pass around the main gate and a reception area opposite it, and converting the sauna (one of the few buildings to survive intact, excepting the huts) into a museum. Gilbert's reaction to these proposals was one of bewilderment, and in his view 'no doubt admirable from the museum curator's perspective, but incongruous after what [he and his students] had just seen' (1998: 173).

Signposts and symbols: It is important that the engaging, accurate museum displays aren't left alone in presenting troubled pasts (Schofield 1998), though they do of course have an important role to play. While these displays do contain touchstones through which visitors can gain insight into ordinary lives and personal experiences, the places themselves can be more powerful still in achieving these objectives, both in terms of the atmosphere or character of the place, and in its material remains. The open ground at District Six has extraordinary character, and has retained its sense of place and identity, a point reinforced on the 1997 Heritage Day holiday, when several thousand people 'reclaimed' District Six, to look at art and listen to music (Hall 1998). The ground also has the potential to be powerfully symbolic, the bare red earth acting as a reminder of the physical act of forced removal.

The general point here is that sites (in the sense of monuments and places) documenting troubled pasts, and especially those that involved human suffering, should attempt to 'bring the place alive' for visitors, and most of the examples given in this chapter achieve that, provided the visitor is suitably informed. To talk of ghosts may seem unscientific, but it is a valid point. A final example from Gilbert's *Holocaust Journey* illustrates this, quoting from the *Jewish Chronicle*, John Izbicki's account of the reinauguration of the restored Orianenburger Strasse Synagogue in Berlin on 7 May 1995, where he had prayed as a young boy before emigrating to Britain in 1939:

> We all sat outside, on the ground where two-thirds of the original building once stood. This empty space, where the main hall of the synagogue used to be, is to be left as a lasting scar of history. It is the remaining one-third that has been transformed into a museum, a place for researchers to come and study the history of German Jewry. The roof of that one-third is adorned now, as it was before, with two golden cupolas that shine like beacons across the Berlin skyline. As I listened to the speeches of eminent personalities and looked up at the windows of the restored building, I thought I saw — and certainly felt — the presence of so many others who had once prayed there.
> (Quoted in Gilbert 1998: 36)

To return to the opening quotation, it is argued here that for the interpretation of past troubles to be affective and thereby effective, stories should be presented that have characters to whose lives the visitor can relate.[8] With the recent past we have those people in abundance, real people whose lives and activities, whose sacrifices, heroism or evil deeds, give the stories a strength that could never be generated in fiction. We should make the most of this resource in our presentations. We should also remember the important fact that the buried archaeology contains another aspect of those people's lives, and one that's worth conserving in some form. Their artefacts lie in the soil; and the nature of their community continues to influence the character or 'feel' of the place. This is exemplified by District Six, where the history of the area makes it an important heritage site. With the museum displays and the literature available, it illustrates the way recent troubles can be presented to a public who increasingly want to know. At the time of writing, the future of the District has yet to be resolved, but given strength of opinion and the depth of commitment locally, a sensible and sustainable solution will surely be found serving as an example to others, both in the new South Africa and beyond.

Afterword

This essay was originally written and presented for publication in 1999. Subsequent amendments have been restricted to one or two obvious updates and the addition of some specific bibliographic references. It is likely that some of the examples will be somewhat out of date.

Acknowledgements

First of all I owe a considerable debt to Sandra Prosselandis, Director of the District Six Museum, for commenting on this chapter, putting right a few errors, misconceptions and misinterpretations, and suggesting some new avenues to pursue. Sandra declined the offer of joint authorship, so I should stress the point that some of her ideas (and words) are included in the text. I am also grateful to Haajirah Esau of the District Six Museum for supplying the photographs, Graham Fairclough for commenting on an earlier draft, and to my employer – English Heritage – for enabling me to visit South Africa and experience briefly the legacy of the apartheid regime.

Notes

1   Contra Lowenthal (1998: 19), who stated that, 'to reshape is as vital as to preserve. As Orwell bluntly warned those English he saw mired in compliant reaction, "we must add to our heritage or lose it" . . . we add by fabricating'.

2   One lady wrote: 'When I die scatter my ashes at busstop 100 Constit[ut]ion Street.'

3   What is surprising is that there are still many Capetonians who don't know of the Museum's existence, and many former residents who haven't yet visited the Museum for a variety of reasons, some because it is simply too painful to visit their past. The initial target group for the Museum was former residents and they remain the priority, but there are now many more overseas and local school visitors than before.

4   People always spoke of being able to read the time off the city hall clock.

5   This comes at a time when history students are abandoning ancient history for modern, and when historians accept that for periods such as the Dark Ages it is 'very difficult to engage the imagination'. At both A and degree level, the Second World War, and specifically Hitler, is currently heading the popularity stakes.

6   Recent press reports have described proposals to extend the Robben Island experience to include overnight stays in prison cells, though how much 'comfort' will be afforded to paying visitors isn't clear.

7   Similar difficulties may be encountered in Northern Ireland, where in the context of peace talks and optimism about a lasting peace in 1998–9, discussions about how to commemorate the Troubles are being held (Jarman 2002) and whether, indeed, to preserve anything of the Troubles, and what effect this might have on the success of any future peace agreement.

8   Which is why the Anne Frank Museum in Amsterdam is so successful, despite her story not having a deportation in it; of course it is in the context of Auschwitz, and her subsequent deportation that we read her Diary (Gilbert 1998: 76).

■ ■ ■

References

Anderton, M. and Schofield, J. 1999. Anti-aircraft gunsites, then and now. *Conservation Bulletin* 36, 11–13.

Ballantyne, R. and Uzzell, D. 1993. Environmental mediation and hot interpretation: a case study of District Six, Cape Town. *Journal of Environmental Education* 24 (3), 4–7.

Bell, M. 1997. The ghosts of place. *Theory and Society* 26, 813–36.

Ben-Ze'ev, E. and Ben-Ari, E. 1996. Imposing politics: failed attempts at creating a museum of 'co-existence' in Jerusalem. *Anthropology Today* 12 (6), 7–13.

Calder, A. 1969. *The People's War 1939–45*. London: Cape.

Clark, K. 2002. In small things remembered: significance and vulnerability in the management of Robben Island World Heritage Site, in Schofield, J., Johnson, W.G. and Beck, C.M. (Eds), *Matériel Culture: the archaeology of twentieth century conflict*, 266–80. London: Routledge: One World Archaeology, 44.

Dobinson, C. 2001. *AA Command: Britain's anti-aircraft defences of the Second World War*. London: Methuen.

English Heritage 1998. *Monuments of War: the evaluation, recording and management of twentieth-century military sites*. London: English Heritage.

English Heritage 2000. *MPP 2000: A review of the Monuments Protection Programme, 1986–2000*. London: English Heritage.

Fortune, L. 1996. *The House in Tyne Street: childhood memories of District Six*. Cape Town: Kwela.

Fransen, H. 1996. The architecture that Cape Town lost, in Greshoff, J., *The Last Days of District Six*, 19–21. Cape Town: The District Six Museum Foundation.

Geiryn, T.F. 1998. Balancing acts: science, Enola Gay and history wars at the Smithsonian, in Macdonald, S. (Ed.), *The Politics of Display: museums, science, culture*, 197–228. London and New York: Routledge.

Gilbert, M. 1998. *Holocaust Journey: travelling in search of the past*. London: Phoenix.

le Grange, L. 1996. The urbanism of District Six, in Greshoff, J., *The Last Days of District Six*, 7–15. Cape Town: The District Six Museum Foundation.

Hall, M. 1998. Cape Town's District Six and the archaeology of memory. Precirculated paper presented to the World Archaeology Congress's Inter-Congress on damage to cultural property, Croatia.

Hall, M. 2000. *Archaeology and the Modern World: colonial transcripts in South Africa and the Chesapeake*. London and New York: Routledge.

Hall, M. 2001. Social archaeology and the theatres of memory. *Journal of Social Archaeology* 1 (1), 50–61.

Holmes, R. 1997. *War Walks 2: from the Battle of Hastings to the Blitz*. London: BBC Books.

Jarman, N. 2002. Troubling remnants: dealing with the remains of conflict in Northern Ireland, in Schofield, J., Johnson, W.G. and Beck, C.M. (Eds), *Matériel Culture: the archaeology of twentieth century conflict*, 281–95. London: Routledge: One World Archaeology, 44.

Jeppie, S. and Soudien, C. (Eds) 1990. *The Struggle for District Six: past and present*. Cape Town: Buchu Books.

Linenthal, E.T. 1995. Struggling with history and memory. *Journal of American History* 82, 1094–1101.

Lowenthal, D. 1998. Fabricating heritage. *History and Memory* 10 (1), 5–24.

Malan, A. and van Heyningen, E. 2001. Twice removed: Horstley Street in Cape Town's District Six, 1865–1982, in Mayne, A. and Murray, T. (Eds), *The Archaeology of Urban Landscapes: explorations in slumland*, 39–56. Cambridge: Cambridge University Press.

Malan, A. and Soudien, C. 2002. Managing heritage in District Six, Cape Town: conflicts past and present, in Schofield, J., Johnson, W.G. and Beck, C.M. (Eds), *Matériel Culture: the archaeology of twentieth century conflict*, 249–65. London: Routledge: One World Archaeology, 44.

Noakes, L. 1997. Making histories: experiencing the Blitz in London's museums in the 1990s, in Evans, M. and Lunn, K. (Eds), *War and Memory in the Twentieth Century*, 89–104. Oxford and New York: Berg.

Perkins, G. 1999. Museum war exhibits: propaganda or interpretation? *Interpretation* 4, 38–42.

Schofield, J. 1998. Character, conflict and atrocity: touchstones in the landscapes of war, in Jones, M. and Rotherham, I.D. (Eds), *Landscapes – Perception, Recognition and Management: reconciling the impossible?*, 99–104. Landscape Archaeology and Ecology, Volume 3. Sheffield: The Landscape Forum and Sheffield Hallam University.

Schofield, J. 1999. Conserving recent military remains: choices and challenges for the 21st century, in Baker, D. and Chitty, G. (Eds), *Presentation and Preservation: conflict or collaboration*, 173–86. London: English Heritage and Routledge.

Smith, C. 1997. *Robben Island*. Mayibuye History and Literature Series No. 76. Cape Town: Struik Publishers.

Uzzell, D. 1989. The hot interpretation of war and conflict, in Uzzell, D. (Ed.), *Heritage Interpretation Vol. 1: the natural and built environment*, 33–47. London: Belhaven Press.

Uzzell, D. and Ballantyne, R. 1998. Heritage that hurts: interpretation in a postmodern world, in Uzzell, D. and Ballantyne, R. (Eds), *Contemporary Issues in Heritage and Environmental Interpretation: Problems and Prospects*, 152–71. London: The Stationery Office.

Chapter 11

THE USE OF NEW TECHNOLOGY IN THE INTERPRETATION OF HISTORIC LANDSCAPES

Brian Bath

At first, the ideas of high technology and historic landscapes do not seem to go together particularly well. But when faced with the problem of how to interpret those landscapes without creating unsightly intrusions, new technology offers some remarkable help.

In the long development of plans for the Stonehenge landscape there have been many different suggestions as to how it can be conserved and interpreted to the highest standards. Of course, with a World Heritage Site of such emotional and archaeological significance to many different parties, there is little hope of everyone ever agreeing on any one solution. However, there has been demonstrated an evolution of thinking in relation to the interpretive approach taken to such a site.

Stonehenge is not just the monument itself, but a ritual landscape including over 450 scheduled monuments spanning many millennia and sited over many hectares. As archaeologists have moved away from the study of individual elements in a landscape to a more holistic approach that considers the complex web of links and relationships between the elements and the landscape itself, it has become more important to convey this approach to visitors. In the case of Stonehenge, diverting the attention of visitors who have come simply to see and absorb something of the world's best known 'mystery' is something of an uphill task. The same problem applies to some extent at Avebury, which is distant, but still part of the same World Heritage Site. Avebury however has the benefit of consisting of a number of more visually striking monuments, such as the Avenues, Silbury Hill and West Kennet Long Barrow in addition to the henge itself.

Conserving Stonehenge

It is not possible to talk about the interpretation of Stonehenge without talking about its conservation. One of the major problems all such sites face is that everyone wants to see it and be there, even though they would prefer that all the other visitors were not there as well to spoil the view and the atmosphere. The temporary solution has been to rope off the henge to give everyone a clear view. But what would happen if the ropes were taken down and visitors could access the site again, as English Heritage have set as one of their main objectives in improving the access and interpretation of the site?

If the same number of visitors came as before there would be a threat to exposed surface archaeology and to the protected lichens on the stone surfaces at ground level. A crowd in the stone circle would obliterate the view and no one would be able to take photographs easily. It does not take long to create a spreadsheet that demonstrates that crowding would reach uncomfortable proportions on a large number of days throughout the year. If you accept that all visitors have the right to see and visit the stones, as English Heritage does, how can you allow access, reduce numbers of visitors within the stone circle and retain visitor satisfaction all at the same time?

The proposal, and most likely the solution that will be implemented, is to create a distant visitor centre with full interpretive and visitor facilities, and to provide transport to a point from which visitors can walk to and from the stone circle. This has the benefit of allowing virtual reality experiences and any other entertainment or interpretive technique to be used without running the risk of being accused of littering the landscape with visitor facilities. It also allows visitors to bring media with them, and take it away again, creating little or no intrusion on the overall atmosphere of the place other than their presence. This is very similar to the approach that has been developed towards litter in historic settings, certainly at Audley End and many other English Heritage sites in the Midlands, where no bins are provided so that you have to take your rubbish away with you. If you bring interpretation into the landscape, then take it away with you when you go.

The overall approach then can be summarized as permanent off-site facilities, and only temporary on-site media. If the same principle is applied to footpaths and directional signing, then the absolute minimum only is provided, and that should only be visible when sought out. Technology could be the key that allows the removal of all footpaths and signs. You simply link a Global Positioning System (GPS) to an audio tour and every visitor can be told exactly where they are, and where everything else is, at any point on the landscape. This is an example of satellite technology helping to rid the landscape of unsightly signs and helping to conserve the landscape by allowing (or even encouraging) visitors to take different paths through the landscape in order to reduce wear and tear on the fragile downland. A new postage stamp sized GPS chip has just been launched in the US and will be selling initially at about £60. In a year it will be half this, and there will be no economic reason not to include them in audio wands where required.

Audio wands

There is a conventional, but highly successful audio wand being used at Stonehenge at the time of writing. It was supplied and produced by Soundalive Ltd. The solid state system allows information to be retrieved by entering any number from 1 to 999. When sections of information are linked together by continuous numbering, different tours and different levels of information within tours can be accessed. The most visitor friendly aspect of such technology is that it allows random access. You create your own tour, if you want to, by selecting only the information you want. This is particularly important at Stonehenge because everyone seems to have different and very set views about what they believe about it. These wands, similar to older mobile phones in appearance and use, can also cater for multiple languages easily as they can be re-programmed with another language in only three and a half seconds. If a coach arrives unexpectedly and 40 people want Japanese tours, it does not take long to provide extra tours in that language.

A major benefit of digital wand technology is that the interpreter can develop many different approaches. At Battle Abbey, three different characters are used, a Norman, a Saxon and Edith Swanneck, Harold's common law wife. Each tells the story of the battle from their point of view. The visitor chooses which story they want to hear. At the beginning of the tour they watch a video of the battle and as they come onto the site they are introduced to the characters and given a choice of routes around the site. They can then choose how to visit and who they want to tell them about the site. In practice the great majority of visitors listened to all the options, providing a wider understanding of the different perceptions of what was happening at the time. Cast aluminium panels show scenes of the battle and give numbers and symbols for each of the characters and for further levels of information such as arms and armour and Norman tactics.

Video wands

Working for the National Trust in the Lake District, I carried out a survey of responses from visitors relating to the use of audio and video wands in such a sensitive setting. Video wands are, in effect, small hand-held computers that provide audio information, as well as having a small screen that can provide graphics, text and images. For visitors to the area it would provide complete orientation with maps, images and information on potential destinations. It could also choose destinations that they might not know about but which the computer believes will be of interest (based on the data entered at the start). Such a device would have the benefit, not only of fully interpreting the landscape, but would, as it could at Stonehenge, help to spread the visitor load at peak times. Combined with GPS, it could be a very powerful device indeed.

Our initial expectation was that the visitor profile in the Lake District would not welcome the intrusion of this technology into such a setting, and this proved true for a small group of dedicated fell walkers. However, to our surprise, the great majority of visitors to the valleys, mostly older visitors taking shorter excursions at certain points such as Aira Force, welcomed the idea and thought it would add greatly to their enjoyment of the area. The findings were produced in advance of cost effective technology being available, but all the components are now in use or being used at other sites.

Extending audio tour capabilities

Antenna Audio, innovative audio tour suppliers and developers, have been working with Renault cars for some time now to incorporate GPS into an in-car system that would provide interpretive information to people as they drove around a town or through a landscape. Extending the route information already available, the GPS would allow the system to tell people about the buildings and locations around them, as well as guiding them to the type of destinations they had registered an interest in. A GPS system has also been incorporated into an emergency phone link by the RAC, to help them find stranded motorists. A similar function could be added to an audio wand used in remote areas.

Siemens explored the potential of using mobile phones as audio-guides at Fountains Abbey, a rich landscape of historic buildings and gardens in a superb setting. The project did not take off, but the application of phone technology to interpretation is intriguing. Any amount of information can then be stored on servers and relayed to the user. Given the rapidity of growth in the mobile phone market, it is entirely possible for companies such as Pitmans, the guide book producers, to create audio interpretations for sites and towns around the country that users could access from wherever they may be for the cost of a phone call.

There is, of course, even more potential in the use of mobile phone technology to link to the web. More and more mobile phones can do this, and information can be streamed to an individual wherever they are. As communications technology advances and costs come down, this must certainly be one of the most potent tools for the interpreter of large landscapes and destinations in the future. One recent development in 1999 was the introduction of the X-plorer audio tour device from Antenna Audio, which will upload audio files from the internet and yet still fit into your pocket.

Audio tours of a wider landscape

In the here and now, audio tours are being used within very large areas. In South Wales the Teclyn audio wand has been used on a county-wide basis in Carmarthenshire. This device is based on a hard disc drive, and can currently store up to 40 hours of information, but much larger volumes will be possible in the near future. Visitors are given a fold out leaflet with many attractions and sites featured in the area, each keyed to a number. Visitors can listen to information about a variety of destinations and choose which to visit. When they get there, they can use the wand tour to tell them about the site itself. There are many different themed tours that can be followed, linking aspects of different sites. The wands can be taken from one site to another and dropped off at Tourist Information Centres or back at hotels, wherever they were taken from. The scheme seems to have been a great success, as discovering the breadth of attractions in the area has led to visitors staying longer. Most hotel owners who are part of the scheme now give the tours to guests as experience has shown they will generally extend their stay or book again for the following year.

Portable PC and web-related interpretation

At the Whitney Museum in New York an exhibition opened in May 1999 called 'American Century'. In collaboration with the Intel Corporation the museum has been offering visitors a museum tour based on a new application for a Mitsubishi Pad PC – a more powerful version of a Palm Pilot, a device originally designed for taking inventories in warehouses and factories. Carrying the Pad, which is connected to headphones, through the museum, visitors can access audio, text, high-resolution colour video and film to accompany specific works of art. An entire multimedia gallery of interpretive material is immediately accessible. The Pad PC will eventually incorporate a web browser to link to the museum website through a wireless network inside the museum. Apple Newtons have also been modified for similar tasks. Soundalive produced a demonstration model in Britain, while Paul Trapido developed a device from an Apple Newton called Arif that incorporates a web browser and can run animations. It is being used in a Science Museum in Kuala Lumpur. This machine can also save a record of items you are interested in and print them out at the end of a visit. Photographs of visitors can be loaded into the device and their image used to personalize explanations of exhibits.

There are many examples now of innovative audio and hand-held computer interpretation to demonstrate the growing use and potential of this medium. There is a growing diversity of audio tour equipment now available, and every year new machines with ever expanding memories and abilities appear. Suppliers such as Soundalive are always ready to develop devices specifically for particular needs, and it is always worth talking to suppliers to check the next generation of equipment that will be available. It goes without saying I hope, that other media such as guides, guidebooks and leaflets are also an important part of any non-permanent interpretive mix.

Off site interpretive technologies

Off site interpretation of a landscape offers an immense range of possibilities, as any technique that can be used in a museum or attraction can be considered if it is appropriate and the funding available. Here, I want to concentrate on some of the digitally based techniques that can be applied to landscape applications. There are two main growth areas in particular, multimedia, including virtual reality as the most rapidly growing aspect of computer generated graphics, and the related web-based application of such programmes.

One of the more innovative applications of digital technology to landscape interpretation is the Timeframe viewer, developed by John Sunderland. This is a permanent installation in which a digitally generated reconstruction image is seen against the actual landscape through a television sized viewer. What appears to be a window on the landscape is actually a video image with the graphics mixed in, and in perspective. The device is available commercially, but is only really suitable for specific areas where security and maintenance are regularly available.

The technology to drive digital technology development improves almost weekly, and applications are seen in almost all areas of the world. At Stonehenge, the brief has been for some time to develop the visitor centre as a major attraction in its own right. It is hoped that many visitors would consider a visit to the centre a fulfillment in itself. That may be open to dispute, but it is certain that an attraction can be developed, using virtual reality worlds, to create a sense of being at Stonehenge, in its relevant landscape setting and at each of the major stages of its development.

Virtual landscapes have been developed mainly for military applications and used in training simulators. Some of the best early models formed the basis of helicopter and jet fighter trainers – full-scale versions of the flight simulators familiar on home computers. One of the main problems with simulating a realistic landscape is the reason why the direct experience of the landscape is so often so breathtaking, that is the sheer variety of colours and textures that contribute to the overall visual image. However, recent developments in the rendering of such images has meant that they are now much improved. Technologies that allow progressive zooming of the viewed area allow immense detail to be brought into the field of view. This has mostly been applied to photorealistic virtual models of historic buildings and art works, as in the model of the Sistine Chapel. Similar techniques can also be applied to natural settings, but these need animated movement to make them convincing. (The wind blowing through a field of long grass is far more complicated than a masterpiece by Michaelangelo.)

Virtual Stonehenge

For Stonehenge, an accurate model of the entire World Heritage Site does not yet exist, but in 1996 a large section of the site around the henge was modelled using satellite data to give an accurate map of the general topology. However, this did not show any details more than half a metre in height, and actual detail had to be modelled by hand from photographs. The stones themselves were modelled independently from photogrammetric data that had been mapped by English Heritage, and the stones rendered using the photographic record from the same study. The initial model suffered from the fact that the photographs were not taken specifically for it, and colour balances and lighting changed in different sequences of images. Even the very advanced facilities provided by Intel, who sponsored the model, could not fully re-balance the images. However, the model has been further developed since then.

These accurate models can be viewed on a monitor, through a headset, in virtual projection domes, or in fully immersive environments in which the imagery is projected onto all the surfaces around you. Given the advances in 3D modelling that the film industry has been funding over the last few years, it will not be too long before this filters down to a level at which heritage sites can consider their use. Realistic animated characters will soon be able to interact with you in realistic historic settings, (although not at Stonehenge I suspect). Hollywood directors are already generating film actors from scratch based on the success of the Lara Croft character in Tomb Raiders. (Perhaps a virtual Aubrey or Stukely might be appropriate for Stonehenge come to think of it!). Advanced research is being carried out by Nadia Thalmann, the pioneer of virtual humans, at MIRALab in Geneva on the ways in which these 'avatars' as they are called can interact with viewers in the real world.

Photorealistic models of built structures and landscapes can provide more than a fun piece of computer modelling. In the first place an accurate model can be used and accessed more easily than hundreds of photogrammetric images to make comparisons with the monument as it changes over time. The Stonehenge model incorporated accurate astronomical data, so that the changing positions of the stars could be plotted against the positions of the stones. Linked to a geographic database it could also be a user friendly access point to massive amounts of data on the monument and its surrounding landscape. With some modification such facilities could be accessed by the public to provide an educational and interpretive database. The Wroxeter Hinterland Study has linked ongoing research and its findings to a geographic database, and made elements of this accessible to visitors at the site. This allows a wider and more detailed understanding of the landscape beyond the existing visitor perimeter.

Simple 3D modelling, as a form of reconstruction, has been made highly popular by the television programme *Time Team*. At the end of most programmes the reconstruction of the site or building is the highlight of the show. New knowledge made easy. These simple models have many uses, but can be put to great effect when showing the developmental stages of a building over time, or of the changing elements within a wider landscape. INTEL also sponsored the development of a Stonehenge interpretive website. The programme was created by Superscape and

English Heritage. The idea was to show the entire World Heritage Site at each of ten different stages in its evolution, from the earliest totem pole like structures thought to exist in clearings, through to Stonehenge in the future.

It was possible to move from one era to another by moving a slider on a timescale, and to watch the evolution of any of the major monuments in the area as they changed, developed or disappeared with the passing of time. This made understanding the relatively complicated changes at the henge site itself very easy. While the modelling was relatively simple, it was very effective for the purpose of exploring the site through time. Each of the eras could be navigated as in any virtual world and viewed from any height or distance. Clicking on any highlighted element in the model brought up information about it. A virtual sunrise was added for the summer solstice so that anyone logging on could see the sun rise virtually over the Heel Stone from the centre of the circle. It was also possible to take a tour of the main features of the landscape, view it by night, or find details of how to get there, prices, where to stay in the region and so on.

Virtual tourism

There has been extended debate about whether virtual tourism would affect visitor numbers at the real site. The simplicity of the Stonehenge model was not really a contender here, and visitor numbers did not change at all. However, some recent information from the Science Museum in London suggests that up to 40 per cent of those who access its website did go on to visit the museum itself. While web-based sites allow anyone anywhere in the world access, it seems they do not stop a visit to the real thing, or affect income from admissions. As the web becomes the place to be and to buy, some serious content from heritage sites would not be amiss (even if they must also have their e-commerce elements to fund them).

The Stonehenge website has links to other relevant and serious sites about Stonehenge, but a project in Scotland has recently taken web links for interpretation a step further. Ossian is a major database of available interpretation and related websites for visitors to the Highlands. Touchscreen units are available in Tourist Information Centres, and many others will be provided. Advances in virtual reality tours have been mainly in built up areas, such as the Bury St Edmunds Virtual Tour, which is linked to tourism development in the town. However, there are a growing number of websites calling themselves 'virtual' that use only 2D graphics.

The digital landscape of Avebury on CD-ROM

Given the increase in the power of home computers, increasingly ambitious programmes can be provided on CD-ROM or DVD formats and linked to the web. The National Trust is currently developing a multimedia CD-ROM to interpret the historic landscape of Avebury, and it will hopefully contain details of the newly discovered Avenue first recorded by Stukely. It will also contain links to the main National Trust website for details of visiting and other related matters. The programme is focused on a full 3D reconstruction of the Avebury henge and Avenue as well as the surrounding area in the Later Neolithic. The henge and Avenue model was created by a group of archaeologists who have begun to use virtual modelling as a way of better understanding such monuments. Dr Wheatley, based at Southampton University, and his colleagues, have been making frequent trips to Avebury to accurately measure the topology of the stones, and to create a photogrammetric record upon which the model is based.

The 3D landscape can be explored through a series of 'hotspots' that can be touched or clicked on to reveal layers of information and links to related topics and sites. A major educational tool is Alexander Keiller's Study, which can be found housed in the Alexander Keiller Museum at Avebury. Entering the 3D model of the study, users can access a range of topics to help them explore the significance of Avebury. On the wall is a painting of the Later Neolithic landscape. Clicking on this allows the user to access a timeline and to change between views of Avebury at different periods in time. The views are not digital reconstructions, but superb paintings. Areas of change or interest in the views can be clicked on to give further information and links. Back in the study, Alexander Keiller will show you around. Drawers can be opened to explore the collection of artefacts (some of the objects will be in 3D and fully rotatable) or a turning globe can be investigated to find out about the global context of Avebury, while paintings of archaeologists reveal information about themselves and archaeological techniques used in the past and the present. There is access to information about the people at Avebury during various periods of time, as well as a comprehensive index. For those who do not want to explore on their own, they can simply take a guided tour of the site and the programme.

While the CD was made available for sale at some time during the year 2000, material from it also featured in a new exhibition about the development of the Avebury landscape in the Great Barn, just opposite the Alexander Keiller Museum itself.

Looking to the future

By the time this chapter is published, there will be yet more technological breakthroughs that will allow even more scope for interpreters. The overall trend in digital technology is convergence, the coming together of mobile phone technology, television, personal computing, digital video, web browsers and audio replay. Portable computers will be easy to handle and offer a powerful interpretive tool for interpreters of historic landscapes. Such applications offer the ultimate potential to provide accessible interpretation over wide areas, even over entire countries.

Wherever you are, you can access an interpretation of the significance of a place in a way suited to your learning style and level.

Even now, web access through television screens will bring the possibility of armchair tourism, with remote video cameras relaying live pictures of potential destinations, just as they do to PCs. You could watch a reconstruction of the Battle of Hastings in its actual setting. As animation techniques improve, it will not be long before historic events and characters can be digitally modelled and viewed in actual locations. It will be an interesting debate on the accuracy of such events, especially as viewers will have the capacity to join in and take on roles themselves.

Over and above all the possibilities, of course, is the fact that the entire engine of technological development and application is driven largely and necessarily by companies who need to make a profit to survive. Only those applications that can successfully generate income will see the light of day and succeed. However, those interpreters that can offer the technology developers new applications may well attract some help initially.

As always, the imaginative use of the potential of the technology is far more important than the technology itself. A well written guidebook or an excellent personal guided tour is far better than a bad audio tour or virtual model.

Chapter 12

Bryant

TILDEN'S CHILDREN: INTERPRETATION IN BRITAIN'S NATIONAL PARKS

Margi Bryant

Interpretation has a special relationship with national parks. As every practising or would-be interpreter knows, the concept of interpretation was first explicitly presented in Freeman Tilden's *Interpreting Our Heritage*, based on approaches and techniques developed by the US National Parks Service (Tilden 1957). Tilden's central thesis – 'through interpretation, understanding; through understanding, appreciation; through appreciation, protection' – offered a resounding rationale for interpretation in the service of conservation.

It should come as no surprise, then, that the national parks of England and Wales were among the first organisations on this side of the Atlantic to take interpretation on board. The Peak District introduced regional strategies for site interpretation as early as the 1960s, while Pembrokeshire Coast pioneered 'turn up and go' guided walks for the general public at around the same time.

Tilden's vision, however, was not merely a matter of installing outdoor panels or organising guided walks. It was a thought-through approach with a coherent set of objectives and principles (provoking curiosity, relating to everyday life, revealing an answer, and so on). Crucially, Tilden was adamant that interpretation was much more than – and essentially different from – straightforward factual information.

Despite their quick takeup of interpretation, British national parks were not early exemplars of this approach. Through the 1980s, when many museums and heritage sites were developing innovative new ways of engaging with the public, much national park interpretation remained information-led, formulaic and uninspiring. This reflected both a lack of resources for interpretation and, as the National Parks Review Panel concluded in 1991, a 'lack of coherent policy' (Edwards 1991).

Figure 12.1   Understanding, appreciation, protection: Tilden's Formula has been a guiding principle for interpretation in national parks

But all that has changed. Since the mid-1990s, fostered by a very different social and political climate and a new generation of talented specialist staff, the national park sector has made huge strides forward. In the first few years of the twenty-first century, Britain's national parks were producing some radical, effective and award-winning interpretation.

This chapter is an overview of interpretation in Britain's national parks: its background and context, organisation and delivery, constraints and opportunities, past shortcomings and future potential. My analysis is based on knowledge of the sector, first-hand experience as a national park interpretation officer and numerous discussions with colleagues in other parks. My examples of good practice are necessarily a small selection, and apologies are due for the many excellent projects not included. Ultimately, this chapter reflects a personal viewpoint.

Park perspectives: interpretation in context

Created in principle by the 1949 National Parks & Access to the Countryside Act, the first ten parks – all in England or Wales – were set up between 1951 and 1957. Their dual purpose was to protect areas of countryside selected for their outstanding natural beauty, and to provide recreation opportunities for the general public.

The demand for recreational access – with passionate and well-organised campaigning by organisations such as the Ramblers Association – was a driving

Figure 12.2 Map of Britain's national parks: most of England and Wales' national parks were created in the early 1950s. Scotland's two parks came into being in 2002 and 2003

force behind the 1949 legislation. National parks were the post-war Labour government's gift to the nation, and from today's perspective can be seen as an important step in the democratisation of the countryside. Little attention was paid at the time to the potential incompatibility between recreational access and national parks' other primary purpose, conservation.

Furthermore, Britain's national parks – unlike their American counterparts – were not nationalised parks. The land designated for protection remained mostly in private hands and continued to be a working, commercially productive environment. The main tool available to the fledgling park administrations in carrying out their conservation remit was their control over development – housing, industry, infrastructure, etc. – within the park boundaries.

From the outset, then, two implicit conflicts lay at the heart of Britain's national parks: conservation versus recreation, and private ownership versus public access. These tensions have never been fully resolved.

When the American concept of interpretation crossed the Atlantic, British national parks were barely ten years old. Only two of them – the Peak District and the Lake District – were managed by independent boards with staff numbers in double figures. The others were 'little more than names on the map', each run by one or two staff in county council offices. Britain's parks lacked the identity, value-system and central organisation of the American model (Freeman and Haley 1993).

At the same time, the 1960s were a decade of affluence and mobility. Tourism and the leisure industry were growing, car and caravan ownership increasing, major road-building, electricity, telecommunications and other infrastructure programmes were under way nation-wide. All these factors meant mounting pressures on national parks and an increasing need to communicate with the public. The new American concept of interpretation seemed a timely arrival, and was hastily harnessed to existing mechanisms of information provision.

The first major review of national parks was carried out by a committee chaired by Lord Sandford between 1971 and 1974. The resultant report recognised the potential conflict between conservation and recreational access, and recommended that where this could not be resolved, conservation should prevail – a rule subsequently dubbed the 'Sandford principle'. However, echoing Tilden's interpretation-to-protection formula, the report welcomed interpretation as a means of promoting both conservation and visitor enjoyment 'at a single stroke' (Sandford 1974).

The second comprehensive assessment was carried out from 1989 to 1991 by the National Parks Review Panel chaired by Professor Ron Edwards. The panel's report, *Fit for the Future*, had a major influence on subsequent policy and legislation (Edwards 1991).

While commending much of the interpretive work being done by individual parks, the report identified a lack of coherent policy and a widespread confusion between information, public education and public relations. The report was critical of the multiple roles taken on by information services, which had become 'a mixture of park interpreters, tourist information points and shop-keepers'. It called for proper interpretation strategies with defined target audiences, monitoring systems and performance indicators. At the same time, it recommended that parks should try to widen their influence by communicating park values to all sections of the community.

The Review Panel's recommendations formed the basis of the 1995 Environment Act, which gave the national parks of England and Wales a revised legislative framework. This confirmed conservation as the first statutory purpose, but added the new element of 'promoting public understanding and enjoyment' as a second purpose. An additional 'statutory duty' – not quite so compelling as a 'purpose' – was also added, that of fostering the economic and social well-being of local communities.

The administrative framework of national parks changed at the same time. They became 'single-purpose authorities', distinct from local councils but continuing to exercise the key power of development control within the park area.

The new emphasis on public understanding was, at policy level, a significant boost for interpretation. Though its impact was not felt for some years, it laid the foundation for important developments, such as the creation of new interpretation officer posts and the routine inclusion of interpretation in park management plans.

Scotland's first two national parks, which came into being in 2002 and 2003, were based on a different legislative framework with four statutory aims: conservation, public understanding and enjoyment, local economic and social development, and sustainable use of the area's resources. The stronger emphasis on economic and social matters makes engaging with the public a high priority for Scottish parks, and interpretation has had a recognised role from the outset.

Who does what: how park interpretation is organised

Given the autonomy of each national park, and the way interpretation – in England and Wales, at least – was grafted on to information services, it is not surprising that different parks have different concepts of what interpretation involves. The interpretation portfolio can include publications, exhibitions, outdoor panels and signage, activities and events, community projects, public art, electronic media, information centres, merchandise and corporate communications.

No two national park interpretation officers have exactly the same range of responsibilities. Publications, for example, are a central feature of the portfolio in some parks, while in others they are completely outside the interpretation remit and are handled by a publications or communications officer. Guided walks and other events are seen as central to interpretation in some parks, while in others they are the responsibility of rangers or education officers.

In the late 1990s some parks still did not have any interpretation posts as such, while others had an interpretive team of three or more full-time staff. But the trend was clearly towards the creation of dedicated posts. Snowdonia and the Peak District appointed their first interpretation officers in 1996, the Lake District and Pembrokeshire in 1997. By 2004 all the parks had someone with 'interpretation' in their job title.

Numerous other individuals also contribute, in most parks, to delivering interpretation. These include designers, rangers, information centre staff, freelancers and volunteers. The number of people, especially in the latter two categories, may run into dozens or even hundreds.

This broad-based approach to defining and delivering interpretation has both advantages and disadvantages. Ideally, it offers scope for interpretive principles to permeate all the many and various ways in which national parks communicate with the public, as well as drawing on a wide range of skills and experience. On the other hand, it can create an overall vagueness about the principles and practice of interpretation and make it hard to achieve coherence, consistency and quality.

Some interpretation officers still feel that the essential principles of their craft are not all that well understood within their park authority. One of the most widespread and frustrating problems is the confusion – identified in the Edwards report – between interpretation and information. Though Tilden made the distinction crystal-clear, interpretation staff can find themselves labouring this point on an almost daily basis.

Another problem is the variety of functions and objectives within any one park authority. Interpretation staff may be located within the park's visitor services, information services or communications division, but are often working to a brief from an internal 'client' representing nature conservation, historic buildings or footpath management. The situation is further complicated when funding for the project is channelled through the 'client' from an external source. In these circumstances, interpreters may find it hard to establish clear and agreed objectives, messages and audiences, or even to be sure who is setting the agenda.

The next few sections take a closer look at the main interpretive media and techniques used in Britain's national parks. This is an area of rapid and exciting change. For convenience, I have grouped interpretation delivery under four broad headings: visitor (and information) centres, publications, on-site interpretation and face-to-face interpretation. While these 'traditional' categories still have relevance, it should be noted that they do not do justice to the current reality of many imaginative projects that mix and match techniques and defy classification.

Magic carpets and nautical knots: interpretation in visitor and information centres

Visitor centres and information centres are generally the most visible and instantly recognisable way in which national parks engage with the public. Though the number of centres varies from twelve in the Lake District to only two in Pembrokeshire

Coast, their combined throughput – somewhere in the region of 3.5 million people a year – makes them highly significant.

They are, however, a classic case of interpretation having to fight its corner amid a multiplicity of functions. The Edwards Committee clearly had national park visitor centres in mind when it spoke of 'a mixture of park interpreters, tourist information points and shop-keepers'.

Many centres are fully fledged tourist information points, offering a wide range of services for visitors, including accommodation and travel bookings, free leaflets about local attractions, and advice on a multitude of topics from tides and weather to the location of the nearest public toilets. Centres also have an important income-generating function as retail outlets, selling national park literature and corporate merchandise alongside Ordnance Survey maps, glossy commercially published books, postcards, fine china, pencil-sharpeners and teddy-bears.

Interpretation has, until recently, been the Cinderella dimension of this service, especially where space is in short supply. There are still a number of small information centres where the interpretive element is limited to a couple of formulaic panels on a poorly-lit wall. Financial rationalisation, however, means that many small centres with a low visitor throughput are being closed down. The current trend is towards fewer centres but better ones, with significantly increased interpretive potential.

There has also been cross-fertilisation from other heritage sectors, such as museums, where the trend is towards major investment in imaginative, engaging exhibitions. The Lake District's visitor centre at Brockhole, a good example of this trend, reopened in 1998 after a £1.1 million refurbishment assisted by the Heritage Lottery Fund. Brockhole now has a state-of-the-art interpretive exhibition developed by a leading design consultancy. Planned as separate modules, so that new elements can be introduced in the future, the exhibition includes a magic carpet ride and numerous other interactives, while the adjacent film theatre shows a highly original audio-visual compilation about everyday life in the national park, using the unscripted voices of local people.

Some smaller information centres – if strategically placed and with healthy visitor numbers – have also enjoyed a makeover putting much more emphasis on interpretation. Snowdonia's little centre at Aberdyfi, on the west Wales coast, has an annual throughput of over 40,000 and was refurbished in 1994 at a cost of £15,000. Using a small space imaginatively, the exhibition area suggests the deck of a cargo ship carrying slate from Aberdyfi in the nineteenth century. There are panels about local history and legends, a push-button audio facility playing songs about local characters and life at sea, and an interactive area where visitors can learn and practise nautical knots.

Increasingly, too, visitor centres are expanding and diversifying their role. Many are now a focus for community activities, a setting for children's workshops or evening entertainment, a start-and-finish point for guided walks. The new Gateway Centre in Loch Lomond and the Trossachs National Park is typical of this trend.

Not only does it have a first-rate interactive exhibition, layered to engage both adult and child audiences, but visitors can also join in an imaginative range of activities from dog management to drumming.

On the shelf: publications in search of a future

Well into the 1990s, publications were widely regarded as a mainstay of interpretation in national parks. Most visitor and information centres, as well as numerous other local outlets, had racks of look-alike circular walk leaflets or species identification guides. Despite steady improvements in design, most of these publications relied heavily on tried-and-tested formulae and seemed immune to the new ideas and approaches beginning to permeate other forms of interpretation delivery.

This was partly caused by the subject-matter. Leaflets or booklets describing self-guided walks have always formed a substantial chunk of the overall publications output, reflecting the linked purposes of public access, enjoyment and understanding. The self-guided walk leaflet has its own built-in conventions: there must be a map, a general introduction, information on how to get to the start point, an easy-to-follow explanation of the route and a description of points of interest. This offers little scope for a provoke–relate–reveal approach and little space to address wider issues.

The other traditional mainstay of national park publications is the 'special interest' booklet, describing the wild flowers, birds, seaweeds, castles, prehistoric tombs or Victorian chapels to be seen within the national park. These too rely on predictable formulae, so that applying a truly interpretive approach would mean a radical departure from expectations.

However, national parks have sometimes managed to break free from these constraints, or at least to find imaginative ways of working within them. Northumberland's Hareshaw Linn leaflet is, at first glance, a classic self-guided walk, but it draws on a community oral history project to include local people's thoughts and feelings about the area, resulting in a very different experience for the reader. The Peak District has involved local communities in collecting stories about the past and present of their villages, and brought these together in publication form. This approach points to an important future direction for national park publications, where creative engagement with the local community can harness a unique perspective.

Without a special dimension of this kind, national park publications simply cannot compete with the increasing quantity of excellent commercially produced literature on the countryside. The days are long gone when poorly designed, badly written national park leaflets had a guaranteed readership because there was nothing else available. One strategy tried successfully by some parks has been to work with the commercial sector in an advisory role, resulting in publications that carry a national park 'seal of approval' but without the park footing the bill.

Figure 12.3 Touch and sound: Yorkshire Dales' alternative approach to site interpretation features a carved message encouraging people to listed to the sounds of nature

The rapid growth of electronic media suggests a possible new dimension for published material. All the national parks now have websites, which are rapidly becoming an important channel for visitor information, especially at the pre-visit stage, and for promoting and explaining the work of national park authorities. However, the web's role as a medium of interpretation – as opposed to information – is problematic, due to its essential separation from first-hand experience. Even so, some parks are actively exploring the web as an alternative way of delivering interpretive literature.

Blots on the landscape? the pros and cons of on-site interpretation

On-site interpretation, especially in its traditional guise of outdoor panels, probably divides opinion in national parks more than any other interpretive medium. In some parks there is a general presumption against on-site panels, except – and then only sparingly – in built-up locations. Championed by planners and conservationists, this view regards panels as an unwelcome intrusion into the scenic beauty of the park landscape.

However, many park interpreters appreciate panels for their immediacy and for the large, previously uncommitted audience they can reach. At the same time, new developments in panel design and construction, and the variety of materials now available – from slate to sacking – can minimise any negative visual impact.

Panels tend to be popular with funding agencies – cynics would say this is because they display the agency's logo – and with local communities, who take pride in such a visible statement of the special qualities of their area. Given the increased necessity of external funding and the commitment of national parks to work in partnership with local people, panels are unlikely to drop off the agenda completely.

Panels seem to have their own particular pitfalls, however. There can be huge divergences of opinion as to what makes a panel interpretive (Veverka 1998). Pressure from various directions – external funders or internal 'clients' – can lead to a multiplicity of objectives, messages and target audiences, resulting in panels that try to do too many jobs and succeed at none. A good example of this confusion is the series of panels produced by Pembrokeshire Coast for their long-distance National Trail footpath. Each panel ended up with six main objectives, eight separate categories of information and over 800 words of English text (and the same again in Welsh). Subsequent evaluation showed that people were reading very little of these panels and retaining even less (Bryant 1998).

The Peak District is unapologetic about panels, which have played an important role in its interpretation partnership project. This project – an unusual collaboration of residents, parish councils, local authorities, voluntary organisations and the private sector – saw the installation of around 50 panels between 1997 and 2001. But panels form only one ingredient of the Peak District mix, and have increasingly given way to alternative forms of on-site interpretation such as art and sculpture, developed through community projects.

Yorkshire Dales has also side-stepped the problems of panels through a radically different approach to outdoor interpretation. Aimed at non-traditional sectors of the audience – especially younger children and the visually impaired – the interpretive 'stopping points' in Freeholders' Wood use sculptures in unobtrusive natural materials, with minimal text, to convey a series of messages. Local community input was achieved through discussions, workshops and open days led by the commissioned artist. Projects of this kind, using visual and tactile communication rather than text, point to an interesting future direction for on-site interpretation.

'The highest and best': face-to-face interpretation

Britain's national parks were early and enthusiastic pioneers of face-to-face interpretation, predominantly in the form of guided walks. A regular feature of US parks since the 1920s, guided walks were piloted in Britain by Pembrokeshire Coast in the 1960s, and rapidly became a must for national parks on this side of the Atlantic.

Figure 12.4 The way we were: authoritative leader and respectful audience on a guided walk in Pembrokeshire in the 1960s

Tilden saw face-to-face interpretation as 'the highest and best form of interaction, and the . . . best use of visitors' time' (Tilden 1957). Subsequent research in the US established that visitors remember 90 per cent of what they do, 50 per cent of what they see, 30 per cent of what they read and only 10 per cent of what they hear (Lewis 1988). Guided walks would appear to be in the 'do' category, and should therefore be one of the most memorable forms of interpretation. However, if they are really just an outdoor lecture, they belong in the low-retention 'hear' category.

Since the early 1990s, guided walks have attracted a great deal of criticism. In a special issue of its bulletin in 1992, the Centre for Environmental Interpretation (CEI) faced up to the charge that guided walks were 'old hat, boring, costly [and] preaching to the converted' (Diment 1992). CEI rose to the challenge by presenting examples of exciting, innovative walks from all over Britain, involving drama, dance, literature, ghost-stories and communication techniques for all abilities. None of the examples came from a national park.

Most parks have recognised the validity of such criticisms and taken a long hard look at what they do. Since the 1960s, guided walks had generally followed a tried-and-tested formula: an authoritative leader talking to a respectful audience about the intricacies of the subject-matter – ornithology, botany, archaeology or whatever – with little interaction or participation, and sometimes little regard for the audience's ability to comprehend.

This may once have been quite acceptable, but public expectations and attitudes have changed. A new generation of younger adults has grown up experiencing an interactive rather than didactic approach to learning, and can choose from a wide range of high-quality options for spending leisure time. As the museum sector has found, 'authoritative condescension' is no longer appropriate (McManus 1999).

Furthermore, audience profile research in national parks has confirmed the charge of 'preaching to the converted'. Guided walks attract high percentages of well-off, well-educated, well-informed participants, mostly over the age of 40 and already fully committed to heritage conservation. By the late 1990s, national parks were recognising the need to reach new and wider audiences by adopting a more populist approach.

For most parks this has meant developing a broad-based programme of activities and events, in which guided walks are just one element. Guided horse-rides, bike-rides and canoe trips, costumed walks and living history, storytelling, creative writing, arts and crafts, music and dance, traditional country skills, puppet shows and family fun days have all found their way on to the agenda. Guided walks now account for less than half of all events organised by national parks.

North York Moors was one of the first parks to put a particularly strong emphasis on new kinds of events, developing an innovative programme in the late 1990s with the help of substantial European grant aid. From the outset, the programme had a low percentage of guided walks but many alternatives, ranging from 'Meet the Vikings' and 'Murder at Robin Hood's Bay' to male voice choirs, sheep-herding, canoeing and raft-building. Pembrokeshire Coast realised through an internal review in 1998 that it had fewer family-oriented events than any other park, and within a year had upped the percentage from 6 per cent to 23 per cent of the total programme.

Events, of whatever kind, need more personnel at the sharp end than any other form of interpretation. In some parks, all events are led by fully paid-up staff members: rangers, education officers, ecologists, historic building specialists and so on. Others rely heavily on unpaid volunteers or paid freelancers, usually local people with extensive knowledge of the area's wildlife, geology, history and so on.

The sheer range of people involved can make it very difficult to ensure consistency and quality. Parks that use particularly high numbers of volunteers or freelancers have explored new ways of keeping everyone on-message. Pembrokeshire Coast, for example, runs a six-day compulsory training package for event leaders, covering communication skills and national park messages as well as risk assessment and first aid, while Yorkshire Dales uses both self-evaluation forms for leaders and questionnaires for participants.

The increased focus on working with local communities has given rise to a new kind of face-to-face interpretation: events staged not by the national park for the public, but by communities – with help from the park – for themselves. Such projects often include a public event, performance or festival that visitors to the area can attend, but that is not their central aim. Northumberland's Hareshaw Linn project, which included oral history, storytelling, art workshops and the creation and performance of an original drama, is a good example of this trend. So, too,

Figure 12.5 Halloween in the North York Moors: guided walks have given way to fun events aimed at a younger audience

are numerous local projects within the Peak District interpretation partnership, such as the Pilsbury Castle costumed walk and the Ashover Rock Art project.

Wagging the dog: the role of interpretation in national parks

Most of Britain's national parks have been in existence for over half a century. No-one seriously disputes that they have played an important role in the guardianship of the country's natural and historic heritage. Their importance was given new recognition in 1999 by the announcement of proposed national park status for the New Forest and the South Downs, and by the creation of Scotland's first two national parks, one covering Loch Lomond and the Trossachs, and the other the Cairngorms.

But national parks have still not sorted out their priorities. The revised mandate contained in the Environment Act and the National Parks (Scotland) Act added new responsibilities without resolving the potential conflicts embedded in the old ones. With public access firmly back on the political agenda since the Countryside and Rights of Way Act, and the increasing demand for public bodies to be effective and accountable, national park authorities face some tough questions.

Are they primarily conservationists or communicators? Is their most important function planning control, countryside management or public education? Are their prime constituents local residents or the millions of city-dwellers who visit national parks for recreation and spiritual regeneration? Even these very basic questions provoke sharply divided opinions among those who work for, live in or actively support national parks.

All this can leave national park interpreters with a confusing set of parameters within which to operate. They can be faced with situations that seem to question the very legitimacy of their profession: for example, when national park planning departments oppose any kind of site-based fixture on the grounds of visual impact, or when wildlife managers insist that telling the public about a rare species will mean its immediate destruction.

Nonetheless, national park interpreters have built up an impressive accumulation of expertise and credibility. One of the challenges they have taken up is to demonstrate the usefulness and effectiveness of what they do. Systematic monitoring and evaluation is a relatively new phenomenon in the interpretation profession as a whole, although some sectors – notably museums – have been using it for years. National park interpreters are making sure that evaluation becomes a routine element of interpretive projects and services. In today's political and social climate – reinforced by a newly rigorous approach to performance management across all local government agencies – this has put interpretation well ahead of the game.

National park interpreters have also made new and important headway in forging links with local communities. Though local residents often have a jaundiced perception of park authorities – usually due to a bad experience with the planning depart-ment – interpretation can offer a much more positive perspective. The Peak District interpretation project, involving seven main partner organisations and extending out-side the park boundaries, may owe some of its success to its semi-independent iden-tity. But it also represents a real commitment to working with local communities and a flexible approach to the potential range of interpretive media and techniques.

Community projects are much more than just good public relations. By involving local people from the start, as the main source of ideas, stories and creative energy, these projects turn traditional interpretation on its head. Instead of national park 'experts' explaining the significance of local heritage to an unaware public, local people themselves become the interpreters. There is an important caveat here, however. Community enthusiasm will not produce good interpretation if it ignores accepted standards of best practice. National parks therefore need to make a strong commitment to providing guidance, training and support.

Where this has happened, the results have been lively and original. Drama and dance, environmental art, photography, oral history, interpretive sculptures, poems carved on benches and practical archaeology have all featured in recent projects. Community-led interpretation seems uniquely appropriate to the British context – there are, of course, no local residents in American national parks – and means that projects and initiatives started by park authorities can become truly sustainable.

There is another challenging dimension to working with communities. The Edwards Committee's recommendation that national parks should seek to reach 'all sections of the community' underpins recent attempts to engage with new and different audiences – such as ethnic minorities, low-income families, people with mental or physical disabilities – who have so far been conspicuously absent from national parks. Real progress in this direction will need commitment and concerted action by every park authority, but interpretation has a key role to play. In some parks, interpreters are taking the lead in promoting social inclusion by organising 'taster days' in collaboration with the relevant grass-roots associations. These enable people from under-represented sections of society to visit as a group and enjoy a day of interpretive activities.

It is generally recognised that interpretation is of demonstrable value to the national park agenda. For several decades interpreters have presented and explained the highlights of national park landscapes, wildlife and history; they have informed, entertained and educated the public; they have encouraged visitors to spend time and money in national parks and thus helped the strained economy of rural Britain.

Should that be the summit of their ambitions? Or should they help set the agenda for how national parks engage with the public and what issues need to be explored? The recent success of community-based interpretation projects suggests there is a lot of mileage in a more open-minded approach. Many interpretation professionals would agree with Roy Ballantyne that they should use their craft 'to address major social, political and economic issues in such a way as to encourage [people] to think about and consider different futures' (Ballantyne 1998).

National park interpreters are ideally placed to take this approach, because major social, political and economic issues – sustainable development, environmental protection, cultural diversity, access and inclusion – lie at the heart of the national park debate. The Peak District has taken up this challenge in its partnership interpretation strategy, which says: 'There is more to the Peak District than thousands of years of history and stunning landscapes; interpretation can get people thinking and raise awareness of real-life, current-day issues' (Peak District Interpretation Project 2001).

Ballantyne also argues that interpreters should not be merely 'hired hands . . . skilled in the techniques of presenting the messages of other people and organisations' (Ballantyne 1998). It is highly significant that Northumberland's multi-faceted Hareshaw Linn interpretation project has been, in retrospect, seen by the park authority management as having changed the way the authority relates to local communities. This is a clear case of interpreters setting the agenda.

Interpretation may have become well-established as a useful tail that can communicate the mood and messages of the national park dog, but it may perform an even more valuable role when it does more wagging in its own right!

■   ■   ■

Bibliography

Ballantyne, R., 'Problems and perspectives for heritage and environmental interpretation in the new millennium', in D. Uzzell and R. Ballantyne (eds), *Contemporary Issues in Heritage and Environmental Interpretation*, The Stationery Office, 1998.

Bryant, M., 'Trial on the trail: monitoring and evaluation of interpretation panels on the Pembrokeshire Coast Path', *Interpretation* 3: 1, 1998.

Diment, N., 'Show, tell and move on', *Environmental Interpretation* 7: 3, April 1992.

Edwards, R., *Fit For the Future: Report of the National Parks Review Panel (Chairman Prof R. Edwards)*, Countryside Commission, 1991.

Freeman, P. and Haley, T., 'Integrated strategies in national parks', in J.M. Fladmark (ed.), *Heritage Conservation, Interpretation and Enterprise*, Donhead, 1993.

Lewis, W.J., *Interpreting for Park Visitors*, Eastern National Park & Monument Association, 1988.

McManus, P., 'Getting to know your visitors', *Interpretation* 4: 3, 1999.

Peak District Interpretation Project, *Peak District Interpretation Strategy*, 2001.

Sandford, J., *Report of the National Parks Policies Review Committee (Chairman Lord Sandford)*, HMSO, 1974.

Tilden, F., *Interpreting Our Heritage*, Chapel Hill, NC: University of North Carolina Press, 1957.

Veverka, J.A., 'Planning truly interpretive panels', *Interpretation* 3: 1, 1998.

Chapter 13

THINKING ABOUT INTERPRETATION: CHANGING PERSPECTIVES AT ENGLISH HERITAGE

Alison Hems

With its sister organisations in Wales and Scotland, English Heritage is the government's principal advisor on the historic environment, with statutory responsibilities to both conserve and foster understanding of it. It discharges its responsibility to promote understanding in a variety of ways — through publications, education programmes, lectures and workshops, and through the development of some form of permanent interpretation at all of its 400 or so historic properties. More 'temporary' forms of interpretation — guided tours, story-telling or re-enactment — supplement and enhance the permanent displays, and provide new opportunities for audience development and marketing initiatives.

These 400 properties vary enormously in scale and in type. They range from remote archaeological sites to fortified manor houses, from roofless abbeys to furnished country houses and once royal residences. The houses often sit in gardens designed by some of the best-known landscape architects of their day, and may contain important collections of furniture, paintings and domestic ephemera. English Heritage is responsible for extensive archaeological collections, some of which are displayed in context at the appropriate property while the remainder is available for study in a series of regional stores.

Interpreting these buildings, the collections they contain, and the events and personalities associated with them is a collective responsibility, shared by site staff and education officers, curators and inspectors of ancient monuments. Responsibility for drawing together the threads of history and heritage, and for reconciling the demands of the expert with the expectations of the visitor rests with a small interpretation team; its role is to manage interpretation projects on behalf of English Heritage and to develop good practice across the organisation as a whole.

Until 2002, the Interpretation Department formed part of a large Marketing division, and sat alongside guidebook editors and education officers and with retail, promotions and special events teams. Its work united the academic and scholarly activities of English Heritage with those intended to generate income. In 2002, the organisation was restructured into five large directorates, with Interpretation forming part of a new department called 'Property Presentation', itself part of a new Research and Standards division. Rather than marketing, education or outreach, the department's immediate colleagues became curators and conservators, historic buildings researchers and, briefly, specialist project managers. One of its roles, however, continued to be to contribute to the organisation's commercial activities, by helping to create properties that people want to visit. As government grant-in-aid is reduced, so the need to generate income through admissions, retail and events programmes increases. Ensuring high levels of visitor enjoyment is seen as a way of generating additional income, primarily through secondary spend. Attractive shops and good catering are part of this equation, but encouraging visitors to use them also depends on the quality of the rest of the visit; an appropriate mix of interpretative techniques and telling the 'right' stories is essential to this. New interpretation might be developed, therefore, with the aim of increasing visitor numbers at a given site or, more often, in order to enhance the 'visitor experience' at key historic properties.

Effective interpretation, however, sensitively developed for both its audience and the site for which it is designed, is also about encouraging access in the widest sense. It is about making sense of often fragmentary buildings, and making apparent the stories hidden behind fine architectural detail or carefully conserved paintings. It is about making connections between the monument and its locality, and making visible the significance of that monument for those who live in its real or symbolic shadow. It offers a means by which we meet income targets while also reaching new audiences and exploring new ideas about the nature and value of the historic environment.

As with buildings, so interpretative techniques vary enormously from place to place. English Heritage intends that all its properties are interpreted to a 'minimum standard' that offers basic information about who, why and when – and why significance persists into the present. Each property should have a 'guardianship panel' that states English Heritage's responsibility for its care, sometimes in partnership with a local manager, and which sets out a limited amount of information – an illustration, some key points about that property, and details about access arrangements. In addition, a further panel may contain a site plan, a reconstruction drawing or a historic image which provide a little more contextual or background information.

The majority of English Heritage sites, to which admission is free, will have no more fixed interpretation than this, although further information may be available through publications or, increasingly, through related web pages. At paying sites, however, the visitor may find an audio tour, an exhibition, more graphic panels, interactive displays for families, models and games. Elsewhere, the fragments of the past may be recreated virtually, through computer-generated models. On the Headland at Whitby, for example, English Heritage commissioned virtual recreations of the abbey at key periods in its development and linked these to other monastic foundations in the north east; it created virtual restorations of the interiors of the seventeenth-century 'New House' in ways that would have been impossible within the shell of the building itself.

English Heritage has also begun to develop initiatives aimed at interpreting our buildings at a distance from the property itself. Books, CDs and videos have always offered a way of doing this. 'Historic properties on line' offers another, and represents a major initiative to extend and enhance access through the web site. Making connections between related properties and interpreting all of them in the most accessible location, perhaps in conjunction with other agencies, suggests another approach. As well as being better history, and more challenging heritage, such projects support intellectual access to those properties where physical access remains difficult, and helps to protect those sites that are particularly vulnerable in environmental terms – repointing crumbling masonry is one challenge, resurrecting lost species quite another. Thus Wigmore Castle, one of the great fortress castles along the Welsh border, has been painstakingly restored and reopened to the public. But it has been conserved as a ruin and as an important ecological site, rather than as 'a place to visit'. Those who brave its steep slopes and the prickly plants that surround the Castle's remains will find relatively little information there, but the wide range of information collected during the archaeological and consolidation phases of the project formed the basis of a wider access and learning project with local schools.

Elsewhere, the focus may be less on interpreting the properties in guardianship and rather more on making sense of the wider historic environment and their place within it. The Department talks only rarely, and with caution, of 'bringing the past to life', and rather more of engaging interest, stimulating the imagination and instilling a sense of self-discovery. The challenge here, therefore, is to signpost possibilities for further exploration and engagement.

The interpretative techniques used at these properties, and at those presented unequivocally as 'visitor attractions', will emerge from an understanding of the site itself and from an awareness of its actual or potential visitors. The building itself will suggest or limit particular techniques; those aspects of its past and present that make it significant will suggest themes and stories. In both cases, we look to the conservation plan to help us disentangle the possibilities and identify solutions.

Conservation plans are a relatively new tool in the management of the built heritage, but they seem likely to become an increasingly familiar one. In interpretative terms, they are important because they seek to define *significance* and thus provide the raw material for developing interpretation and for preparing an interpretation plan. That significance might be ecological, archaeological, cultural, historic or economic. It might be all of these things, in which case the conservation plan will attempt to create a balance between them and to establish an order of priority across a large, complex and often multi-period site. The plan should contain a review of all available information, and will identify gaps in our understanding of a particular building. It documents sequences of change – phases in the development of a building or landscape – and so helps to identify the points at which we might seek to conserve, restore or move on from an earlier period in that building's life.[1]

Having established significance, it becomes possible to draft policies for the conservation, development and management of that property. These policies might identify a range of possible future uses, and provide guidelines on how to make the changes and adaptations that new use will necessitate. They will clarify issues relating to the building's care and protection, from which maintenance regimes and mitigation strategies can develop. All of these will have an impact upon the ways in which a site is interpreted although, rather than absolute prohibitions or recommendations, the plan should provide a framework around which creative solutions and responses can be found. Conservation plans do not, as a rule, deal with audience expectations or with the ideas and assumptions that visitors bring with them, and so cannot determine how a site may be interpreted.

Significance can be expressed in terms of personality and events, rather than architectural excellence or the survival of period detail; relatively ordinary buildings can have extraordinary associations. This is the case at Down House near Bromley in Kent. Built in the eighteenth century and remodelled in the nineteenth, Down is a substantial house set in extensive grounds, but it is not particularly remarkable architecturally. It was, however, home to Charles Darwin and his family for some forty years. It is this that lends the house its significance and thus underpins its interpretation.

Darwin moved from London to Kent in 1842, seeking escape from the distractions of town life. The house remained in the Darwin family until the 1920s and was subsequently bought by Sir George Buckston Browne, who intended that it be 'preserved intact in memory of Darwin for all time and for the good of science'. Using existing furnishings and artefacts donated by the family, Sir George restored the five main rooms on the ground floor 'as far as possible in the condition in which he left them'. It was here, and in the garden, that Darwin had done so much of his thinking, collating the material he collected during his voyage on HMS *Beagle*, carrying out new research, and ordering his theory of natural selection. It was here that he wrote *On the Origin of Species*, and it was here that he finally decided to risk its publication, correctly anticipating the fury that would greet its appearance. It was here, too, that he and his wife brought up their large family, and where Darwin played with his children, an affectionate and familiar father.[2]

The idea of 'keeping up the study and garden for pilgrims . . . furnished as he left them; or at any rate . . . filled with memories of him' was raised as early as 1898 by Sir Joseph Hooker, then Director of the Royal Botanical Garden at Kew. Buckston Browne went some way towards achieving this through his miscellany of

Figure 13.1   Darwin's study in Down House, Kent, has been refurbished, so far as possible, as he knew and used it

display cases, souvenirs, manuscripts and ephemera, laid out in the hallway and four ground floor rooms. The house passed to the Royal College of Surgeons in 1953, to the Natural History Museum in 1993 and finally to English Heritage in 1996. The fabric of the building was then repaired and the ground floor rooms restored to their appearance in about 1877. This involved conserving surviving pieces of furniture, extensive research into appropriate paint finishes and textiles, and the careful laying out of Darwin's notes, specimens and scientific equipment, walking stick and hat. The judicious purchase of a small number of period items – cushions, parcels of books, a dog basket – added further signs of life and humanity to the recently refurbished rooms. These new acquisitions also acted as a peg on which to hang the recollections of Darwin's children. The stories are retold by David Attenborough on a random access audio tour which guides the visitor from room to room and highlights key objects within them.[3]

It is as though the family has just stepped out into the garden to admire some discovery, while the visitor has crept in to peer at Darwin's desk and puzzle over the skeletal birds arranged on the billiard table. It is a sleight of hand of course, because it is not 1877 and because we know what came next – Darwin's death in 1882, the twentieth-century validation of so many of his ideas, the continuing debate surrounding the theory of evolution, and its political use and mis-use. Some of these issues are raised on the first floor of the house, where a lack of material evidence made it impossible to recreate even sketchy period interiors. Down House thus appears to have no bedrooms; instead, there is a series of small displays that investigate more fully the stories hinted at in the study and drawing room down-stairs. One room is devoted to the *Beagle* and to the specimens Darwin collected on his five-year voyage; it recollects his experiences at sea and the miserable times he endured as a sailor. Another display seeks to convey the sense of anger and outrage that the *Origin of Species* provoked. There is space for small changing displays that will focus upon family material not accommodated within the permanent exhibition, on new acquisitions, and on the continuing relevance of Darwinism in contemporary science and philosophy.

The decision to devote the first floor of the house to an interpretation of Darwin's ideas, their origins and impact, rather than to a presentation of its interiors, was a pragmatic one. Had more of the rooms' contents survived then Down could have been restored more fully as a period house, with more nods towards the taste of its owner and his wife. The decision was, however, entirely consistent with the notion of significance, and with the logic of using that, and not the accidents of survival, as a basis for interpretation. Darwin's choice of bedroom wallpaper may have been fascinating, but it matters far less than the experiences that informed his thinking and the conclusions to which he finally came.

At Down House, the interpretative approach was driven by a story of enormous power and significance. The decision was a relatively easy and straightforward one; more difficult is the interpretation of those buildings whose significance relates to more than one period or more than one personality. More difficult still for an organisation charged with conservation is to acknowledge and interpret a building's contemporary significance, or to present its meaning in the present alongside those from the past.

Lots of English Heritage properties have more than one story to tell, and different interpretative techniques are adopted in order to do so. Dover Castle, for example,

contains Roman and Anglo-Saxon remains, a medieval keep, later medieval forti-
fications, an eighteenth-century barracks and Napoleonic defences. Its underground
tunnels served as the operational heart of the Dunkirk evacuations, and later as a
potential seat of regional government in the event of nuclear war. The castle's tag
line refers to 'Two thousand years of history', which is easy enough to say and
difficult to convey or makes sense of. Interpretation ranges from the simple naming
of parts to a theatrical evocation of the siege of 1216, when the 'Key to England'
threatened to fall, and the recreation of the wartime tunnels of the Second World
War, complete with operating theatre and snatches of overheard conversation. To
an extent, the castle's history has been broken down into manageable chunks of
time and experience. We have yet to consider its contemporary significance, and
what it might mean to the town it so dominates.

Part of the conservation plan process is to consult with those who have a particular interest in a particular building. Taken to its logical and necessary conclusion,
consultation means creating opportunities for local residents, community groups
and key stakeholders to think about what makes a building or landscape meaningful to them. It is this that makes the process so potentially exciting and which,
in interpretative terms, allows us to explore new meanings and alternative
stories. Traditionally, meaning has been defined and then articulated by the expert.
Increasingly, however, English Heritage has declared an intention to encourage
people to 'participate more actively in the exploration and conservation of their
past'.[4]

This commitment raises important questions about the nature of that past in a
socially and culturally diverse society. The challenge here is to find ways of introducing themes and stories that acknowledge the existence of other pasts and other
meanings – black history at Kenwood House, for example, or a focus on Indian
crafts and culture in the redisplayed Durbar Room at Osborne on the Isle of Wight.
In Great Yarmouth, fluctuating economic prosperity became the basis for the redis-
play of Row 111 and the Old Merchant's House, two houses built in the seventeenth
century by those who prospered on the back of Yarmouth's trade with Europe, the
Far East and the Americas. The story is contained within the architecture, as once
grand houses down by the South Quay were subdivided to create homes for families living in increasing poverty. Until the 1990s this story, in so far as it was told
at all, related only to architecture – the partitioning of a room with a magnificent
plaster ceiling or the insertion of a new staircase – and not to the social and economic
changes that led to these alterations, or to the experiences of the fishermen or
herring girls who lived within these rooms. The themes that underpinned the new
displays were there all the time, but they were drawn out through English Heritage's
work with local people and the local museum service, and a collaborative attempt
to interpret Yarmouth's 'Maritime Story' and 'Rich and Poor through time'.[5]

Kenwood House, by contrast, offers the visitor a commentary on wealth,
expressed through its architecture, its estate, and the paintings the house now
contains. Kenwood is probably best known, and is certainly actively promoted, as

Figure 13.2   Osborne House on the Isle of Wight was, for Queen Victoria, 'a place of one's own, quiet and retired', although this did not stop the flow of state papers or the need to deal with them

an important Adam house now home to an equally important collection of paintings, including works by Rembrandt, Vermeer, Turner and Gainsborough. The house and paintings were given to the nation in 1927 by Edward Cecil Guinness, the first earl of Iveagh. High on Hampstead Heath, with stunning views across London, the house is a popular destination for local people enjoying an afternoon stroll or for visitors seeking out the late Rembrandt self-portrait or Vermeer's *The Guitar Player*. Elsewhere in the house, visitors will find portraits of eighteenth-century society beauties or of absurdly pretty children with birds and small dogs, as well as important paintings drawn from the seventeenth-century Dutch and Flemish schools. They will also find what survives of Adam's Kenwood, although the paintings and furniture he arranged for his patron were dispersed in 1922 and further alterations were made when the house was converted into a gallery for Iveagh's collection.

Kenwood was remodelled by Robert Adam between 1764 and 1773. He transformed a modest brick house into a splendid neo-classical villa for William Murray, the first earl of Mansfield. Adam designed the portico on the north front, and built a third storey and the wing to house his 'Great Room' — Mansfield's magnificent library. He then encased the whole building in white stucco and added his own decorative signature to its interiors.

Figure 13.3 The Durbar Room at Osborne House was built in 1890–91 as a place for state receptions. It reflected Queen Victoria's long-standing interest in India, and represents a starting point for further exploration of an ongoing relationship in the present

Mansfield sat as Lord Chief Justice for more than 30 years, and was regarded as one of the great judges of his day. It was Mansfield who presided over the Somerset case of 1772, and who cautiously attempted to define the status of black slaves in England. His famous judgement has frequently been misinterpreted as meaning the emancipation of black slaves in Britain, when all he said, but could not enforce, was that a master could not compel a slave to leave England; advertisements for the sale of black slaves continued to appear in English newspapers long after the Somerset case. Nonetheless, his verdict was greeted with cheers by those who saw it as confirmation of an earlier declaration that 'a toleration of slavery is, in effect, a toleration of inhumanity' and who believed with 'that excellent lawyer Lord Chief Justice Holt that *as soon as a Negro comes into England, he becomes free*'.[6]

The visitor will find relatively little about this at Kenwood, unless he or she decides to take the audio tour which provides an introduction to the house and a more detailed account of some of the major paintings. Since relatively few visitors do choose to take the tour, this story is lost to them, as is that of Mansfield's own family connections with the West Indies and with black history. A family portrait by Zoffany, no longer at Kenwood, shows Elizabeth Murray, a niece to Mansfield,

(a)

(b)

Figure 13.4   (a) The south front and (b) the library at Kenwood House, London, are fine architectural and artistic achievements, but the house has other stories to tell and other connections to make

sitting on the terrace while Dido Belle, her companion, slips quietly by, an enigmatic smile on her face. Dido Belle was black. Her father was John Lindsay, a captain in the Royal Navy and Lord Mansfield's nephew; her mother, a black slave captured in the Caribbean. Dido was born in England and eventually came to live at Kenwood. She remained there when Elizabeth married, and continued to help the family as

Mansfield became increasingly frail. When he died in 1793, Mansfield left Dido £500 and an annuity of £100. He also confirmed her own freedom from slavery.

As at Great Yarmouth, these connections with other histories have always been there, quietly and implicitly made. Dido Belle is introduced to the visitor to Kenwood through its guidebook, rather than in the house itself.[7] Given the difficulties involved in inserting new interpretation into a relatively small and very busy house, the omission might be forgiven. Yet Kenwood's significance is not confined to the Adam library or the paintings in the Iveagh collection. Less comfortably, it has other associations and connections that English Heritage will need to make apparent if it is to be truly representative of something we might label 'England's heritage'. A white wedding cake of a house speaks to us in the present about current issues and concerns; the task of the Interpretation Department is to find ways of giving them voice.

This brings us back to the importance of understanding the significance of each building, *and* the needs and expectations of its audiences. Understanding both contributes to the development of themes and the selection of techniques – perhaps a permanent display or audio tour, but also a temporary exhibition programme, community arts project, or holiday learning scheme with local schools. The same understanding leads us to ask other people to interpret our properties for themselves, adding to a body of knowledge and understanding previously accumulated by architectural historians and curators. This, in turn, will enable us to see the properties in new ways, in relation to their historic and contemporary significance. Interpretation is already part of the process that explains and makes accessible a diverse range of historic buildings and monuments; it can also help identify and make visible new meanings. We may, by thus changing perspective, come to talk with some conviction not of 'bringing the past to life' but of bringing real life into buildings from the past.

Notes

1   Kate Clark (ed.), Conservation plans in action: proceedings of the Oxford Conference (English Heritage, 1999)

2   Alison Hems, 'You haven't got any Rembrandts . . .', Interpretation, 2, no. 3 (July 1997)

3   Julius Bryant, 'Darwin's Down House: creating the lived-in look', Collections Review (English Heritage, 1999)

4   As, for example, in the strategic plan for 1999–2002

5   Sara Lunt, 'The houses at Great Yarmouth and the heritage partnership', Collections Review (English Heritage, 1999)

6   Peter Fryer, Staying Power: the history of black people in Britain (Pluto Press, 1984)

7   Julius Bryant, The Iveagh Bequest (English Heritage, 1995)

INDEX

Numbers in **bold** type refer to pages containing illustrations.